The Slave Son
by Marcella Fanny Wilkins ("Mrs. W. N. Wilkins.")

Address:
HardPress
8345 NW 66TH ST #2561
MIAMI FL 33166-2626
USA
Email: info@hardpress.net

THE

SLAVE SON.

BY

MRS. WILLIAM NOY WILKINS.

LONDON:

CHAPMAN AND HALL, 193, PICCADILLY.

1854.

PRINTED BY
JOHN EDWARD TAYLOR, LITTLE QUEEN STREET,
LINCOLN'S INN FIELDS.

DEDICATION.

———◆———

MY DEAR MRS. JAMESON,

I had some thought of dedicating this work to those ladies who have laboured courageously and unremittingly for the emancipation of the African race, and many distinguished and revered names occurred to my recollection : this would also have been in harmony with the intention of my tale. Yet if homage there be in a Dedication, I feel it ought surely to be rendered to her who has cheered and encouraged me through the difficulties which have beset my labours,—to her whose kind and generous sympathy throughout has been to me like a beacon in the midst of darkness.

To you therefore, my dear Mrs. Jameson, I beg to inscribe this little book, as the best expression of my respect and affection which I have to offer.

I have endeavoured to describe Slavery under a different phase from that which has hitherto come before the Public. The slave saints and martyrs, of whom we hear so much, I believe to be more poetical than real. I hold moreover, that, were it otherwise, and slavery produced many such, the system would be a good rather than an evil, or only of that kind of evil which pertains to physical suffering; but there lies hidden within it a deeper woe than this,—the debasement of the mind, the deadening of every virtue, the calling into action those weapons of defence which nature has given to the weak—cunning, deceit, treachery, and secret murder. Root out therefore, ye who call yourselves Christians,—root out and utterly destroy a state of things which is the occasion of such ruin!

All are born free and equal, whatever differences may afterwards arise, and all are equally placed here to tread a path which has Heaven for its goal. It therefore becomes a question which concerns, not the Negroes alone, but all nations,—Shall one half of mankind crush beneath the wheels of their gilded car the other half who humbly toil their way on foot? Or shall not the humbler half lay claim to space upon the road, that they, as well as their more fortunate brethren, may win the Heaven to which God invites them? Ay, truly they shall. The grey light is in the sky; the dawn will soon appear; the day is coming, when the wrongs of crushed humanity shall find a voice in every heart, and every Christian hand be stretched forth to help.

With esteem and affection,

I remain, dear Mrs. Jameson,

Yours,

MARCELLA FANNY WILKINS.

CONTENTS.

—◆—

THE

SLAVE SON.

———◆———

INTRODUCTION.

THE following pages were written about six years ago, but it was thought advisable to alter the narrative, then consisting of detached pieces, to one consecutive story; even then being little encouraged, as the subject of slavery had passed away from the public mind with the days of Wilberforce, I threw it aside, until the appearance of Mrs. Stowe's work removed the objection, and the cessation of family cares and the return of health enabled me to listen to the suggestion of my friends and submit the work to the Public.

For the sake of truth I have placed the scene of my story in the Colony, and at the period, in which the principal events took place. I might equally well have transferred it to any other slave country, and to any more recent period, for the same causes are ever followed by like effects.

I did not start in life however with any particular sympathy for the Negroes.   There were no scenes of cruelty or oppression in our homestead to awaken my pity,—far otherwise; and while our domestics presented all those features of an enslaved people so repulsive to the free, I learned from the first to regard them, as the children of all slaveholders do, in the light of a species of cattle,—I do not mean because they were bought and sold, and their labour unrewarded, I mean something worse still,—I mean that neither their total dismissal of all the proprieties and decencies of life, nor their immorality, ever shocked my principles or affected my mind any more than the habits of the beasts of burden working with them ; and yet the Negroes were always with us and about us, so also were the domestic animals belonging to the house.   I record these facts the more willingly, as it may help to show the nature and extent of the influence which slavery holds over man.

But the mixed race, the coloured population, early enlisted my sympathy : first of all, through their innate abhorrence of slavery and constant struggle after freedom ; and then, when free, through their constant, yet vain and impotent upheaving against the social weight which keeps them down as Pariahs.   I speak of the prejudice of caste.   None but those who have lived in slave countries are aware of the cruel extent to which this prejudice is carried.   I saw them longing for education where no school would admit them, —yearning after excellence where no right to excel was allowed them,—at the same time ready to kiss the feet of those who only made a show of teaching them on friendly terms, and never stopping to inquire whether this passing condescension was not for the sake of the money which they freely and generously gave. The devotion and gratitude of these poor creatures was too touching ever to forget; but a circumstance arose which fixed their wrongs indelibly in my mind.

There came to the Colony where we lived a young lady of colour from Europe,—a lady, I repeat the word. To a refinement of breeding which only belongs to the best society, she added accomplishments and manners of the first order; she was spoken of as a wonder. But soon it was understood that she would not receive gentlemen unless they presented themselves respectfully, and as they would to white ladies. Instantly society was in a ferment. Ladies who customarily made closet companions of coloured women whose life was an open acknowledgment of their degradation, were here all amazed at the impudent assumption of virtue by this coloured girl; and although crowds would gather at night opposite her window to hear her sing, in the daytime she was avoided as if struck with the plague. Those who met her in the street would turn back, or cross to the other side; and every invention was put in play to show her how completely she was thrust from the position she had dared to assume. I was then very young, scarcely better than a child, and just at that age when the heart is fresh and open to all the most generous feelings of our nature; and, romantic as it may seem, in my room that night I made a vow that it should be my one great task through life to raise the coloured race to social emancipation and respect. In my youthful enthusiasm I felt persuaded that my one little feeble voice would shame away prejudice from the millions of white people who entertained it; and I came to England full of my subject and elated with my hopes of doing good, in spite of the ridicule which was often thrown on my endeavours and remarks. Of course such illusions passed away with growing years and riper judgement, but I never once lost sight of my subject, even when the cares of life were thickening around me. I prepared a series of stories (of which the following is the first) calculated to show what these people are, and to create such an interest in their behalf as might lay the groundwork for their future rising; and I still hoped on through it all, that the time would come when I should have leisure and opportunity to finish what I had begun.

And the time is come, thanks to Mrs. Stowe! when my subject is no longer irrelevant to the topics of the day.

I present myself however not so much to take rank among the champions of civil emancipation (for they are numerous enough already), as to invite supporters for its completion in the social advancement of the coloured race; for slavery can never be said to be abolished where prejudice of caste keeps the people degraded. It is the blight which remains when the simoom has passed, quite as deadly and as poisonous, and at this day holds influence as fully and forcibly in the free northern states of America as in the south. I need only refer to the circumstance of Douglas being horsewhipped for walking between two white ladies to prove this.

Nay, in the British Colonies, where eighteen years ago one half of the population was beggared to emancipate the other, prejudice against the emancipated race influences even the local authorities, just as much as at the period of our story.

It was an easy matter for statesmen at the head of Government in England to pass, for their political and commercial ends, an Act for favouring a distant people who never come across their feelings either to annoy or perplex: but how comes it they have never directed their appointed governors to open the colonial offices and departments to the deserving and the capable among the coloured race? How comes it they have never given encouragement to place them on an equal footing with the white? Have they never once thought of doing this? It is really poor justice, —a mere mockery of a great deed, more boastful than real.

But it is different with the American statesmen. *They* are surrounded with coloured people in every relation of life, and they have to wrest from the very growth of their minds a prejudice of no common force, before they can give that heartfelt, earnest labour to emancipation which can alone obtain success. None can tell but those who have lived in slave countries what a hold it takes of the mind, and how far and wide its influence spreads throughout all the feelings and actions of life, till it forms part and parcel of one's very nature, like the creed we have learnt from our mothers; and often, when boasting of having risen superior to it, we find ourselves suddenly as much under its sway as ever.

This happened to myself. I had been already a few years in England, still full of my subject,—talking of it by day, dreaming of it by night,—when I went with some friends to a party. I had not been long seated when I saw entering the room a young man of colour. It was the first time in my life that I had seen a person of colour enter a room on equal terms with myself; and my surprise and discomfort were by no means diminished when the daughter of our hostess introduced him to me as partner for the next quadrille. If the footman had presented himself for that purpose I could not have been more startled, and had I met this gentleman of colour at Court it could not have saved him from the feeling of aversion and contempt with which I instinctively regarded him. This, no doubt, was very absurd, as the hue of his complexion was the only circumstance against him; but it illustrates the force of a prejudice which interferes with the social welfare of a whole race.

There is no more fatal extinguisher of genius, of talent, of worth, of all that is noble in the mind of man, than this general blackballing,—no surer means of crushing the mind, of fettering the intellect, of lowering the morals, than this scourging rod of prejudice, which indiscriminately condemns the coloured people to the condition of brute and Pariah. Read what the Irish were in the days of the penal laws, and it will give some faint idea of what the coloured race at this day suffer, not by written law, but social custom; for nothing in England can.

It is true that this is a country of castes, but it is also true that the wall which encircles each may often be climbed, not only by casual visitors, but constantly by strangers who come for affiliation; and where the upper classes exercise their selecting power judiciously, it acts wholesomely, and imparts to the people a vigour of exertion which has the best effect upon their children and upon themselves. But for the coloured man there is no hope: the barrier which separates him from intellect, worth, honour, greatness, reaches high up to Heaven, far beyond his power of surmounting, and all that is left him is to sit down in its shade and mourn!

But what though it requires the powerful effort of a powerful mind, dictated by a still more powerful heart, to overcome a feeling which has rooted itself in our very nature, still I do not despair. The whole matter rests with the American ladies, and of all the women upon the earth there are none superior in in-

dependence of spirit and benevolence of heart.   The
political emancipation of the coloured race is a deed
for the men ; their social emancipation is an heroic act
worthy of the American ladies, and I dare promise
them a glorious reward.   The coloured people, with
their patrimonial heritage of intellect grafted on the
warm strong temperament of their mothers, exhibit
while yet children, all the elements of fire, imagination, and genius.   What may not they henceforward
become under genial influence and encouragement ?
The women of caste are modest in their demeanour,
faithful to their homes, fond mothers, and true generous friends, and have a refinement of feeling which
is astonishing in the low condition to which they are
condemned.

In their physical constitution too they are an ex-
tremely interesting race.   The French, whose re-
search in science is greater than ours, have discovered
an affinity between their various castes and those of
the Asiatic families, particularly among the women.
The Mulattoes, born of white and black parents, bear
a marked resemblance to the Copts or Egyptians, the
people who first gave civilization to the world.   The
Terzerons, born of the Mulattoes and whites, have the
golden complexion, straight nose, and slender forms
of the Persians, the most refined people of the East.
The Quadroons, born of the Terzerons and whites,
have eyes like houris, regular features, and the languid expression of the Asiatic Turks,—many indeed
with perfect faces like the Greeks and the Romans,

who once bore sway over the nations of the earth in philosophy, science, and warfare. While closer again to the Negro, the caste called *Capre*, sprung from the Mulattoes and blacks, show the rounded proportions and plump faces of the Hindoos.

I do not apprehend that the mixed race will ever form a nation apart. In these days of swift travelling and increasing interchange of thought, it is more likely that exclusive nationality has seen its best days, than that it should spring up anew with another people. But I look forward to a thorough equalization of races, which shall procure for all equal rights by written law, social law, and the law which comes from Christ; when man shall owe his greatness to his own striving,—to the exercise of the talents he has received from God, not to the hue of his complexion, or rather, I should say, to the complexion of his parents; and when the coloured man, ·taking place among his fellow-men on earth, may do credit to the generous and glorious nation which has freed him. To quote the prophetic words of Burns,—

"And let us pray, that come it may, and come it will for a' that,
    When man to man, through all the world, shall brothers be and
    a' that."

I have done; and it only remains with me to say that I repudiate all personal responsibility with regard to the sentiments I have put in the mouth of my hero: I have drawn him such as I have seen him,—the type of his race,—and such as may be found

in every slave country; and he speaks here as every
slaveholder speaks when irritated by the observation
of strangers or the reproaches of the abolitionists. I
have only to add my grateful acknowledgments to
Mrs. Jameson, whose large warm heart found place
for sympathy with my subject and earnest encouragement for my labours in the very midst of her
then pressing labours on Legendary Art; and also to
Mr. Patten, the philanthropic Librarian of the Royal
Dublin Society, a man whose liberal heart and mind
will ever be admired by those who know him, and
who, like myself, have derived their best ideas and
happiest suggestions from the stores of his intellect.
And having spoken thus much for myself and for
those to whom I am indebted, I beg at once to in-
troduce my Story.

CHAPTER I.

A SHORT REVIEW OF THE HISTORY OF TRINIDAD—
AND A LITTLE GOSSIP.

OF all the Colonies ever visited by the Abolitionists there is none where the slave was found so happy in his condition as in that most fertile and beautiful of the Antilles, the fair island of Trinidad. It lies southernmost and last of the band of isles called West Indies, and just in the delta of the magnificent Orinoco, of whose shores, from its close resemblance to the mainland in point of geological formation and natural production, it is supposed to have once formed part, and to have only been rent therefrom by some comparatively recent convulsion of the earth. But fertile and lovely as is the isle, it was nevertheless the latest known and the latest cultivated of all the Colonies, for reasons I will explain, and which, with a short review of its history, may go far to account for the somewhat easy life which the Negroes enjoyed.

It had the honour of being named by Christopher

Columbus himself, who discovered and visited it during his third voyage to the West. It was on a Sabbath-day he first caught the outline of its mountains, from which circumstance he dedicated this new land to the Santissima Trinidad,—Sunday being set apart by the Spaniards for the particular worship of the Trinity. And as the gale from the shore came loaded with perfume, and the opening vista disclosed, as he neared it, a richness and magnificence of vegetation hitherto unknown, he called it exultingly the Indian Paradise.

But his glowing descriptions were doomed to pass unheeded, for the great discoverer had fallen under the displeasure of Royalty, and the island was suffered to remain as wild and uncultivated as when first proclaimed a Spanish conquest, till the year 1783, when by a romantic adventure it was suddenly brought into notice.

About this time Roume de St. Laurent, a French inhabitant of Granada, happening to visit its shores in quest of natural curiosities, he was struck with its aspect,—its grandeur, its fertility, its large and numerous rivers, and, above all, the advantage of its situation. He became enthusiastic ; he imagined himself a rediscoverer of the colony, a benefactor of mankind, and forthwith taking passage to Spain, he succeeded so well in advocating his views with the Ministers, as to win from them that celebrated Royal Schedule which soon after resounded throughout all Europe, inviting Catholics of every nation to establish themselves in the new colony, under promise of free trade, exemption from taxes, protection during five years from creditors left behind, and many other immunities equally encouraging and important.

Meanwhile St. Laurent was not idle, but continued visiting all the great commercial cities of Europe, rousing the indolent, interesting the speculative, holding forth golden prospects to the ruined, and so eloquently speaking on his subject, that in a short time were seen emigrants flocking from all quarters of the globe to this new land of promise : the Colony soon acquired a political and commercial importance equal to its geographical position.

Much of all this success was owing to its first Governor, Don José Chacon. A wiser and more benevolent man, a truer Christian, was never chosen to hold that despotic power which is vested in the hands of a Spanish Governor. He carefully watched the carrying-out of every law which protected the slave, and more than this, he set the fashion of mercy and kindness towards them, which afterwards, even under British rule, never entirely disappeared from the Colony.

We are apt to revile the Spaniards. Let us take a glance at their laws, such as bear upon our subject : perhaps we may find something to admire, perhaps even to learn from. Chivalrous nation ! Though feudal and despotic their government, they nevertheless framed their laws studiously to protect the friendless ; thus were women, children, vassals, and slaves, all attended to, their various cases considered, and officers provided for their protection.

Among other privileges of the slaves, they who from tyranny or other cause became discontented with their masters' service, were entitled to require a written pass, good for three days, wherein to seek another owner ; they were also entitled by law to demand and obtain manumission on producing the sum of 500 piastres purchase-money ; and be it observed, that the murder of a slave, a circumstance mostly unnoticed in other colonies, was here punishable by law, and the perpetrator made liable to a fine of fifty dollars (£10) to Government, besides the full payment of his value to the owner.

But here, as elsewhere, that damning clause was in force, which denied to the slave the power of bearing witness against a white man in a court of law ; and all this talk of protection would have been but a mockery, had not the religion of the land, which was formed for a system of feudality and acted ever in harmony with it, stepped in to correct the vices of its enactments. The priests, unable, by the nature of their vows, to hold any personal property or tie, and having consequently but little interest in upholding the slaveholder, easily and naturally acquired the privilege of interference, and became, by means of confession, arbitrators-general between master and slave, thus exercising a salutary check on that irresponsible power which in other colonies has so demoralizing an effect upon society.

The observance of at least thirty Saints' days, besides Sundays, was also in favour of the slave, who had a proportionate amount of time to himself; thus, those Negroes who were in any way inclined to industry might very well contrive to save,—a disposition favoured by Chacon, who benevolently appropriated several acres of Crown-land for the sole use and profit of slaves working out their freedom.

But it was not to the slaves alone that Chacon extended his merciful protection : there were yet two more races over which he watched with equal care— the free mixed race, or Mulattoes, and the Indians. Of the former the number was at first very small, but they soon increased in proportion to the rest of the population; for these unhappy victims of persecution had also been induced by the Royal Schedule to leave their old abodes in quest of a new and happier home, whose Government consented to grant them protection in return for a stipulated portion of their wealth. This indeed was no new thing : arrangements of this sort were commonly practised in all the other French, English, and Spanish Colonies, where, in return for a considerable tribute, they received a very slender and capricious protection ; here, on the contrary, when Chacon made the agreement he kept it, and under his protection they did not so deeply suffer from the disabilities to which, in common with the Negro, they were made subject.

The priests aided Chacon here too. Far from sharing the general prejudice against a tinge of African

blood, they professed it a part of their ministry to
level all ranks and conditions. They had all the dead
buried within the same sacred enclosure, without ex-
cluding (as was the case in other colonies) slaves or
Mulattoes; and permitted in their churches no pews
or any kind of private seats, so that within the precincts of their temples the scene presented was one
of perfect equality, the Negro, the Mulatto, and the
Indian kneeling fearlessly by the side of the white
man, praying to the same God and benefiting equally
by the offices of the minister.

Thus discountenanced by the clergy, caste prejudice lost much of its evil effects, and the free Mulattoes also shared in the general prosperity of the
island.

As for the Indians, they only numbered a handful
at first, having long before been sent to work in the
mines, where they pined away in despair. Government however now considered they might be useful
in the Colonies, and emissaries were accordingly sent
to all parts of the adjoining continent, to bring over
as many Indians as they could persuade, till in a few
years their number in the island amounted to two
thousand. It is true they were still sunk in heathenish superstition, and their habits, manners, virtues,
and vices all partook of the savage life they had been
accustomed to lead; yet, simple and inoffensive, they
seldom intruded on the haunts of the white man.

As soon as they were tolerably settled in their new
abodes, Government thought proper to burden them

with a tax, which Chacon subsequently commuted to a weekly portion of labour on the high-roads then in progress, and he so contrived to time and soften their labours as to avoid inducing despair among them. They lived in scattered villages along the sea-shore or on the banks of rivers, very often in the most picturesque spot; and as each hamlet was formed, Government placed there a Regidor and a missionary, by whose influence the Indians gradually seemed to progress in civilization, as rapidly as their indolent nature and inherent love of savage life permitted.

The island now presented a mass of population congregated from almost every part of the globe, not even excepting China, whence thirty families came to speculate in tea-planting; and as each day brought fresh importations of adventurers, all differing in habits, ideas, grades, and languages, confusion would soon have wrought its worst, but for the affability and wise behaviour of Chacon. He visited all, took an interest in the affairs of all, brought peace and harmony among the discordant masses, and dealt encouragement to their good endeavours; and it is even related that whenever he found a worthy individual too poor to improve on opportunities, he would generously help him with loans from his private resources.

This was the golden age of Trinidad. Its port became the mart for all merchandise going to and from the continent; wealth flowed in abundance to its coffers; and such, it is said, was the simple integrity of the inhabitants, that heavy bags of gold,

c

sealed with the merchant's name who issued them, passed current among all grades of people, and were never either suspected or opened. It was common to see warehouses and shops cleared in an hour by a single purchaser, and a forest of ships from every trading nation of the earth brought life and business to its port.

But this was not to last always: war was proclaimed, the English fleet bombarded the town, and the good Chacon, left without sufficient means of defence, was forced to capitulate; for this he was ordered to be secured in chains, and sent home to his ungrateful king; and many a heart regretted him, and many a tear was shed, and many a child born years after was taught to bless his name as it rose on the lips.

The terms of capitulation were understood to secure to the inhabitants the continuance of Spanish law, the free exercise of the Catholic religion, and all the privileges granted by the Spanish Schedule, so that the Colonists still hoped that their prosperity would not be disturbed. But with British rule came taxes immediately, each one more burdensome than the last, and various enactments, among which, be it recorded, was one proclaiming that no Colonist should be empowered to purchase Crown-land unless he could show proofs of possessing eight slaves wherewith to cultivate it. Moreover the Crown-land appropriated by Chacon to the private use of the slaves was gradually withdrawn, and the laws which protected the Negroes were made, one by one, to give way to other statutes and a different order of things. The English Governors, unfortunately, were not men to soften matters, or to gain by comparison with the lost Chacon; and when to the arbitrary proclamations of the Home Government were added a sensible impoverishing of the inhabitants, a falling-off in commercial relations, and lastly, and most vexatious of all to the Planters, serious threats to emancipate the slaves, it is not to be wondered that disaffection increased, and murmurs were heard in this island more loud and bitter than in any other of the West Indies. Secret emissaries, it was said, were even sent to America, to offer allegiance to that mighty nation; and it was indeed with despair in their hearts and hatred on their tongues that the inhabitants met an unsuccessful answer to their hopes; for the Americans, it was understood, would not consider it worth their while to interfere, unless the whole group of Colonies struck rebellion at once.

But, in the midst of all this ferment and discontent, the spirit of Chacon still prevailed. The Spanish laws, set aside as they were by arbitrary Councils of State and the partiality of the Colonial employés, were still respected by the priests; and the slaves, even though their minds were unsettled, and the ties which bound them to their masters were fast loosening, yet their condition was easy. I refer in this more particularly, and I might almost say exclusively, to the Spaniards; for, to the shame of my

c 2

brother Protestants be it said, they were the only slaveholders I ever saw who enforced the observance of religious service among their slaves and encouraged *the rites of marriage*. With them the Negro married woman bore a recognized title to respect; she had influence with her master's family, and privileges on the estates which were never accorded to the unmarried.

The Spaniard is indolent by nature; he has little ambition beyond the enjoyment of the hour, and his love of power is so mixed up with paternal care, that these become one in feeling as in action. What if, in the evening, after Vespers, the Spanish master would call his slaves around him, and make each kneel down and kiss the rod; in the same tone would he not meet the morning greetings of his own children, by proudly holding out his hand for them to kiss? To both he dealt continual indulgence and mercy, and if in his fits of anger his actions often bordered on cruelty, still, as a matter of feeling, it was understood and submitted to, and the unoffending might still remain happy.

Not so with the money-loving races of Jews, English, and Dutch, and some of the French. Unchecked by their own free laws, unrestrained by the mandates of their own free religion, and swayed only by the ambition of fortune-making, the Negroes were with them worse than beasts of burden; souls were nothing, bodies were cattle-property; and the cold, hourly, continuous tyranny of these masters, who treated them like the cane-plants subjected to their mill, was such as to work its own destruction, even had emancipation never come to the aid of the oppressed. Something of this it is my purpose to show in the course of the following narrative.

Affairs were still in a state of considerable ferment in the year 1832, when, about midcrop-time, several rich planters and some merchants from Port Spain (capital of the island) were observed suddenly to leave their residences, to flock to a very obscure hamlet on the south-east coast, where the country is wild, little cultivated, and less frequented. Of course each, as he arrived, offered some plausible excuse for his journey,—the curiosity of the villagers demanded it; but whatever was said, it seemed upon the whole to fall very far short of satisfying the gossips of the place, and the subject was thus discussed by a group of females returning one evening from Vespers; when, after the usual Spanish greeting of the hour,—

"You know," said one, after listening to all the various surmising, debating, examining, and wondering, "all this can betoken nothing but a visit from the Governor. His Excellency is a quiet Hidalgo, liking to travel without much noise or fuss."

"Ave Maria!" exclaimed another, struck with the grandeur of the event, "don't say that; for if the Governor comes here we shall certainly receive an invitation; and my *niñas* (daughters) have not a thing to appear in. It was but yesterday I was turning over our stock of flowers, fringes, and feathers: *bargame*

Dios ! they all fell in powder as I touched them,——devoured, I tell you, by the white ants; and the cockroaches have got to their laces; so what we are to do I don't know."

"Don't talk!" said a merchant's wife, "I have got some book-muslin down here which I can sell you, and you can get Laurine to trim it. She has the prettiest way in the world of gumming down green leaves and flowers in all manner of patterns upon book-muslin. I recommend her as a workwoman. I assure you whenever there is a ball in Port Spain she is sent for expressly to help to make the ladies' dresses; and through her taste your daughters will look beautiful."

"Or," observed another, "you can trim the muslin as the lady of our good Governor Chacon once did, —quilt it all over with fireflies within the squares."

"*Sí, sí*, I remember my mother talking of that," interrupted the first speaker; "when the Señora sat down to converse the fireflies fell asleep and their lamps went out, so the dress looked as if spotted all over with black; but when the Señora but moved, or danced, or shook her dress, it was something to see the thousands of living diamonds which sparkled all over her dress: it was a clever device. Why don't you do the same, *caramba ?*"

"Because," replied the complaining lady, "this is crop-time, don't you know? and I have no spare hands to catch all the necessary flies."

"Well then," resumed the other, "I daresay I can

lend you something, for my daughter is laid up,—she can't appear for many a day. Poor thing! her complexion is so fair and tender, like a *niña Inglesa*. Just think, *mira !* she sat at a window overlooking a cottage with a slated roof; the sun was shining on this roof,—mind, not on the window at which she sat,—and the glare of the roof caught her face, and the skin has actually peeled off like a mask. Ave Maria! but she is careless, the fair little creature. We brunettes don't suffer so much, you see; we are not like the fresh European ladies—obliged to shut ourselves up in dark rooms during the noon-tide heat, or to wear masks like some of those *Inglesas* when they only just put their nose out in the morning."

"That reminds me," observed Maria, a young lady with some pretensions to good looks, "I had better put on my gloves : I have let my hands grow so coarse and brown lately that I am ashamed of them, and just because it was too hot to cover them. I think my gloves must be in my bag ;" and diving into the profundities of a black silk affair which hung from her arm, and which also contained her missal and pocket-handkerchief, she withdrew the gloves, and commenced pulling them on. The operation however was quickly cut short. " *Santos mios !*" she screamed, as she convulsively capered about, and made efforts to pull off her glove, while a very respectable centipede, five inches long, crept from within the warm cavities of the glove, and coolly made its way up her arm.

And now behold the pocket-handkerchiefs, books,

bags, parasols, sticks, all flourishing about in every
direction! and, kindly belabouring the invaded arm,
they soon brought down the intruder and put him for
ever out of all pain and pleasure of this world.   But
it had set the company nervous.   One fancied she
felt a deadly scorpion down her back; another thought
she felt a black spider on her knee, and under her
arm she was sure there was something creeping, and
without another word off she tore her sleeve and
grasped at the offender, which proved this time to be
nothing but a string,—a harmless bit of tape left to
hang unused.

In the course of a few minutes tranquillity was
restored, the ladies' nerves grew calm, and the conversation was resumed this time with many a tale
of like rencontres : how one gentleman got bitten by
a tarantula, and died two hours afterwards; how a
friend's Negro was killed with a bite from a coral-
snake; how a lady went to bed and found it occupied
by a brood of boa-constrictors; and then one of the
company laughed, and told how another had gone to
mass with the edge of her bonnet presenting one
continued fringe of long disgusting black millepedes;
and audible symptoms of merriment were still going
the round when a new comer came in sight, and
brought back all their wandering thoughts to the
point whence they started.

"*Bargame Dios!*" they one and all exclaimed,
"there's Mr. Hinde; who would have thought to see
him here? It must be that the Governor is coming."

"Do you know Madame Hinde?" inquired Doña Juana: "she is a fine woman, with such an excellent heart! Have you heard how she went to the sick stranger who was left ashore, they say, in the town of Port Spain, dying in a miserable room? Well, she took him to her house, had a doctor and a nurse, and tended him herself till he recovered: there's a good heart for you! And has she not a spirit too? Does she not manage her Negroes? *Caramba!* they are not impudent, I warrant you, in spite of all those horrid Orders in Council; I tell you they jump and waltz about if she but holds up her little finger. Now there is her man-cook Achilles. *Ahí,* Señoras! the last time I was in Port Spain I saw her flogging that man herself with a cowskin in the open yard: there's for you!"

"That must be some time ago," said the young Maria, "for town servants may not be flogged now, since that Order in Council."

"*Sencilla!*" exclaimed Doña Juana, looking pitifully at her companion, "do you think Madame Hinde is to be baulked by Ministers or their servants? Not she! That man Achilles had the impudence to go out gossiping in the middle of cooking the dinner: that's what those Orders in Council bring, teaching the Negroes to rebel. Well, Señoras, Madame Hinde saw what was going on, and she waited. She expected seven guests that day, to whom she sent an apology, and a request for postponement of their visit; meantime the dinner-hour came, the bell was rung, and

Achilles sends up the dishes raw, Señoras. So Madame Hinde calls up Achilles,—he had just eaten his own dinner,—and there she seats him and makes him eat up the whole dinner for seven, every bit, raw and burnt. In vain Achilles begged and prayed : there she was at his elbow, and he knew that if he but showed sign of resistance he would be sent off that instant to the estate, where of course his mistress could do anything she liked with him. Achilles, Señoras, was laid up ill for a week afterwards, and they were obliged to have a doctor to him; but I promise you it was a lesson : he won't forget that he is not to mind English Orders in Council more than his mistress."

"Bravo!" cried the company, "I like that. How different she is to her sister Angélique, Madame St. Hilaire Cardon! she is a fool, and a martyr to her servants."

"Ah, don't talk! I tell you she is broken-hearted since the death of her son."

"Poor thing! poor thing!" cried the commiserating ladies, "it is all the English people's doings, God help us! I hear all the Colonists say it is the way with them wherever they plant their sway. It is well for us we have such a man as St. Hilaire Cardon himself; he is here, by the bye,—I saw him this morning."

"Indeed!" cried Maria, delighted, "then of course it is the Governor that is coming."

"*Sencilla, qué locura es esto!*" snapped Doña Juana,

"don't you know they don't speak? Don't you know the Governor is afraid of him,—that St. Hilaire is his sworn enemy,—that he writes in the newspapers against him and the Government? In short, he is the lash that keeps them all in order, those tyrants—*demonios*; and he is the bravest, the cleverest, the richest, and most respected man in the Colony. You should see him as I have seen him when travelling on the high road: off goes every man's hat as he passes, his Lordship the Bishop's as well as the meanest Mulatto's. They could not do more to the Governor, and the Governor himself is afraid of him!"

Maria replied tartly that she had seen that doughty hero with an Englishman that morning, and she, for her part, did not like either Frenchmen or Englishmen: the Frenchmen were *traidores todos*, and the Englishmen were *borrachones todos*.

"Who says Englishmen are *borrachones todos?*" said a gruff voice behind them.

The suddenness of the question caused the ladies to start; some of them called out " Ave Maria!" then crossed their hands upon their bosoms and gasped; others elevated their voices to an angry pitch, and frowningly cried out, " Who is that?" but in another second they had all gathered round the speaker, with questions innumerable.

" Don Duro!" " Don Duro Harding!" " You too?" " Why all the world is coming here nowadays!" " What is the matter? what is going to be done in our little village?" " Is there a gold-mine

discovered? and who discovered it, and whose is it?"
" Or is the Governor coming? When will he come?
Will he be here today? Will he stay long? Will
he give a dance?"

To all this volley of interrogatories Don Duro
made no reply: how could he, indeed, when he was
not given time? He only thrust his hands into his
pockets, and looked profound.

He was a dark little thin man, half Spaniard, half
English, that is, his father was an Englishman and
his mother a Spaniard, and he had all the long-head-
edness and reserve of the former mingled with the
deep passion of the latter; but he knew how to dis-
semble at all times, and he owned a good place as
manager of the Palm Grove, then belonging to St.
Hilaire Cardon.

" Come now," said the ladies, " you can tell us if
you like; there must be something, or you would not
have left the estate to come here today; now say, *de
verdad, palabra de honor*, what is it all about? What
has brought Mr. Cardon down here?—at least you
can tell us that."

" To look about him and see this part of the island,
to be sure."

" Then what is that Englishman with him for?"

" Why, don't you know it is to show that new
comer this part of the island that Mr. Cardon has
accompanied him? Probably they will go all round
the island; he is his friend, and may be his partner."

" *Bargame Dios!* but now I know why you took

part with the English. *Hombre*, you ought to be more attached to your mother's nation."

Don Duro turned his eyes upon the speaker with the slightest possible sign of displeasure.

But without noticing the look, or caring one straw, the lady took up the interrogatories with renewed vigour.

"Then what is Mr. Joseph Hinde here for?"

"He is come to visit his friends hereabouts."

"Well then, Don Juan Faxardo—he has no friends here—what is he come for?"

"Well, I will tell you : he wants to lay out some money in land; they say he can get land here cheap and productive."

"Hem!" said the ladies, "well then, what brings Don Lopez Mendoza?"

"Ask him," said Don Duro impatiently; "they are all most likely of the same party, and probably will go on board the same little vessel which will touch here today, and they may coast round the island in it."

"Oh," said the ladies, rather chap-fallen, "so there is no gold-mine after all, nor no Governor coming!"

"I shall go and ask Mr. Cardon myself," said Doña Juana, drawing herself up proudly after a moment's pause, "I can ask him anything I like. I knew him when his son was that high," she said, holding her hand some feet from the ground; "I knew the boy when he was sent to France for his education."

"*Ahí!*" interrupted Maria, "my father saw him

there with his little valet behind, and, *bargame Dios!*
I declare he said that there was so little difference
between the two!"

"Listen to that! listen to that!" exclaimed Doña
Juana, almost dancing with virtuous indignation;
"Santa Maria! and are things come to this, that
comparisons are drawn between master and slave?
And even resemblances spoken of! Do you not
know, for the matter of that, Niña Maria, that all
men resemble one another in having legs, and arms,
and noses, and mouths, and so on? but are we for
that to be comparing Mulattoes with white men?
Jesus Maria! but the world must be coming to an
end. I never heard such things,—did you, Don
Duro?"

To which the latter responded with a whistle long
and clear, looking the while steadfastly another way.

"I but hazarded the remark," urged Maria, quite
conscience-stricken, "I meant no harm."

"*Sí, Señora,* but things should be said cautiously
when the roads are full of Negroes, and one of them
may be at this moment at your elbow, listening to
your mad words, — sucking in ideas of rebellion
thereby. Is it not enough to have the English *demonios* meddling with us, without our own young *locas*
(madcaps) turning against us? Ask Don Duro there."

"*Muy de verdad, Señora,*" observed the Manager,
"sapiently, most truly spoken, a dangerous thing
such speeches indeed!"

"And if we begin teaching Mulattoes to compare

themselves to us, it is as much as to teach them to consider themselves equal to us," spoke the lady, with increasing warmth.

" My dear Doña Juana, consider——"

" Particularly in this case, where the Mulatto has turned out the most abominable *demonio*, a *vaga-mundo !*"

" Doña Juana !" entreated the offender.

" A vile Mulatto, who showed so little gratitude to his dear young master as to run away from him in France too, leaving him without a valet, and, when the dear young man was dying, never to come back to receive pardon, but to keep like a wild beast in the woods, where every one knows he is at this moment ! If I was Mr. Cardon, I would have the island scoured, I would ! And I will tell him so, for I can say anything I like to him."

" Really," said the younger lady pettishly, " one can't say a word, I'm sure."

At this moment the party had reached the central part of the hamlet : they had loitered long, and the dews were too heavy to remain out, they separated therefore, some to go into their own homes, others to join more gossips, in order to discuss the all-absorbing subject of their curiosity, though with what success we shall not pretend to say just now. We must only crave permission to pass over that night, and lead our readers to the opening of that day on which most of the individuals here spoken of will begin gradually to figure.

CHAPTER II.

LOVERS' QUARREL.

THE dawn was rising over the heights of Trinidad, and, in a sky fair and serene as that which spanned the valleys of Paradise, a few stray stars of the south were seen to sparkle brightly, even while yet the tints of Aurora were fading delicately and more delicately away before the morning breeze, which now arose soft, cool, and lusciously fragrant. The landscape, at this early hour, was still as though wrapped in sleep; the mountains were veiled in mist, through whose broken tissue occasionally shone the green of a highland midground, while the blue of more distant scenes, catching a reflection from the rosy dawn above, appeared to melt into the faintest lilac. As the light increased and the atmosphere warmed, the white vapours, which had rested so still over the ancient forests, now faded from the view, and the broad summits of the highland ridges appeared capped with lustrous gold, from which long streaks of rich colouring began to glide, softly though perceptibly, down to the highest points of the valleys beneath, where the barbs of the tall cocoa-nut glanced green and silvery, or where clusters of orange, tamarind, and coral mingled their tints with the bignonia and locust.

The scenery was richly tropical. Plantations of colonial produce chequered the view on all sides; young groves of cinnamon on the heights, dark green fields of indigo in the hollows; pleasant slopes, here reddened with the berries of the coffee, there white with snowy flakes bursting from the nuts of the cotton, while yonder, gracefully winding round the base of the hills, might be traced the gorgeous coral-tree which shelters the tender chocolate-bush, while in the plains vast sweeps of cane, now bursting into bloom, shone in the slanting ray like sheets of waving gold shot over with silver and purple.

In front of these, and on the sea-shore, was a small hamlet, which we shall call Sant' Iago. It was still quiet; not a soul was stirring, save in one cottage situated on the wharf, where, through the open shutters of its little front room, the inmates were seen moving backwards and forwards in a very busy manner. One, with broom in hand, seemed occupied in sweeping, while the other, after various arrangements, set a tray upon her head and tripped along to a neighbouring enclosure, with that gay elastic step which tells of youth, innocence, and a happy mind. To hear her warbling in there among the flowers—

D

for it was a garden she had entered—was like music of the birds, her voice was so clear, sweet, and silvery. Evidently the individual she sang to, dwelt somewhere in that huge forest-clad mountain which rose at a little distance to the back of the hamlet; for as the young girl returned from the garden with her tray all laden with flowers, her eyes often wandered in that direction, not with sadness however, but with a hopeful, joyous, trustful look of affection. View her near, you will find that she is a simple girl of caste, that is, one of those despised race of beings who bear in slave countries the appellation of Mulattoes. Nevertheless she has attractions of no mean description. Her eyes are large, dark, and lustrous, her hair silky, black, and wavy, and her small round nose and pouting mouth are by no means unpleasantly turned, particularly when moved by a soft dimpling smile, rich in its own innocent sweetness. Then her costume is such as greatly to enhance her southern beauty. A bright Madras shawl twisted fantastically round her head, another thrown modestly over her shoulders, and a chintz skirt gathered in ample folds about the waist, so as to fall rather short in front, but let to sweep the ground behind, completed her costume,—the same which was adopted by all women of caste after they were prohibited by law the use of bonnet, shoes, stockings, long sleeves, or bodied skirt. The white ladies of course affected to despise it as a garb of degradation, but the truth is, it far surpassed their own stiff fashions in graceful and picturesque arrangement. But Laurine was not only pretty, she was also naturally gifted : everything she touched bore the marks of ingenuity, from the embroidered pockets and plaited sleeves of her holiday costume, to the crisping and fashioning of the cakes she sold. She was unquestionably the most graceful dancer in the whole island; and there are many yet living who remember the songs of Laurine's composing, and the inimitable sweetness with which she warbled the wild melodies of the Negroes. Yet she seldom joined the dance, was seldom seen with companions of her own age, and, although scarcely seventeen, she had the reputation of being a miser : at least she was censured for it by the uncharitable gossips of the neighbourhood, because the love of gain is so stigmatized by the Negroes, whose simple generous natures can never tolerate such a vice. Just look at her now, how busily she adjusts her flowers, forming them into bouquets! there is reseda and roses, pinks and myrtle, sweetbriar and English daisies, with every other flower considered rare within the tropics; and there she goes now to arrange the blooming fruit and hot crisped cakes which an aged woman has brought in from some out-door place, probably one of those brick ovens of simple construction which are often seen attached to the buildings of a West Indian domicile.

"La Catalina," said the young girl, addressing herself to her companion, and using the Martinique patois, which is spoken in all the Colonies,—a sort of mixture of French, Spanish, and Indian,—" I really think I am doing well; I have been reckoning my hoard, and I find I have nearly completed half the sum,—what do you think of that? Five hundred piastres is what the law binds me to : let me but offer that sum and Master Cardon can't refuse my mother's freedom ! and so now I have only two hundred and fifty more piastres to make, and my mother is free. Thank God ! Oh, Catalina, how happy I shall be to take her home to my little hut, wherever I have it, and to take care of her myself !"

"One, two, three reals, these mangoes will fetch," murmured the other, who was a walking arithmetical table,—" five reals of rose-apples, two of balatas, and seven of sappodillas."

The young girl did not seem to heed her reckóning,—she had already satisfied herself about the profits of all, and, busying herself among her flowers, she continued to form them into bouquets, as she spoke aloud her thoughts.

"Yes, and when I brought my little offering of flowers to the altar of our chapel last evening, Padre Martino met me by the way. ' Ah, Laurine,' he said, ' this is all very well, but I fear you are what people say.' What is that, good Father? I asked.—' Nothing but a little miser, my child ;' and so I just whispered into the Padre's ear what my motive was, and then the good priest blessed me, and bade me go

on and prosper. Oh, now I am sure I shall succeed,"
and, with the same breath, she broke out into a little
song of her own composing.

Oh! how hap-py to feel I am free, To think and to breathe in
sweet li - ber - ty! sweet li - ber - ty. I look on the
earth, and I look on the sky. And I send up to Heav'n the
sound of my joy. So all the day long do I sing mer-ri -
- ly, So mer-ri - ly, mer-ri - ly, Sing mer-ri - ly, Oh!
Sing mer-ri - ly, Sing mer-ri - ly, Sing mer-ri - ly.

Bis {
  And oft do I watch the gold-bird fly,
  And, listening, catch its wild melody ;
  But never, sweet bird, would I prison thee ;
  Oh no, little bird, I love liberty !
  So all the day long do I live merrily,
    Sing merrily, merrily, sing merrily,
    Oh! sing merrily, sing merrily.

Bis {
  And I love to look at the forest tree,
  Where it stands afar in its majesty ;

For I know that its boughs are the haunts of the free,
And it gives them a home for their sweet liberty ;
So all the day long do I sing merrily,
  So merrily, merrily, sing merrily,
  Oh! sing merrily, sing merrily.

Bis {
And oft, on a fair and a sunshiny day,
To the wide savanas I roam far away,
To be with the birds and to feel I am free,
For this is my bliss, and the song of my glee ;
And all the day long do I sing merrily,
  So merrily, merrily, sing merrily,
  Oh! sing merrily, sing merrily.

She had hardly finished these words, when she became aware of the presence of a third person, and she started as she recognized a young Mulatto, who, with his arms resting on the window-ledge, stood gazing in at her with intense admiration and delight. Smiling at her surprise, he entered the cottage, and, seating himself at once, he prepared himself to listen to the chiding of the damsel.

"Belfond! you here?" she exclaimed, with reproving eyes,—"in broad day,—the place full of white people!—your master himself here too! Oh, Belfond, what madness! you can have no real love for me, if you act so rashly; you must begone, indeed you must."

"Never fear," replied the youth, still speaking the patois of the Colony, but in terms so finely modulated and with such choice of expressions as to betray a romantic mind refined by a European education,— "don't be alarmed, Laurine, the white men are not abroad yet. But you say true," he said, assuming a more serious tone, " I must be on my guard, for what am I but a runaway—an outcast—an outlaw? suspected as a rebel—watched as a thief. Yes, I know they are on the look-out for me."

" Then why did you come? It is so rash!"

" I know it is; and I have braved all danger, Laurine, to come and plead my cause with you this morning."

" Hush!" said the young girl, holding up her finger as a warning, "don't you know you are never to speak of that till my mother is free; and oh, Belfond, La Catalina will tell you we have reckoned up just half the sum!" and as she spoke, her sweet face brightened as with the joy of a little child.

Belfond shook his head. " It will never do, Laurine; it will take too long to make up that other half, and the promised time will never come for me if you delay our union longer. It's of no use, I can't keep away from you, Laurine; I hover round this village day and night like one crazed. I shall be caught at last, I know. But come, Laurine, pack up your things, put up your money, and come; there is a good priest down yonder who will bind us together directly, without asking any questions, so do come, Laurine! It is such stuff, doing righteous where there is no righteousness recognized. I tell you we shall have a shorter, better way of making your mother free. You and I and La Catalina will pick her up on our way, and we shall be as happy as kings."

Taken by surprise, Laurine opened wide her beautiful eyes, and fixed them on Belfond. "And where shall we live?" she asked,—"not in the trunk of a tree?"

"No, my bright star," said the youth, insinuatingly putting his arm about her, "I have a prettier place for you than the trunk of an old tree. Look out at the back there; do you see that mountain? Its forests look thick, don't they? Yet there, on the top, where no white man's foot has ever trod, I have cleared a space and built you an ajoupa, Laurine, which the Governor's lady might envy." Laurine looked wonderingly in his face, as he continued, "I don't say it is covered with gold or lined with silver, but I think it is prettier. The roof is thatched with the leaves of our own forest palm, the walls and doorway of cocoa-nut basket-work, and the windows are trellised with liana fibres, fine as lace, to keep out the vampires and all ugly flies while you are asleep. Then it has its trees and its garden,—a large spreading tamarind on one side, beneath which you may sit in the evening, and sing to me some of your own pretty songs, and on the other side there is an ancient cotton-tree, quite bare of its natural leaves, but covered all over with those fly-mocking flowers which you are so fond of—it is quite a hanging-garden; then within the lowest fork is a large tuft of the fairy-fringe, with its silvery and silky hairs all tipped with pink, and higher up is the blue-winged blossom which hangs its garlands even to the ground, and hundreds of others that you will rejoice in. Wherever I found a pretty plant, I brought it there to adorn the place for you, from the large changeable rose to the great cactus and the modest little *four-o'clock*, which will tell you the hour of the day."

Laurine stood entranced, and with a smile playing about her open lips, which gave fresh enthusiasm to her lover.

"And for provisions, Laurine, we have such abundance of them! you should just see our fields of maize and purple cassava, hedged all round with bushes of the Angola pea, or wild fences overgrown with the climbing koosh-koosh and sweet potato, and all in bloom already; so that they will be ready for the game I shall bring home from the chase, before another moon comes round: meantime we have stores and stores of plantain and cassava-bread——"

"Who are *we*?" asked the young girl, turning round.

"Oh, did not I tell you? Why, there are about thirty brave fellows like myself, all enemies to slavery, who have settled with their wives up there, and built them green huts all round about yours, so that you shall live among them like a little queen."

"Oh, but," objected Laurine, "those terrible dark woods without any paths: suppose you were to lose yourself some of these days while at the chase, and never come home?"

"Oh, bah! no!—no fear of that! we foresters, we want no beaten track, we make paths for ourselves; we cut notches in the trees as we go, and mark them."

"But suppose you lost your hatchet, Belfond?"

"Well now, Laurine, suppose I did lose my hatchet; there are other signs for us, and he must be a stupid fellow who does not know that the roughest tree shows a smooth side to the south, and shape his course accordingly."

"Oh, but the bush-rangers,—the bush-rangers!" cried Laurine, with a look of alarm.

"The bush-rangers! pah! let them come, we can give them a reception; but they won't come near us —we know how to detect them miles off; trust me for noting where the dried leaves are flattened by the tread; where the festooning liana has been snapped; where the overhanging branches have been roughly handled! Trust me too for hearing sounds at any distance; and when I put my ear to the ground, I can tell, even in the valleys below us, the creaking of a white man's shoe from the treacherous approach of a naked foot. It is only a little pleasant excitement for us. Oh, but a mountain life is a glorious thing! Come, Laurine; now, Laurine, make up your mind to make me happy at once."

La Catalina, who had been roused by the eager words of the young man, had gradually come round to where he was, and stood listening with all her might.

"And you too," continued the young man, looking at her, "you must come now at once, we can't do without you. It is such a busy, merry life up there! What do you suppose the women are doing now? why, gathering up and melting down the fat of an aboma we killed last night: the fat is for lamps, and they have already laid in a good store of wax of the wild bees for candles, so that we shan't want for light; then we have cut down heaps of the beebee-wood for tinder, and oh, such a pile of lianas, for twisting into ropes! Yesterday we felled a royal palm, and the day's work for the women was to ga-ther the sap to ferment for wine, to collect salt from the ashes, to make brooms from the leaves and mat-ting with the bark; and by-and-by, when the vonvon beetle has laid its grubs in the pith, our women will melt them and clarify them for butter. Always some-thing pleasant to do! it is so delicious to do without white people! Say, Laurine, is it not charming? You yourself will be inventing some new plan every day: come, do come, Laurine, my angel, my bird, my star!"

"Indeed, my child," slowly put in La Catalina, "when the fruit is sold, I think we may go; there is one, two, three, four dozens——"

This passing allusion to the shop sent all those fine dreams vanishing into air, and brought Laurine back directly to her senses. She started: "Oh, Belfond! Oh, La Catalina! what a foolish girl I have been! Don't you know, Belfond, what a wicked thing it would be of me to make my mother a runaway?"

"What!" ejaculated the young man with surprise.

"Oh," replied the young girl, "don't think it; I am not finding fault with you,—indeed, indeed not; I daresay you were excusable in leaving your master; you have much to excuse you, I know. You had been in the white man's country, and you couldn't work again like a slave: yes, I understand that; still—"

"Still you think I am wrong?"

"No, I don't say that; at least I don't clearly know; at least my mother is different, and if she ran away to come with us, it would be stealing, you know —a horrible theft!" and in saying this, Laurine spoke from sincere conviction; for, in slave countries, it is not by law only that the fugitive slave is punished, but contempt and horror are everywhere inculcated by the white people against the culprit.

"Yes," continued Laurine, "stealing herself from her master is very wicked; Padre Martino told me so, and everybody says so,—it would be a great disgrace."

The young man threw back his head, and laughed long and loud,—so loud that Laurine, alarmed for his security, significantly imposed silence, and looked out at the door to see that there was no danger in the way; then, with an expression earnest and imploring, she entreated him not to treat the matter with levity, but to have patience a little, till she had earned the price of her mother's freedom fairly and honestly, as the law permitted.

"Well," said the young man, assuming his former

gravity, "I had some misgivings about your scruples, and I have come prepared even for that; saying which, he unfastened the leathern belt which confined his waist, and he drew forth a large blue bag, which he placed jingling on the table: "There!" he exclaimed with an air of triumph.

Laurine looked in his face, not with her wonted simplicity, but with a keen searching eye, that went inquiring into his very soul.

La Catalina leaned her elbows upon the table, and bent over the bag, longing to reckon its contents, while Belfond still grasped the neck tight in his hand, in order to hold it upright for the inspection of both. "There!" he said, looking steadfastly at the bag, to avoid her eye, and pounding it down upon the table with emphasis, "there is enough money to buy twenty mothers; take it—take what you want, and buy your mother now—this day—this very hour—this minute, Laurine, if you don't wish to drive me mad."

Laurine placed her hand gently upon his shoulders, and gazed up intently into his eyes. "Where did you get it, Belfond?" she asked.

"Get it? Ha, ha, ha! get it? If you knew how I got it! so cleverly, Laurine! it was my master's last night—it is mine this morning."

"Only say you did not steal it," she said, her fingers grasping convulsively the arm she had touched.

"Well, what if I did? You know I am a slave," he said bitterly, "no good is expected of me, surely:

what right have I to be honest? I only stole it from the man who would use the strength, the labour, the blood of his eldest child, to turn them to gold for his younger ones,—who would make a cowardly slave of his brown son, creeping and crawling before his fair son. You would not have me treat that man honestly, would you?"

" Belfond, dear Belfond," said Laurine, "it is not for us to judge others, or to be good only when we see others good; and other people's wickedness is no excuse for ours. Dear Belfond, I can't reason like you, but I know those little things, and this is stolen money, dearest, and I could not touch it, it would never prosper. Do take it back, put it where you found it, and let us be honest; be sure God will help us in another way."

The impetuous young man rose up, and, indignant at the suggestion, "What! and are we to lie down like worms, and meanly say 'thank you' for all they rob us of—for what they do to us? Why, child, that money ought to be mine, and mine it shall be, were it only in payment of the long weary years of service I have given him. Why, look you here" (and he drew the maiden to the door), "do you see yonder, on the horizon, where the sun is just peeping from its couch in the sea, leaving behind it a part of its own brightness? Look well, you will see a spot darkening the light,—it may well be dark—it's a slave-ship. It is to meet it, and to bargain in the human cattle it brings, that so many white gentlemen are come down to this quiet place. The slave-trade is forbidden by law, and the creatures it brings are contraband goods; yet what matter? white men can always evade the law, for they protect and shelter one another. Suppose any coloured man were to inform against them, do you think he would be listened to? How would he be treated? Kicked out of the tribunal, I tell you, flogged—perhaps killed. Every one of those poor wretches in that ship has a home in Africa, and little ones many of them have left behind; but they are black, and of course it does not matter. Oh, Laurine, you are not safe,—even you! I know from good sources that the manager of the Palm Grove has been looking over the registry, and is questioning your right to be free, and if once they imagine to deprive you of the blessing of freedom, who can stand against them? What will you do then? Do you know, Laurine, what it is to be a slave? Have you ever thought of all you would be exposed to? Ah! even I, passionately as I worship you now, I should hate you, if once you were a slave. Why should I waste my precious affections upon the slave of another man? Cursed would be the day for you and for me which should see you a slave. See, Laurine," and he threw himself on his knees before her, " by the worship you give at the holy shrine of the Virgin, the protectress of maidens, Laurine, I conjure you keep me from crime, for I cannot answer for myself; don't condemn me any longer to the torture of seeing you, day after day, the standing butt of every

white villain's jests,—I cannot punish their insolence.
Say you will come; say so now," and he drew the
young girl's hand passionately to his breast.

Laurine was weeping; her tears fell one after the
other heavily down,—not indeed for the ills which
her lover foretold to herself, but for the pain her
conscience required her to inflict upon him.

"Belfond, don't ask me to do what is wrong," she
sobbed; "I could not make a runaway of my mother; I could not use stolen money. God bless you,
Belfond! The Holy Virgin protect us! but let us be
honest."

He did not wait to hear more, but, dashing away
the hand he was holding, he rose quickly and proudly
to his feet, and as he seized his rejected present, his
lips all blue and quivering with suppressed passion,—
"That is not it, Laurine," he said, with a sarcastic,
demoniac expression of his mouth, "but you love the
white people,—you love to sell to them—you love to
listen to their insulting jests—you prefer them to
me, a poor hunted slave; farewell!" and ere the last
word was uttered, he was already in the street.

La Catalina, in surprise, hurried to the door to
look after him; she could not understand what was
the matter all so suddenly; and Laurine flew to her
room, where, throwing herself on her little tressel-
bed, she gave way to an agony of tears. This was
the first quarrel she had ever had with her lover,
and it was a serious one; not that his late robbery
had at all altered her opinion; she had long known

him to be, though scrupulously honest towards his own race, yet somewhat lax in his ideas of right and wrong towards the white people. But, like many a nobler damsel, his errors only attached her the more to him, and she fondly hoped that by her sole influence she might yet lead him back to what was right. "No matter," she said, as she endeavoured to comfort herself, "he will think better of all this by-and-by, and love me all the more for it. He is so hot! but when the fit is over, he will reflect upon it, and in his own good heart I shall find love greater than ever."

CHAPTER III.

LAURINE.

A WORD concerning this interesting girl. The picture is not overdrawn : to that quick sensibility and warmth of feeling which is common with those of her caste, she added a strong attachment to duty, or principle, such as she understood it to be. She was strictly just in all her dealings, and while her pleasant manner attracted customers from every quarter, she was never known to charge unfairly to either white or black.

It may be asked how it happened that the child of a poor slave had found money enough to set up a shop; or, further, as the children of slaves always follow the fortune of their mothers, how it happened that she was free. Something of her history will explain all this.

She was born on the Palm Grove estate,—not when it belonged to Mr. Cardon, for his possession was comparatively recent, but in the time of its first owner, Mr. Perrin. There were a great many children of caste born on this estate much about the same time, and, as they all bore a great resemblance to one another, scandal assigned them to one and the same father, even to the master himself; but as this has little to do with the tale in question, we shall pass it over, and proceed. Among all these children Laurine was considered to be the prettiest and the most engaging, and therefore was she chosen to play with and attend upon her mistress's only child, a sweet little girl of four or five years old. From Laurine's earliest childhood the characteristic feature of her disposition was that of devotion. Long before she knew what piety was, she reverenced authority in every form, and her heart was filled with affection for those who ministered to her kindly. Nothing could exceed her love for the little girl whom she was taught to call her mistress : she anticipated every wish the child could form, dispelled every gloom, made peace where there was crossness, and created interest out of the very spirit of dulness. Of course the little child became used to her, as they say; and when at a subsequent period it was decided to sell off the children that had been grown (for Mr. Perrin made a great deal of money by raising human crops), and Laurine was put down among the number to be sent away, little Eleanor Perrin filled the house with such loud and continued lamentations that her father was forced, for the sake of peace, to make the little slave an exception, and keep her as perpetual playfellow to his white child. This was not lost on Laurine, and her

affection to her little mistress became greater than
ever.   Some time after, little Eleanor took ill of one
of those terrible disorders common in the tropics; and
now was Laurine's devotion appreciated.   She attended upon her night and day—knew no fatigue of
body or mind—was at the pillow at the slightest
movement—made the room cheerful and pleasant as
it was quiet and orderly, and if she ever left it for a
moment it was only when her mistress watched the
patient's sleep, and then she brought in the prettiest
bouquets the garden could afford.   But all the care in
the world could not avail; the doctors were forced to
acknowledge the uselessness of medicine, and the
little life, which had so often given joy to the household, was now seen to ebb slowly and gradually away.
In one of those lucid intervals which immediately
precede death, little Eleanor fixed her eyes steadily
upon her young slave.   She did not thank her, she
did not express affection, for she was never taught to
think that either the one or the other was to be felt,
but simply whispered a wish that Laurine should be
freed.   The little slave of course did not expect that
this desire would be complied with, and when her
dear little lady was gone, whom she was accustomed
to care for and to love, she mourned for her alone,—
not for remaining still a slave, for she never dreamed
that it could be otherwise.   By-and-by her master
died also, and Laurine was left alone with her mistress; but the latter had never completely recovered
her little girl's death, and after the last misfortune

she took to her bed, from which she never got up again. One day she called the young girl to her: "Laurine," said she, "I am going to my long home, and I wish to say a word to you. You have been faithful to me and to my child who is gone before me, and I could not meet her in the other world unless I had complied with her dying wish; for this reason I have left you free in my will. I don't know whether it is for your good,—I am afraid not, for no one will take care of you like a mistress; but as you have been a faithful slave, so I hope you will be a faithful freedwoman; and may God bless you! Pray for me fervently when I am gone."

The will was perfectly good, though if it had been otherwise, the heirs of the estate being people living in Europe, it was the interest of no one near to contest it, and so Laurine received the announcement of her freedom. She was thirteen when this happened. She had lost a kind mistress and a home, but she had gained that which gave her new life, new spirit, new thoughts, new powers, and self-respect. She felt like a bird escaped from a cage, not knowing what to do with herself, but bewildered with the joy. The world was all before her, with its strange vastness, with its toils and its dangers, its troubles and trials; but of these she knew little and cared less, she only felt to breathe more freely, and she knew she had none to obey, none to fear, none to flatter; and in her wayward fancy the first use she made of her liberty was to go off early in the morning to the woods, where she remained the whole day gathering flowers, picking berries, and watching the birds.   As she often said afterwards, it was the happiest time of her life, and she would probably have settled down into an idle stroller, but that her warm, loving heart stimulated her to exertion.

This is how it happened.   As soon as her mistress was dead and the will made known, the estate was put up for sale by order of the heirs in Europe, and Mr. Cardon became the purchaser.   Laurine was immediately turned off the estate by the manager, in company with a few more encumbrances, in particular an old man of the Koromantyn nation, of whom we shall afterwards speak.   Not that the young girl cared for being sent off: the forest abounded in fruit, of which she was fond; and for shelter she would contrive to steal into her mother's hut at night, when the white people had all retired to rest; and she cared for nothing else.   But Laurine's heart had been accustomed to hold an object of love, her thoughts to own a point of concentration, and the void she now felt in both became painful to her.   She had never inquired for her father,—no child of caste ever does, for, beyond the lighter complexion, which secretly but surely involves the grafting of European intellect on the warm strong feelings of Africa, it never is of any consequence from whom the Mulatto springs; and although such a slave points disgrace on the unnatural master who first sold him, and his unfeeling accomplice the master who holds him, yet no observation is ever made either by white man or black, for custom has sanctioned the sin. Laurine therefore never knew who was her father, nor ever asked; but of her mother she did think: she remembered the passionate love her mistress had borne for the child who was gone, and she longed to become, even she, the object of as much solicitude and affection. Now the Negro women are either passionately fond of their children, or they are hopelessly indifferent to them, and it was to the latter class that Laurine's mother belonged: she only looked coldly and vacantly upon the little girl as she came in and out, and admitted her to her cabin only as she admitted the cat, without care or notice, not even so much as to ask whether the child was hungry, or where she had been during the day. The slave had fallen to the condition of a brute; her maternal instinct, if indeed such had ever existed with her, had vanished with the calls of the infant, and she had come to look upon her offspring as an alien with whom she had nothing to do.

Thus Laurine, as yet a mere child, found herself all at once without a creature to belong to, to care for, or to love; all her little romance of affection had fled. Never did she look up to the white people with such admiration and respect; never did she consider the African race with such a sense of their low caste and hopeless inferiority. "If I was a white child," she would say to herself, "I should be loved, my mother would care for me; but then she is a Negro, and I am a desolate wretch," and with these reflections she often sobbed herself to sleep on the dry cocoa-nut leaves which she dragged in every night for a couch. But observing her mother more closely, she soon discovered that the Negro slave stood in more need of her child's aid, than the child of her mother's. Madelaine was one of those individuals in whom slavery had annihilated all power of thought, care, will, even self-preservation; she was by no means a rare instance, there were many like her even on the estate to which she belonged, and the late master had been obliged to think and act for these living automatons on the most trivial affairs. Listen to this all ye who advocate despotism! Listen to this, ye who argue the care of physical wants as that of supreme happiness, and see one of the effects of your system! He had to dole out their weekly rations meal by meal as to infants,—to attend to the daily covering of their bodies,—to watch over their cleanliness, and even to examine their persons, lest there should be some hidden sore, by which they would lazily allow themselves to be eaten up. Indeed every phase of slavery points a lesson to the wise of all people; and there are other nations besides the Negroes, who, if they but look, will see as in a mirror occasional reflections of their own condition. Madelaine, as a slave, knew nothing of sorrow; Laurine, free, became thoughtful and sad, and, though yet but a child, care sat heavily on her brow.

The estate being now transferred to Mr. Cardon, he placed Don Duro upon it as manager, and in the

beginning, and before he came to know the peculiarities of each individual, he dealt out their weekly
rations to each, *i. e.* two pounds of salt-fish and two
measures of cassava or tapioca; and in naming this, it
is as well we should be particular in explaining that
each Negro had, besides this, a patch of ground, and
one day in the week to cultivate it for himself.

One Monday evening, when Madelaine had received
her portion at the muster-roll, and Laurine had stolen
in as usual, the mother was eating the customary
salt-fish quite raw, for she was too inert to set her
pot boiling, or even to hold the cassava-flour which
accompanied it, without spilling the most of it on the
ground. Poor Laurine was hungry, and she watched
with eager eyes the wasted food, for she had been less
fortunate that day in gathering wild fruit; but little
did Madelaine care, and she saw her child stooping
to pick up the rejected food with the indifference of
a brute; and, in truth, Laurine was not long in discovering that her mother's was a hopeless case. Returning the next evening, she found her without anything to eat; she seemed indeed as if too lazy even
to feel hunger, for, after picking up a few mangoes
from under a tree, she lay down on her bed and shut
her eyes to sleep. Laurine approached the bed:
"Mother," she said, "have you had any dinner?"
"Let me 'lone," was the cross reply. Laurine guessed
she had not, so begging some plaintains from a
neighbouring hut, she put them on the fire, and in
a little time she was able to produce some sort of a

meal, which Madelaine took without offering a remark; and after having satisfied her appetite, she sat
at the door of her hut to watch and laugh at any one
who should happen to pass. Every day was a repetition of the last, till the next Monday, when rations
were again given out, the same wastefulness was productive of the same want, and was met with the same
apathy on the part of the brutified slave. At last
Laurine began to wish for some other means of pro-
curing food besides begging from the neighbours or
wandering in the woods; she bethought herself of
cultivating the little patch of ground which the custom of the Colonies had assigned to her mother, and
though she worked mostly by moonlight, the neglected
weed-covered ground soon became rich, and she was
able to accompany the Negroes to the town market
on Sundays, where it was usual for them to sell the
produce of their gardens. The profits were so ample
that she felt encouraged to continue, and, confiding
the care of her mother to one of the slaves of the
estate, she often took an odd turn in town, where she
heard of work to do. In one of these journeys she
was fortunate enough to meet with a pious, aged
spinster, who took kindly to the little girl, and set
her up with a small tray of needles and thread, etc.,
to sell; then she was pleased with her industry, and
gradually helped her not only to support herself and
mother, but to lay something by too.

It was not all at once that Laurine conceived the
idea of earning the freedom of her mother,—that idea

suggested itself gradually. By a merciful dispensation of Providence, it is so ordained that the object we help becomes dear to us, and the more trouble we take, so also the greater love do we bestow. Laurine felt this; her automaton mother became dear to her exactly in proportion to her helplessness; she longed to be with her or to have a home for her. Then came confidential conversations with La Catalina, who informed her the law would protect her in the purchase of her mother's freedom if she could produce the legal amount, that is, five hundred piastres; and then followed an enthusiastic desire to obtain the boon, which for three years Laurine never once lost sight of. Such is her simple story, and such the motive of her persevering industry; and it was not mere labour she gave, it was the daily, hourly sacrifice of her own youthful, sociable inclinations, unpretendingly, unostentatiously, and almost unconsciously offered up on the shrine of filial affection.

CHAPTER IV.

DISCOMFITURE.

WE left Laurine preparing for the business of the day. She had no sooner made herself ready than customers began rapidly to drop in, and in a few moments the little shop was crowded.

"Laurine, pearl of Sant' Iago, bring here a cup of mawbee for a poor slave."

"Laurine, my humming-bird, some coffee for an old countryman."

"O Laurine, you help the sun to make the day bright; come, bless a friend with a look, and refresh him with a frothing cup of chocolate."

These requests, gallantly worded in Negro patois, soon however gave place to ruder and more peremptory commands, and the Negroes and coloured people, who are never permitted to eat or be seated in the presence of the higher race, fell back respectfully on the approach of their "superiors." Orders came in with such unusual rapidity, that Laurine, already agitated by the occurrences of the morning, now became almost distracted.

"La Catalina," she said, whispering anxiously to her companion, "I don't know what I am doing; pray come and help me. Santa Maria! there's Mr. Cardon and the Englishman and the manager, all coming in: may the Virgin help me! I am trembling all over."

La Catalina, always thoughtful and composed, readily left her department,—that of receiving the money and giving change,—to help her young friend, and, while the latter retired to her room to recover herself, came forward to serve the customers. The three gentlemen who had excited the alarm of Laurine now entered. The eldest was a tall, portly, handsome man, in the prime of life; the resolute expression of his eye, his imperious manner, and the overpowering loudness and volubility with which he spoke, indicated an arbitrary, irascible, and determined character. One of his companions, to judge from the freshness of his complexion, was a recent importation to the island; he was much younger, and appeared to be a man of unassuming and benevolent disposition. The other was of small stature, had a swarthy, Spanish face, and his manner showed what in Europe would be called utter ignorance of his place. The tallest gentleman entered first.

"Well, La Catalina, how do you do?"

The dame curtseyed.

"Where's Laurine?"

" She is busy inside, if you please, master, she can't
come just yet."

The gentleman fired up. " What! you old baboon," he exclaimed, " do you think I shall be waited
upon by you? Get back to your corner, and make
way for the young one: I'll make her busy with me
if she doesn't come quick. *Pardi!* I am not going
to have your wrinkled hands serving out coffee to me;
just go and fetch her here at once, and make her
bring me three cups of coffee all hot and frothing, do
you hear?"

Poor Laurine was nervous enough already; but
when she heard herself so roughly called for by the
man whom above all others she disliked, she began
to weep; though it was not so much the planter's
overbearing manner, as the contemptuous familiarity with which he treated every coloured woman he
approached, that caused our gentle maiden of Sant'
Iago to tremble.

St. Hilaire Cardon sat down by one of the small
tables in the shop, and, waiting till his commands
were obeyed, commenced drumming upon it as if his
thoughts were busy and impatient. Don Duro, in
the absence of anything better to do, threw himself
into a chair, and with perfect *nonchalance* stretched
out his legs like the open blades of a pair of scissors,
and, with his head resting on the back of his chair,
seemed to be making an attentive survey of the
thatch. The European was the only one of the party
who remained standing : he did so from choice, for

there was an ample number of chairs and stools, but that position was more convenient for observing what was passing around him. "Strange!" thought he, as he looked at the Spaniard, "what odd customs prevail in these colonies, where a mere underling, a low ignorant servant like this, is allowed to sit down on equal terms with his master!"

"Dorset," said Mr. Cardon, suddenly stopping the movement of his fingers, "shall you buy any slaves this morning?"

"No," replied the other, "for, to say the truth, I cannot afford it. I have consented to go on board partly to gratify my curiosity, and partly because you say I may be of service to you in pointing out unhealthy subjects. But I assure you I am diffident of my own judgment: familiar as I may be with European forms of disease, the state of things here is new to me. I am afraid I shall only expose my ignorance."

"Bah!" said the other, "you know quite enough for me,—quite enough for the Colony: it is my belief the doctors who come out to practise were all of them only apothecary boys in England,—nothing else, *parole d'honneur!* Why, you are a treasure of learning here! Ask Doctor Pillstuff what his own name is in Latin, ha, ha!—and as to cures, what, as you say, can European doctors know of tropical diseases? the Indian women know more. Not that I would discourage you, not at all: I know you are a man of honour, and that is something in my eyes; it gives me confidence in what you say. I wish you would come and live on my estate, the Palm Grove, as a regularly engaged physician : I want you to find out the cause of a certain mortality among my Negroes."

" Not on the Palm Grove, my good Sir ; I could not live away from my own place ; but as my little property is next to yours, I can visit it every day if you like."

" Well, that will do : I forgot you lived so near : but you must do your best to find out what is the matter. I will give you the regular salary. *Sacre Dieu !*" and the planter frowned and clinched his teeth, " I have had more losses this year than I can bear to think of : six Negroes died last week, and four the week previous ; no man can stand this," and the angry planter rose, and in a fit of impatience kicked his chair to the other side of the shop ; then stopping short, " Laurine," he called, " when are you coming with the coffee ? do you want me to come after you ? I will, if you don't make haste," he added, winking at the manager ; then suddenly turning to another subject, " Dorset, so you won't buy any Negroes today because you have no money ? It was my intention to offer you a loan, for it is a good cargo and the Negroes will go cheap ; but, *parbleu !* what do you think of this ? I have not a dollar with me ; I was actually obliged to borrow change from Don Duro here ! I'll tell you what happened to me last night : all the money I took with me yesterday from town to pay Captain Hill cash down, all has disappeared ! Some devil's dog got in while we were asleep, and carried it off, bag, box, and all! I'll find out the fellow; I have sent the Alguazils after him already."

"Señor," put in the manager in the midst of a yawn, "perhaps Quaco is the thief: wouldn't it be well to flog him till he owns it?"

"I have flogged him already this morning; not that I think it was he, the black monkey—he cares no more for money than I care for his rags—but all Negroes know one another's tricks, and I would have flogged him till he told me something, only I wanted him with me this morning, and I couldn't afford to make him lame."

"It would be hardly fair to flog him 'on a mere suspicion," observed the stranger.

"I only wish I could find out the real thief," continued the planter in the same strain, "I declare I think I should kill him."

Mr. Dorset met the assertion with an incredulous smile, which the other observed.

"I would, I tell you. How dare any Negro steal into my room at night and touch my money, putting me to all this inconvenience! *Sacre!* let me only catch him today, and we shall have a pickled Negro to show you tomorrow."

La Catalina here interrupted the conversation by bringing in the so oft-demanded refreshment; as she held it out however the cup happened to slip, the coffee poured in a stream upon the floor, and the china following after broke into a hundred pieces. A volley of curses burst from the lips of the angry

F

planter, sufficient to have annihilated the premises had he been gifted with but half the powers supposed to have belonged to the enchanters of old.

In the midst of this scene a fine tall young Negro entered, whose black and shining face wore a good-natured, light-hearted expression.

" Ship come, Mas'r," he said.

" There, see how late I shall be ! Curse the jade for spilling the coffee ! can't you leave your smashes where they are, and go and fetch me some more, instead of standing there blubbering ? And what are you meddling for, you black devil ?" added he as he bestowed a violent kick on the lad, who was stretched upon the ground helping the dame to pick up her broken crockery. " What's the ugly racoon doing ? get up, Sirrah ! run and get the boat ready, if you don't want me to break a chair on your back."

" Es, Mas'r," said the lad, as he stood up with gestures indicative of pain, and rubbing the part assaulted ; " whis boat, Mas'r ?"

" The canoe, you dog, for us ; and get the droguer to bring the new Negroes back ; and when you have got all ready, wait on the beach till I come. Off with you, Sirrah !"

Quaco did not wait for a repetition of the order, but was out of sight in an instant. His suspicious master went to the door to look after him, and at the same time made a telescope of his hand to survey some more distant object. " *Vive Dieu !*" he exclaimed, almost dancing with impatience, " there is the ship coming in as fast as she can, and it will be impossible for me to get there in time for the first picking. That brown monkey knows I am in a hurry, and she does not come! I will teach her to make sport of me."

Whatever may have been the destructive intentions of the planter, they were all forgotten on the entrance of Laurine herself, the sight of whose pretty face and three large cups of coffee on a tray at once dispelled his ill-humour.

"Ha!" he exclaimed, advancing towards her as she placed the cups on the table, "you like to make yourself longed for,—eh, my pretty louis d'or?"

Laurine's hands trembled as he spoke to her,—so much so indeed as to attract the notice of the manager, who, inane as he was, had sufficient quickness of observation where his passions were concerned.

"Mulatto girl," he said, leering at her, "do you know anything of Mr. Cardon's money that was stolen from him last night?"

"I, Sir!" exclaimed she, starting.

"Come, come now," said the planter, reproving the accuser, "she is too good a girl to be bothered. Now don't look so frightened! I will come back by-and-by, and you shall tell me all about it," and with a knowing wink he chucked her familiarly under the chin.

Laurine drew back in terror, and for very shame her eyes wandered to the crowd which had gathered before the door, where, to her great alarm, she saw

Belfond, his eyes fixed sadly and reproachfully upon
her.   A faint cry rose to her lips, but she recollected
herself in time; and Mr. Cardon, who had swallowed
his coffee almost scalding hot, now paid his money,
and with Gallic vivacity called to his companion to
accompany him.

Fortunately for Laurine the haste of the gentlemen prevented any further remarks, and in a few
moments they all left the shop. · She then hurried
to the door, and, straining her eyes, narrowly scru-
tinized every group at every turn and corner, and
where people stood at doors or at ground-floor windows; and then her anxious gaze followed the three
gentlemen, but nothing could she see of her lover,
and, the throng of loungers growing more dense as it
bore towards the beach, all further chance of seeing
him was rendered hopeless.   The crowd increased
each moment, and continually grew more animated
and varied.   There were half-naked Caribs, listlessly
dragging forward their feet and gazing at some distant object, they knew not what; Negro-women with
trays on their heads, pointing to the sea and uttering
exclamations in tones of excitement and wonder;
swarthy freedmen, hurrying on their carts, anxious
to be employed in the expected disembarkation; and
groups of Negroes, sluggishly moving among the
boats, awaiting the commands of their masters, who
strutted amidst the throng, conspicuous with their
neat and snow-white clothing.   From these the eye
passed to the bay, where, upon a calm and crystal

sea, the great object of the day's business, the long-expected slave smuggler, with her black and pointed hull, swelled on the view, and, with her white sails spread before the wind, glided swiftly into port. Craft of all kinds,——canoes, droguers, rafts, luggers,——now pushed out from every point; and the animated scene of the beach was transferred with almost magical rapidity to the bosom of the sea.

CHAPTER V.

A RASH MOVE.

As soon as the beach was deserted by the white men, Belfond, who had secreted himself behind some cottages, now emerged from his hiding-place and slowly walked to the shore. His heart was heavy, and he felt ready to do anything that would cause Laurine to repent of her refusal. In the ardour of his passion he had formed romantic schêmes for the future, without ever dreaming of the difficulties in the way of their realization; now that his plans had failed, he felt disgusted with himself and even with life. Overwhelmed with disappointment, he wandered unconsciously to a distant part of the beach, which was wild and overgrown with brushwood; he walked with hurried and uncertain steps, and at times would stop suddenly and fix his eyes upon the sea, although in reality he saw not its billowy surface, but only the troubled visions of his own mind. By-and-by he came to a little bay formed by a graceful curve in the shore, ending in a headland beyond. It was a lovely spot, where the palm-tops waved above scented shrubs of mimosa, and where the crimson flower of the wild shacshac and the broad disc of the prickly pear reflected their tints and forms in a clear rivulet, which, after meandering through the depths of the forest, as if formed solely to give life and coolness to its beautiful shades, here flowed calmly into the sea. Belfond paused in spite of his agitation, his features relaxed from their stern expression; for here he had often walked with Laurine at sunset, when the golden streaks of light shot along the stream; there, beneath yon bamboo, where its tall plumes waved over the path, they had often watched the shadows of the leaves moving on the moonlit ground, and listened to the music of the wind as it sang its eolian notes amidst the hollow canes; and beyond was the wood where he had first beheld her and loved her as she was carolling blithely to the flowers she gathered. All these things rose to his mind, and the world and its hopes appeared vain and futile as a dream.

These reflections however were interrupted by the appearance of a canoe at a short distance from the shore, directing its course to the spot where he stood. Although it was single-handed, he would at any other time have prudently kept out of sight till he knew whether it contained a friend or a foe; but now, careless of himself, he stood in absent mood, fixedly awaiting its approach. Its occupant proved to be his

friend Quaco, the same Negro lad who came to Mr.
Cardon in Laurine's shop.

"How d'ye, countryman?" said the boatman as he
rowed his skiff to land; for Belfond's mother having
been a Koromantyn, he was often claimed as kin by
the Negroes of that nation. "You no 'fraid they
catch you?" asked the lad solicitously.

"Me!" said the Mulatto, "I don't care for anything."

The Negro youth opened his eyes; "Eh, me Gad,
oh!" he exclaimed, and, resorting to the proverbs with
which Negro converse abounds, asked, "You Belfond
not know *snake that would live has no business upon
road*, eh?"

"I shan't stay here long, Quaco; I shall be off to
Guiria this evening and for ever: I shan't come back
again."

"Eh hey!" exclaimed Quaco in great surprise;
"and Laurine?"

"Oh, she won't care, we have parted for good;"
then, as if to drive away the subject, he hurriedly
stated that he hoped to enlist in the Bolivian army,
where a coloured man had some chance of distinguish-
ing himself. "You know," he said, "General Paez is
of caste blood himself, and so are many of the officers
under him. I have a taste that way, Quaco, and I
ought to be brave, coming of Koromantyn blood."

Quaco leaned upon his oar and fell into a deep
reverie,—a very unusual thing with him, for he was

generally communicative and full of animation; but the truth was, that a chord of the young Negro's heart had been touched by the remarks of his friend. Negro and slave as he was, he had long gazed upon Laurine with feelings of admiration almost amounting to worship. She moved before him like a very goddess, whose lustre held him entranced. He never dreamed however of approaching her; for, besides the distance which caste prejudice placed between the coloured girl and himself,—a prejudice almost as strong as that of the white people against the coloured,—he knew that Laurine's affections had been sought and won by another. He had so trained his feelings that they had settled into a quiet worship of Laurine, without admixture of any wish or thought of a selfish nature. As he could never hope to obtain her for himself, his generous heart found gratification in friendship with the object of her love : hence an intimacy had sprung up between the two youths,—an intimacy however which met with no obstacle in their difference of colour, for unlike other young men of his class, who aped the supercilious airs displayed by their masters towards the Negroes, Belfond prided himself on never entertaining a prejudice which he so bitterly condemned in the white people.

As a pebble cast into a tranquil stream will throw into a mazy confusion the forms of the objects reflected from its bosom, so did the observations of Belfond disturb the thoughts of the Negro lad, and

send them oscillating without rest or shape. He would
have been more than human if there had not arisen
in his mind some faint hope for himself, some half-
formed inquiry "who knows?" and if some little
castle in the air, ill-defined perhaps, yet brightly
coloured, had not presented itself. He leaped out of
the canoe, and eagerly offered his services, although
well aware that a flogging would be the penalty for
his neglect of his master's business. "Hey!" said
he, "neber mind droguer now; me bring it by-
and-by. Hey, go 'way! me sabey very well what
for do."

Quaco was a remarkably good-natured fellow, and
always very ready to help a friend, but just now he felt
more than usually disposed to do so, and even went
so far as to offer to Belfond the use of the canoe.
"Master go to Palm Grove today," he said, "what
he want with canoe, eh? he neber know nothing
't all 'bout he: go 'way! let me 'lone for do all ting."

Belfond felt no scruple in accepting the offer, and
it was arranged between them that the canoe should
be left on that part of the beach as if through forget-
fulness, and that Belfond should wait till the evening,
when he would be ready to make use of it.

"And when is our master likely to set out for
the Palm Grove?" asked Belfond. "Do you think
he is likely to buy many slaves today? for if he does
so, it will keep him there some time. Have you
overheard him say anything about it?"

"Ya, no!" was the answer; "no have no money

this morning, ya hey! Master came down here so big! think to buy half that cargo—maybe all; so he bring down plenty money. But hey! last night one thief come in middle night, fine cleber thief, know too much, and took all. So master get up in the morning—box empty! Ya, ya, yah! go 'way! Then master say, Where's money, you all black debils? then talked too much, calls Quaco, flogs Quaco, and promises more flog every day till him find thief. Poor Negro broad back! *Bird always says worm be thief.*"

Belfond bit his lip: the tide of good emotions which had left his heart now rushed back to their wonted place; and what a sense of right could not effect, even when appealed to by the lips of the loved one, sympathy for the troubles of a fellow-slave obtained.

" Quaco, I was the thief, you shall not suffer for my sins; my last act towards a faithful friend shall not be a bad turn: you shall take back the money before our master returns from the ship."

Quaco looked astonished: " What that? hey!" ejaculated he with that accented expression of surprise, and with those peculiar exclamations which the true African always uses: " yah! how you get in, eh?"

" I'll tell you, if you wish to know. From the news that you obtained by listening at our master's door, I guessed he must have brought money with him. I was determined to have it—no matter now for what use,—so last night, when they were all taking a walk by moonlight, I crept into the house, put the sleeping herb into every body's pillowcase, and then got under the bed. By-and-by they all came home. I saw master, where he put his keys and his box, for he looked at his money before he lay down, and in the dead of the night I took it all: no one heard me,—*sleep has no ears*, you know."

" Ya, ya, yah!" laughed Quaco till his eyes ran tears of joy and admiration; "that's the way! *grand talk not wise talk,* and master's tongue big too much : *fool lets dog eat his breakfast.* Buckra not always a sabey man,—ya, ya, yah !"

" Quaco," said the Mulatto, interrupting him, "don't let us stop to laugh now : come with me down yonder, where I dropped the bag into the hollow of a mimosa-tree : come and help me take it out, and you shall put it on his bed or his table, or anywhere so that he may be sure to find it; and if he says anything about it, you can say, ' Master must have forgotten where he put it :' you shan't be flogged for me again, my poor Quaco."

" Hey, hey ! what that ? put back Buckra's money ? hey cho, go 'way ! *when fowls have teeth,* do you hear ? You think me care for flog,—me Koromantyn ? flog good for Koromantyn skin,—make me feel brave, for no care at all : Quaco back hard too much, go 'way! Come, countryman, don't be a fool now : if you go in a boat to Guiria, you'll want money ; but if you want to throw away money, hearee to Quaco.

See slave ship there? poor niggers there plenty: one of them a poor nigger girl: them tell me from ship's side, she Koromantyn king's child. Well, poor ting, —pretty black shining girl, white teeth,—poor ting neber know worrok. Well now, you Belfond take that money, send somebody for buy her, so make her free."

"Are there any coloured people there?"

"No much; some rich Mulattoes from Port Spain."

"Any that I know?"

"No sabey: wait here till I go see."

"No, I think I'll go and see myself."

"He! he!" again exclaimed Quaco, staring with surprise.

"Quaco, I feel today as if I did not care for anybody, white man or devil, and by the God of thunder I feel as if I could fight them both. I'll wager all the money that remains in the mimosa-tree, that I'll go to the vessel and leave it safe and sound and free as I am now."

Quaco grinned and giggled, but offered no opposition. He was a profound admirer of courage, and the nearer it approached to rashness, the more homage did he pay to its possessor. Now boldness was a trait in Belfond's character which had especially won his regard, and for this too did he love to claim him as countryman, for the Koromantyns are proverbially brave. There was besides a lurking idea in his mind, that if Belfond bought the pretty slave he might carry her off with him to Guiria (the Spanish mainland), and of course leave the field open to him, that he might try to gain Laurine for himself; but this, we ought to say, was but a faint and floating vision, which had assumed no shape in his mind : he said however to himself, " Quaco loves, and loves, and loves, till love comes again, for doesn't sun shine, and shine, and shine, till earth shines again ? But oh !" he added, recollecting himself, " sun never touches earth, he only touches sky : so hey ! Quaco fool too much," and he quickly dismissed the thought. However, he accepted the wager.

The two young men now went earnestly to work. The droguer, for which Quaco was sent back, was got ready, the boatmen called to row it, and the commands of their master duly and properly delivered to them; nothing remained but to settle their own little private affairs respecting the canoe and the money. The latter was not all taken out : about as many doubloons as would suffice for the purchase of one slave were abstracted from the blue bag, and its remaining contents emptied into the hollow of the tree; the sum required was then put into the bag : this Belfond strapped round his waist with the belt which confined his knife, and concealed it with the folds of his cotton garment, for he wore no jacket or waistcoat. The rest of the money they left to chance for the present. " No one will think of looking into the hole of a mimosa-tree for money," said they; " and if any one should, and it is a Negro, we shan't grudge it."

The two boats now set off,—the heavy droguer to fetch back such slaves as should be purchased from the ship, the canoe to bring back the white gentlemen; and into the latter Belfond leaped, caring, as he declared, for not a thing or person upon earth.

In reality he had not much to fear. His master had not seen him for years, not since he had left him in France as valet to his son, who was then passing through the French University, and from whom the coloured youth had subsequently absconded, after picking up by stealth sufficient knowledge to render him for ever disgusted with slavery. Captain Hill, the master of the slave-ship, might, it is true, have recognized him, for it was he who caught him in the streets of Marseilles and brought him back to the Colonies; but he would be too much engaged that morning to think of other matters than the disposal of his goods; the young man also trusted much to his own altered appearance, to favour the chances of his safety.

"The only man I should have reason to fear," said Belfond, "is Higgins, the mate, if he is there still. The villain! I owe him a long account for the agonies he made me endure in the hold, and I suppose he owes me a grudge for my getting away so cleverly when he got drunk, and the Captain had left the ship to him, and they just in port—ha! ha! Well, we don't love one another."

"Hey!" said Quaco, "me knows that man. Hoh! last time he come to Port Spain, hoh! bad, bad too much!" and here, as if the lad was afraid even the waves should catch the import of his secret, he whispered something into Belfond's ear with a look of affright, and then touched a little amulet he wore about his neck, and muttered a prayer, which, as he had been taught by his mother, would preserve him from the power of the Obiah (the African witchcraft).

"You don't mean to say he brings it to Fanty?"

Quaco nodded, and put his finger to his mouth to enjoin silence.

The coloured youth shook his head in silent astonishment; "Is there a God?" he said, curling his lips, as he went on pulling the oars; "ay, is there a God? that's the question;—to see a white man bringing Obiah stuff from the African coast and selling it for money to a runaway Obiah priest, who uses it to destroy white men! nothing but wickedness and confusion!"

"Hush! hush! hush!" said Quaco earnestly.

"Oh, I am desperate, Quaco! I don't care for anything. But never mind now, my dear fellow; here we are approaching the ship. I see they are very busy: plenty of customers! how crowded they are! Near quickly under the vessel, or they will be looking at me. That's it: now for it!"

CHAPTER VI.

THE SLAVE MARKET.——A RENCONTRE.

IN spite of the crowd on board, which obstructed the view from below, it was easy to perceive in what part of the vessel the sale was going on, from the direction in which the people were looking, and also from a signal on the forecastle. The signal was not a flag, nor yet a written notice, but simply a Negro raised somewhat above the surrounding multitude; a female it was too, made to stand on a hogshead against the foremast, to which she was chained. Poor creature! she was the flower of the whole cargo, the healthiest and most comely, and was put in this conspicuous place, not only as a favourable specimen of the commodities offered for sale, but also that she might fetch a high price on account of her appearance; and truly her rounded yet delicate proportions might have served as a model for the finest sculpture, and were not the less striking for being set off by a skin black as ebony and shining as polished marble. Her dress

G

was completely African, if that could be called a dress which consisted only of a strip of dark blue cotton folded round her person, then passed above her left shoulder, to be knotted in front at the waist, and thence falling down as a skirt. A single string of red beads confined the close curled hair which covered her small and well-turned head; beads of the same colour also adorned her neck, arms, and ankles: these were her only ornaments. She looked picturesque, standing there in her gay and primitive costume, her head leaning gently against the mast, which she held embracing for support, her eyes closed, and her full but well-formed lips slightly parted, the effect of faintness and exhaustion. Her companions in misfortune were none of them shackled as she was, but all had the same blue cotton scarfs twisted round their loins; the women decorated with beads of showy colours, and the men with their hair cut out in various shapes, as circles, squares, triangles, and crescents. With all these adornments however, the slaves presented a spectacle which, to say the least, was pitiable and disgusting: the horrors of the middle passage, the effects of scarce and unwholesome diet, and diseases engendered by a crowded hold, were all too evident. The best of them were thin as spectres; some were covered with loathsome ulcers and marks of deformity, the consequence of long-continued crippled postures; and all were calculated rather to appal the beholder than to induce the most unwary to venture a speculation on their miserable lives. They had been hastily arranged in lots, according to the value set upon them by the Captain, but, from not clearly understanding his wishes, or perhaps from other motives, many had strayed from the places assigned to them. The Mandingos, Foulahs, and Mozambiques, known by their more regular features, stood obediently enough in front. The effeminate race of Loango, distinguished by certain raised figures in the form of dice all over their bodies, and by their long pointed teeth, which appeared at every motion of their lips, reclined listlessly on the boards. The stupid-looking Eboes, Quaquas, and Mokos crouched despondingly behind the coops and lumber; while the Koroman-tyns, with tattooed cheeks and fearless brow, looked on in dogged silence, as the multitudes continued to gather on the deck.

Meantime the confusion around them was great, and the noise increased. Voices of every pitch, from the hoarse bass of the rude Corsican, passing through the various tones of Englishmen, Germans, French, Spaniards, Italians, and Danes, to the whining drawl of the Creole, were all trilling, twittering, chattering, and sputtering their several claims to the attention of the Captain, who on his part was busy enough with giving commands to the men and treating with his customers.

" Here, lend a hand, one of you boys, and haul away that black devil from the bulwarks; he'll be food for the sharks if you don't look out. See that nigger wench to the leeside there; give her a shove

G 2

for'ard, will you ? I wonder what she is after. There is another abaft the coops. The nigger beasts ! after all the work I have had in setting 'em square, to go drifting about in that way ! Take the rope-end to 'em if they won't move ! The devil ! give it to those nigger men laying on the boards there : make 'em stand up here near !'' and then the bluff commander of the schooner '' Venus'' composed his features to a less troubled expression, as he turned to his favourite customer and exclaimed—

'' Why, St. Hilary Cardon, my friend, right glad I am to see you. Look at this sight of niggers : by Jove, I've shoals enough to supply half-a-dozen estates if you have 'em. Now an't they jolly goods as ever you come in hail of? Come, now you shall have your choice.''

The coffee-planter nodded and crossed his arms on his breast, while he slowly stepped here, stooped there, or bent aside, whispering to his manager or nudging his friend to call his attention to the human articles displayed for his approval.

'' And see here,'' continued the Captain, approaching the foremast ; '' look up there, Cardon,'' and he pointed to the object we have before noticed, he speaking the while with considerable emphasis. '' This here, I say, is a prize bit : just look what a Venus she is ! *the soul*, as I call her, of my vessel,—ha ! ha ! —but isn't she a perfect beauty in a black skin as ever you set eyes upon ?''

Mr. Cardon directed his eyes upwards and seemed

to muse, but did not take the bait, and was about to turn his back to the mast, when the confusion on board rose to such a height as to interrupt further negotiation. The multitude, too densely crowded on a small deck, were all jostling together, and complaining in no very gentle terms; but louder than the hoarse murmurs and manifold grumbling of the discontented crew, and than all the gabbling din, was heard the whining nasal voice of a young Martinique planter, drawling out in Colonial patois—

"Quo faire Mulâtres ca venir oti bequés yé? Insolents, yo ca pousser mo par derrière! Sortiz là, mo dire ous, Mulâtres effrontés, sacres pendus!" (How come Mulattoes here among white people? the insolent wretches are pushing me behind. Be off, you impudent Mulattoes! And then followed an oath which may as well remain untranslated.)

"I beg pardon a thousand times. I am humbly sorry!" was the conciliating apology of the offender, uttered in the same dialect, but in a voice peculiarly sweet and well modulated: it was that of our Mulatto. Even in the midst of his haughty masters, Belfond stood well and handsome; and though his garments were cast loosely and negligently about his brawny shoulders, and his glossy raven hair hung in wild ringlets about his face and neck, yet there was something about him strikingly superior to the generality of his caste. He had none of that humble, cringing appearance, stamped upon them by their low condition. His proud dark eyes were full of meaning, his bearing was dignified and such indeed as would have challenged respect had he been a white man, but this, in one of his outcast race, testified of a rebellious spirit, and consequently conveyed an insult to every white man who looked upon him.

To understand the scene which followed, it is necessary that the reader should be made acquainted with the condition of the class of people who come under the denomination Mulattoes—a term usually employed to designate the free coloured population, the offspring of white and black parents. The laws of the various Colonies, however much they differed on other matters, according to the constitution of their several governments, all agreed at least on one point—they were all framed to keep down the mongrel race. And even where legislation was more lenient, the social customs of the white population became only the more oppressive, and the unhappy wretches were persecuted with such unrelenting severity as entirely destroyed their self-respect and prevented even the wish to rise. More than twenty years have elapsed since the events of this story, and nineteen have passed since the emancipation in the English Colonies, but prejudice against colour prevails there still. This prejudice is the bulwark of slavery in the Southern States of America; and in the Northern States, which claim to be the head-quarters of liberty, as well as in the French and English colonies, it forms the barrier to real freedom.

But let us pass now to the period of slavery in the British Colonies, when those laws were in force which laid the foundation of the still existing tyranny of society. Never did the Jews, even in the times of Richard and John, labour under more grinding oppression than did the much-injured Mulattoes in our own boasted era of civilization. They were forbidden by law to stand covered or to remain sitting in the presence of a white person, to dress like him, to bear witness against him in a court of law, to resist when assaulted by him, to answer him in terms implying equality, or even to repose after death within the same place of burial. Volumes might be written on the restrictions to which they were subject; but we think enough has been said for our present purpose, and we hasten to resume the thread of our narrative.

"What is that yellow devil saying?" inquired a gentleman near. "What brings Mulattoes here?"

"Out with them!" cried several voices at once, among which Don Duro's harsh tones were loudest. "Drive out the Mulattoes."

"I suppose," observed a facetious customer, "they are come to buy their mothers. I saw a Mulatto a little while back buy his own grandmother for a slave?" This announcement excited much laughter among the company, and probably our Mulatto might have been forgotten, for the southerns are as variable as they are impetuous; but Mr. Cardon, who was always proud and authoritative, turned on the offender, and called out domineeringly, in much the same tone as he would have used in speaking to a dog, "Get out, there!"

In this there really was nothing unusual. It was Mr. Cardon's way of addressing people of colour, and he had a hundred times bestowed upon them much more substantial marks of his displeasure for smaller offences; but in the behaviour of the Mulatto there was something unusual. Stung with rage and jealousy, he forgot his position as a man of caste, and with unexampled audacity stood erect before the white man without stirring an inch. The Captain saw in a moment what would be the consequence, and, being little inclined either to encourage a brawl on deck to the injury of his sale, or to drive away the Mulattoes, whose presence he had rather invited on account of their reputed wealth, he interposed to make peace.

"Easy now, easy!" he said, coming forward, "he is a harmless fellow, and the Mulattoes will stand back in a minute. I say, holloa, you yellow-skin, just wear a little aft there until I have time to treat with you."

The young man thus addressed moved in the direction indicated, and took his place at the side of the vessel, to which all those of his class then on board were fast making their way amid the jeers of the white people. What the feelings of the Mulatto were it is hard to say, but the scornful expression of his face at this moment gave to his features such a striking resemblance to the proud planter himself as to cause many a smile and a whisper among the bystanders. Mr. Cardon did not perceive this, but he

saw something else which provoked his displeasure : he
caught the Mulatto's eye fixed upon him with that
keen, steady, proud air, which tells of anger and rebellion in the soul.   At any other time the planter
would have visited even this faint shadow of resistance with immediate punishment; but his thoughts
were engrossed with the business on hand, and, not
choosing to prolong an interruption which had
already annoyed him enough, he contented himself
with threatening to throw the offender overboard if
he did not take care. Having thus relieved his mind,
he was about to make his way back to the foremast,
when a voice reached him from the direction of the
coloured man, and the words "Do so !" fell distinctly
upon his ears. The planter turned round quick as
lightning : he could hardly believe his senses, for,
from the expression of the Mulatto's face, it was evident that he was the speaker. What audacity!

"Oh, *mon Dieu !*" cried Belfond's affrighted companions, shrinking from his side. The whole deck
was in commotion.

"The wretch is mad !" vociferated the white men ;
"let him be seized and secured in the hold."

"Captain ! Captain ! if you don't take hold of him,
we'll do it ourselves."

Mr. Cardon was already preparing to do so.
Snatching a stick, a good stout one, from his neighbour, he rushed forward, and aimed such a heavy
blow at the offender's head as must have killed him,
had not the young man, dexterous and strong,

grasped the weapon as it was falling, and held it fast, regarding the planter with a smile of most provoking composure, almost of contempt.

Who shall describe the fury of the white man, and his frantic attempts to disengage the stick from the hands of the Mulatto? Like a madman, he twisted, and pulled, and struggled. The *prestige* of caste kept the Mulatto from retaliation, though he powerfully resisted; and the planter, watching his opportunity, with a sudden and powerful jerk pitched him over the bulwarks. If this had happened in England, or even to a white man in the Colonies, what cries and calls for help would have announced the event! but here, where the consequence of a deed of violence and cruelty affected only a free coloured man, or one who was supposed to be such, it was thought nothing of; and as the water was heard to splash below, Mr. Cardon coolly walked back to the forecastle, amidst a chorus of triumphant voices and clapping of hands, which testified the approbation of the spectators. No one thought of saving the life of the Mulatto.

CHAPTER VII.

BLACK CATTLE PURCHASED.

THE uproar among the white people alarmed the Mulattoes. Each, knowing himself to be an object of hatred, and conceiving himself likely to be the next victim of their vengeance, pressed in terror against his comrades. Some stood upon the bulwarks ready to jump into the boats, others crouched amidst their companions' feet, and a few, more hardy than the rest, begged the white men's pardon, and with ignoble humility craved permission to pass to the gangway and leave the deck.

"Get away with you," cried the white people, kicking them on the shins, as Mulatto after Mulatto passed timidly and hurriedly off. But in the midst of this movement a cry was heard, "A Negro overboard!" New confusion! not derision or insult now, but hurry and solicitude.

"Whose?" cried several voices at once.

"Cardon's," was the reply, and the master was at

his post in a moment, eagerly giving orders for proper assistance : and how cheerfully and quickly did the sailors obey !

It chanced that on the off-side of the ship a canoe had been brought round from beside the gangway,— probably to afford the idle Negro who sat within it a better opportunity of observing the proceedings on board; but Quaco (for it was he) had brought the canoe too near, just below the spot where the contest took place above; and as the Mulatto fell, his body came in contact with the gunwale of the boat, which immediately dipped and capsized.

"Here, one of you sailors !" shouted Mr. Cardon impatiently; " *Sacre, Diable !* why don't you make haste ? he'll be drowned."

His anxiety was not disregarded : " How much will you give me for diving," said one of the men.

" *Sacre!* whatever is fair : where's the use of talking, Higgins, when the fellow is drowning ?"

Instantly the mate was in the water, and, encouraged by the interest manifested by the crowd of spectators, he soon brought the Negro to the surface. His reappearance was the signal for cheers, for he had saved property from destruction; he had rendered a great service. And very edifying was the sympathy shown to the Negro : with what tenderness he was stretched in one of the boats brought round to receive him, rum put to his nostrils and poured down his throat, and his body rubbed by a dozen hands ! At length signs of life began to appear : he

sneezed, spluttered, kicked : perhaps he had pretended
to be worse than he really was, but this the white
men could not tell, and the master, between satisfaction at his recovery and wrath at the accident, thundered forth in his usual style, " *Sacre, Diable !* 'tis
that *maudit Mulâtre :* he fell on my Negro on purpose
to drown him, confound the rascal ! "

While these things were going on, Mr. Dorset stood
by in amazement. He was as yet too new in the
Colonies to share in the prevailing notions concerning Negroes, or rightly to understand the position he
himself held with regard to them, and the scene, so
strange, so subversive of his European ideas of justice and humanity, bewildered him. Here were gentlemen whom he knew to be honourable and kind-
hearted : Mr. Cardon himself was generous to a
fault, often even magnanimous, in his own small
sphere of despotic rule ; and yet these gentlemen all
abetted one another in a total disregard of the rights
of a fellow-creature (he was thinking of the Mulatto),
and more regard was paid to a condemned criminal
in England ; but, thought he, it must be a mistake,—
the coloured man must by this time have climbed up
the ship's side, or perhaps has gained a boat somewhere near. To assure himself of this, he approached
some sailors who were looking over the bulwarks,
and inquired what had become of the Mulatto. No
one answered at first,—people were too busy,—till a
louder and more eager question on his part roused
the Manager, who stood near him, and who replied

with coolness that the drowned man was "only a Mulatto."

With indignant surprise the Englishman looked round: the truth flashed upon him in a moment. "Merciful heaven!" he cried, "make way there;" and tearing off his jacket he prepared to leap into the water; but the Captain tapped him on the shoulder.

"You need not trouble yourself, my good Sir," he said with a smile, "the fellow is swimming to shore as fast as he can;" and pointing forwards to a speck which was visible on the sea, he added, "There! don't you see him? you would have something to do to catch the rascal now. I watched him come up about a cable's length off: a brave swimmer, by Jove; never saw a better." And having delivered himself of this remark, the Captain put his hands in his pockets.

He did not however return to his business, but stood there with his eyes riveted on the sea. Higgins came up with a look of intelligence.

"I know what you're after, Sir," he said to the Captain.

"You do, by Jove?" replied the other, turning quickly round and slapping his side: "it is he, then?"

"Himself, Sir, true as the needle," said the mate.

"Who?" asked a dozen voices.

"What's the matter?" inquired Mr. Cardon.

"What's the matter?" repeated the Captain: "are you so blind that you don't know your own slave? The Mulatto I picked up for you in the port of Marseilles."

Mr. Cardon turned pale with passion. By some movement of anger his foot struck against something, and he stumbled; but instead of looking to see what it was, he violently kicked it forwards,—which, to the surprise of every one, occasioned a loud jingling as of large coins of money. His next neighbour picked it up for him.

" *De par tous les diables !*" exclaimed the planter as he beheld it : " the bag of doubloons stolen out of my box last night !"

" By Jove, then," interrupted the Captain, " the thief was your own Mulatto slave, for I heard something fall when you were thrashing him, and I was just going to see what it was. Come Cardon," continued the Captain, as he looked through his glass, " you won't lose him : the fellow, I see, is just setting foot on land safe and sound. By Jove, he is waving his hand at us," saying which, the rough seaman leaned back to give vent to his boisterous mirth.

Mr. Cardon bit his lip till the blood started, and was about to turn away in disgust, when Higgins came to him.

" Now," said he, " will you give me ten dollars if I catch him for you, besides ten more I expect for saving that boy,—will you, Mr. Cardon ?"

" *Sacre tonnerre !* don't pester me with your English money-worship."

" Mr. Cardon, no one but me can catch that fellow for you,—but me, I tell you : there's no bushrangers about here, nor alguazils, and if there was, I can do

business in that line better than either, I'll vouch.
Now you need not be thinking of how he got away
from our vessel, for I was not on board, I tell you.
Can a man be in two places at once? He would never
have found the use of his legs so soon if I had not
had business on shore that night. Ask the Captain
there how I chained him and tamed him down in the
hold. When we first got him on board, Sir, there was
no keeping the chains upon him : he broke two. He
is the very devil! But I tamed him, I tell you, and by
the time we reached the port he looked like—like—"

"The leanest of these, I suppose," added Mr.
Dorset, who had been listening attentively, and he
pointed to some of the Negroes put up for sale.

"Pah!" said the Captain turning away, and putting
his pipe to his mouth.

"Whew! Señor," observed Don Duro, "I could
tame him without that."

"Come now, Cardon," interrupted the Captain,
"you had better leave him to Higgins : you can pay
him for this and for saving the Negro when you pay
me. I'll go bail he will bring you that cove before
three days are over; he has the eye of an Indian for
tracing a runaway. I remember once, when I brought
a cargo of slaves round to Granada, I sold a lot to a
heavy planter down there, and he sent 'em off directly
to his estate ; but the devils no sooner got scent of the
woods than they tied up the overseer that had the
care of 'em, and cut away to the mountains. Higgins
laid a wager that day he would capture every one of

'em before the morrow, and, by Jove, the fellow was as good as his word, for the black thieves were exhibited in the market-place next morning, cut up with the whip like so many crimped cod. But won't you come and look at those articles of mine? I would rather sell 'em to you than to anybody else, and you can pay me when you like, I'm not particular; I'll give you such bargains as will make up for twenty such fellows as the one that got away. Come here!"

Mr. Cardon followed moodily.

"Well, now," continued the Captain, "I suppose you don't care for that 'ere Wenus; but here are some fine articles, I'll warrant!" and he dragged up one of the men from a sitting to a standing posture. "See this one; just look at his shoulders and his arms, did you ever see any like 'em? Why he'll clear you a forest in a week. I saw him felling wood myself on the river-side; he's a real Samson."

A shout of laughter met this vaunt, for the poor wretch, besides a lean, spare, weakly frame, presented to the beholders a set of features which marked him at once as belonging to the Eboe nation, the laziest and most useless of those imported from Africa.

"Now I tell you," said Mr. Cardon, "I am not going to be wheedled into carting a load of these unwholesome black bones off your deck; they may go to manure some other planter's land than mine. Pah! faugh! they smell of nothing but lamp-oil, horse-beans, and ulcers. I tell you I'm not going to be taken in so: you think I don't know how you

H

rub them down and physic them before they come on shore, to hide their unhealthy looks.''

" Come now, easy now ! it's no use talking; you're as smart a man, and as keen in striking a bargain, as any I've ever dealt with; but goods is goods, and will spoil sometimes, particular when a ship has been tossed about by storms one half of the voyage and becalmed the other. You're a man of acute mind, and you should know that allowances must be made."

" It's the ugliest and most useless cargo I ever came on board to see."

" Odds, Sir ! you do nothing but find fault. The time of year is bad for catching niggers on the Guinea coast; and just look, Captain Gosmore set out at the same time with me for Cuba,—his cargo was all made up of niggers with clabba-yaws, and their legs had guinea-worms peeping out through the skin, you could see them moving,—and I'll wager he has made a fortune by his cargo. Niggers is getting scarce now, since the trade was got to be smuggling work, and the population on the plantations don't increase so as to provide against the scarce times."

" You haven't a single available Negro : I wanted Quaquas or Foulahs."

" There's four of 'em there," said the Captain, kicking some who stood close to him,—not that he was a cruel man, not at all, but it was the way of treating Negroes.

The crowd of customers pressed so closely round that it became difficult to survey the slaves properly. This of course pleased the Captain all the better, as it served his purpose.

" I've got Koromantyns here, the finest fellows you could see."

" I don't like Koromantyns, they give too much trouble. And I see the marks of chains on their wrists and ankles: now slaves that are troublesome on board are just doubly so on land."

" Well now, by Jove, Mr. Cardon, you are hard to please. I have only one price for each of them, and I have given you the first picking, as I promised you last time; now, if you don't choose to take 'em, why, don't, that's all! others will." The Captain was provoked at Mr. Cardon's pertinacious depreciation of his cargo,—the more so, as he knew the planter's remarks would operate greatly against his sale, for Mr. Cardon's reputed wealth, together with his powerful mind and imperious temper, made him the most influential man in the Colony. Endeavouring therefore to meet his difficult customer, the Captain soon brought the bargaining to a close, and Mr. Cardon whispered to his friend to point out the best, "for," said he, "I must buy some, be they ever so bad." Some Koromantyns, Loangoes, and Eboes were indicated, and our planter selected eight of the first, seven of the second, and four of the last. "And now," said he to the Captain in conclusion, "you must throw into the bargain that Venus you have been praising so much, to make up a round number, or I will have nothing further to do with your goods."

"'Sdeath, Sir, my Venus! my beauty! my prize slave! Gad! I think you will ask me for the ship next."

"Ship or no ship, Mr. Captain," vociferated Mr. Cardon, "I'm not to be trifled with, and you've been trying to do that ever since I have put my foot on board. Will you throw her into the bargain, or will you not? for I must be gone,—*sacre!*"

The Captain looked up and mused, and looked up again. "Well, you're a good pay, a brave purse, so as you give me money down."

"But I don't give you money down," interrupted the planter: "I find in this bag only a few doubloons of the large sum I brought down, whatever that cursed thief did with the rest."

A little circumstance happened here, which, though not connected with the story, will show the consideration our planter enjoyed in the Colony. A gentleman advanced from among the crowd, politely addressing himself to Mr. Cardon.

"Allow me, if you please, to pay the demand for you, as I don't care to make purchases this morning, and I have plenty of money by me at your service."

"Very well," said the other, neither surprised nor moved, "I am obliged to you." And while the Captain went hurriedly and petulantly to unchain the girl, Mr. Cardon procured writing materials, and indited a note of hand, which he presented to the lender. But

this the gentleman immediately tore up. " Mr. Cardon's word," he said, " is enough, every one knows it
is as good as gold : I only ask that he acknowledge,
I can appreciate his honour." Mr. Cardon bowed
proudly, and, passing off to the ship's side, he called
Quaco to bring round the boats, and prepared to
descend.

CHAPTER VIII.

HOW GOVERNMENT SERVANTS DO THEIR DUTY IN THE COLONIES.

THE gentlemen took their seats in the canoe, and the droguer was brought alongside the vessel, to receive the slaves that had been purchased. In a few minutes they were all stowed in. The black young Venus, as the Captain called her,—she who had formed the signal at the foremast,—was the last sent down. As she was cautiously descending the ladder, some of the Negroes, those of the Koromantyn nation, rose to meet her with every token of respect, and one of them stooped fairly on all fours, to receive her foot upon his back, as she stepped from the ladder to the boat. Mr. Dorset pointed to the little scene with an expression of interest. " I should never have dreamt," he said, " that the Negroes had so much gallantry."

The planter, whose good humour was somewhat restored by the purchase he had made, turned quickly round. " Bah!" he said, looking at the Negroes,

" that's nothing : I am used to that sort of work : it is not gallantry, how should they know anything about such a feeling,—the black things! The fact is, she was some grandee in Africa, so they will tell you, but I'll soon stripe that out of her."

Mr. Dorset was about to ask whether, from consideration for the habits she had been brought up to, he would not treat her with some indulgence, but was cut short by the impatient planter, who was taking a rapid though searching review of his goods, and directing his manager to make some alteration of their position in the boat.

" Don Duro," he said, addressing that worthy, who of course was in the droguer to attend to the goods, " do you have an eye to those Koromantyns, they are not to be trusted. And as for those Eboes, you must never look away from them till they get down to the estate : they will as likely as not throw themselves over the boat-side before you are aware of it. I would not trouble them now, Don Duro, they are just as well there, lying at the bottom of the boat : at all events, they are safe."

" I know, I know, Señor," replied the other, " I am up to all their ways, Señor ; they will never catch me off my guard, Señor."

Mr. Cardon appeared satisfied with this, and taking his seat, he turned cheerfully to the Negroes at the oar.

" Now, Quaco ! pull away, you rascal, and let us see what a good ducking does, and you shall have a holiday this afternoon, and perhaps a dance tomorrow night, as it is Saturday."

Quaco brightened up, and tucking his wet garments as high as they would go, he took the oar, and, with the other boatmen, set to work with all his might, beating time on the water to an animated song, which the rowers of the droguer took up alternately in a sort of chorus. The words—composed, as usual, for the occasion—were in some African language. Immediately on hearing this, the poor wretches who were crammed in the droguer started up with looks and gestures indicative of the wildest emotions. Some of them fell on their faces and wept aloud; others, unawed by the presence of the white gentlemen, laughed outright for joy; others again gibbered and gesticulated towards the canoe like a set of maniacs; while Quaco, who had caused all this commotion, only smiled, and continued his recitative as if nothing had happened.

"Oh, that's nothing out of the way," said the planter, observing surprise on the face of his European friend; "Quaco, who is a devil's imp if ever there was one, has been singing to them in his own language, and they have recognized it, and hail him, I suppose, as a countryman, perhaps as a relative, who knows? if we choose to grow romantic upon niggers."

"Is their language interesting? Is it worth learning?"

"What!" exclaimed St. Hilaire, "gibberish like that! *ma foi*, I think not."

" Do you know anything of it ? did you ever pick up any words ?   I ask this, because I observe you have a rare facility in speaking languages."

" As for that, every West Indian has ; our tongues are lithe and supple like our limbs, and in a colony like this, composed of people from almost every corner of the globe, we pick up languages in our childhood, as we do shells from the shore.   But as for the African dialects, preserve me ! I would not vulgarize my tongue with such sounds ; besides, between you and me," he added, lowering his voice, " I would not trust them to teach me.   A curious fellow came here from Europe some two years ago, wanting to write about Africa ; so he came to my place, and set himself to learn Koromantyn from the Negroes, writing down the words as they taught him : they would assemble in a circle round him, and with the gravest and most solemn faces tell him the words he wanted. I told him then he was a fool, but he would not believe me.   So by-and-by, when he had got his book full and thought himself learned, he travelled round to the other side of the island, and met some Koromantyn soldiers of the black regiment in *Bande de l'Est*.   Well, he began his conversation as he thought in pure African—not one of them could understand a word ; he went to others—just the same ; at last he found out that he had been befooled and made a dupe of,—a laughing-stock for the Negroes, just think ! I had half a mind to give them all a round flogging, but the trick was so clever that I couldn't

help laughing.   Well," continued the planter after a
pause, while he took off his straw hat to wipe his
forehead, for it was growing hot,—"well, Dorset,
what do you think of our bargain this morning?"

"I think," replied the other emphatically, "that
you have made a woful and most unchristian bargain,
unless indeed you mean to do without the services of
these poor creatures, and send them to the hospital
for a year; for in less than that time they will certainly not be fit for work: they are quite crippled,
their constitutions are broken."

The planter at first looked earnestly and search-
ingly at his friend, but in another moment he appeared
satisfied.   "You little know, *mon ami*," he resumed,
as he passed his handkerchief several times across
his brow, and finally replaced his hat,—"you little
know how quickly and comfortably and effectually
these victims, as you would call them, recruit their
strength.   But you will soon learn,—soon learn: all
in good time, *mon cher.*"

"Then again," quoth the European, "I am amazed
at this Captain, at his boldness in venturing here:
why the slave trade was done away with years ago,—
in 1813, if I am not mistaken."

"*Ce n'est rien, cela*," said the planter; "the pro-
hibition only made the trade more exciting and interesting.   People here see no more harm in illicit trade
of this sort, than Londoners do in smuggling French
gloves."

"I wonder they are not detected and punished."

" Detected !" exclaimed Mr. Cardon, placing his hands upon his sides : "you little know what colonies are. Why a place like this, so far from the seat of Government, scarcely feels its influence at all : the real kings are the officials sent over, and provided the offender has friends at our little Court to hush up and wink at his sins, he need never fear punishment, do what he may. As for abuses,—the unlawful meddling, the neglect of duty, and the unjust favouritism of these officials,—their name is Legion ; and who is to redress them? If the united remonstrances of the whole population cannot get a hearing at head-quarters across the ocean, be assured the sins of a favourite will never reach them."

" Do you mean to say," asked the European, looking steadfastly at the planter, " that the Governor knows of this slaver coming in? Do any of the officials ?"

" *Parole d'honneur*, I don't know, and I don't care," said Mr. Cardon, leaning somewhat aside ; " as for myself, I know they won't meddle with me, not one of them : I am no friend of any of them either, but they all know it is as well to let me alone. For the rest, supposing there was some friend of any of the Government pack sinning here this morning, and the virtuous headman got scent of it, and took notice of it, to make a parade of his principles, *mon cher,—pardi !* a sum of money would soon stop his mouth. Ha ! they are all alike—a parcel of mean, cowardly bullies. Now I will tell you a thing that happened but a short time ago : it will give you an idea of the lax way they do their work. A proclamation was issued in the name of the King, prohibiting the transfer of slaves from one Colony to another, under pain of forfeiture. There was a French widow lady residing here who had an estate on the Spanish main, from which, before the proclamation came, she had brought seven or eight Negroes to Trinidad to hire out. Shortly after the new law came into force, the term for which she had hired out her slaves expired, when she very foolishly, and without consulting her friends, took them back to her estate,—during the night too. Having set them to work under her manager in Guiria, she returned here, thinking herself quite safe. Her maid betrayed her. She was sitting quietly one evening in her little home with her two daughters, young things of fifteen and seventeen years of age ; an Alguazil stepped in, with a message, requesting her to come to a place that was mentioned, to speak on business with some of the authorities. She put on her bonnet, thinking to return in a little while, but, *pardi !* then and there she was walked off to prison. The Negroes in question were sent for at once and set free, together with the traitor, but the lady was kept in that prison for three long years, while her girls were left to the mercy of the world. Although I had not hitherto known her, yet I went to see her, as many others did, to express my sympathy for her misfortunes ; my wife offered to take the two girls, but somebody had been beforehand on the same errand. I found the lady with a bed on the floor in a corner of her room, and one chair,—that was all. I don't know how she fared with regard to food. She was let out at last on the remonstrance of some one who had interest in our puny Court. I must say, by the way, what I suppose will please you, that the Negroes of the Island showed themselves to have a respectable amount of feeling on the occasion. They looked coldly on the traitor, and pitied the lady much; they even made a song of condolence, with a rather pretty chorus, to the effect that she

> ' Lies buried in the depths of the prison gloom,
> The damps beneath, above, around,
> Till the fungus grows rank o'er her living tomb.'

Well, contrast this severe expression of His Excellency's most virtuous indignation with the affair of the Barbadians, which happened but a short time ago. In the face of the proclamation and of many other stringent orders,—such as arrive here as fast as the mails can bring them,—a ship comes into Port Spain, in broad daylight, with a cargo of young female slaves from that overpeopled colony, the island of Barbadoes. Received by the Captain of the Port, passed by the Protector of Slaves, numbered and named by the Registrar, these slaves were offered for sale, and the inhabitants, foolishly trusting that all was right, made purchases, each according to his means and requirements. Months elapsed, and many of these Barbadians were transferred from owner to owner through several hands, and still nothing was

said by the officials; when it occurred to them, for
some reason unknown to any but themselves, that
the Captain of the Port, the Protector of Slaves, and
the Registrar of Slaves were wrong, so instantly they
had all the Barbadians called together and set free.
Do you think the officials were punished?—not they!
they fattened, and the inhabitants were flayed.   This
is but a poor sample of what they do, and I might
fill volumes with accounts of their misdemeanours and
tyranny.   I hate them and despise them."

"But this man, this Captain Hill!" said Mr.
Dorset, as soon as he could get in a word.

"Ah, well, this man. *Oui, revenons à nos moutons.*
This man will carry on the trade till our men in
office find it expedient to trumpet forth their virtue,
and then all at once they will sacrifice him to their
interests.   I don't say myself that I very much
approve of this trade, for I hate cruelty to animals;
mais que voulez-vous? we must have slaves to work,
and the young Negroes die so fast in childhood and
in infancy of one thing or another, that the Negro
population would soon die out altogether if we didn't
find some means of renewing it."

"But how comes this?" persistingly asked Mr.
Dorset.   "Are you sure the Negro children are
taken care of, and that there is no mismanagement?
or unsuitability of climate or of their condition perhaps," he added doubtingly.

Mr. Cardon mused awhile,—then began to whistle,
—and then, after another pause, said—"I must con-

fess I don't understand it myself, for certainly the children of the free coloured population don't show the same decrease. I have often thought of this before, but have never been able to account for it. I have often suspected neglect of the young things, and for this reason I would never have a rearing-house, like so many other planters : I let the mothers stay from the field to nurse their own babies. In my opinion the birth of Negro children is more loss than gain. In Cuba, now, they understand this very well, and many of the estates are manned with men only, with not a woman near them."

" How dreadful !" muttered Mr. Dorset.

" Captain Hill," continued the other, with scarcely a pause, " drives a fine trade there, I know ; and I know moreover that he ventures his worst articles here, for fear some day he should be caught, and his cargo forfeited. Higgins is an excellent help to him."

" You did not seem to encourage him much in his kind offers," observed Mr. Dorset.

" No, but he will bring me that runaway villain nevertheless, just as he said ; but I don't care to encourage him. I hate the man : I hate him for his sneaking, treacherous way : he will do anything for money,—he will cringe, fawn, bully, or betray, if you only pay him for it. I never knew him do a common piece of civility without asking to be paid."

The breeze which had wafted the ship gaily towards the shore had now lulled into a perfect repose, and the ripples had given place to a smoothness like glass.

The boats, as they glided along the unruffled surface, were reflected by the still water as in a mirror, and their shadows met and mingled below with the tall corallines and fucus, which showed clearly and beautifully through the crystal fluid; brilliant shells rested like fruit upon the submarine branches, and glittering fish passed in and out, like fairy forms gliding into their hidden bowers; and shadow and substance, —the real and the unreal,—were blended in one magical picture. The broad expanse of azure above was unbroken by a single cloud. Nature was clothed in the most gorgeous of her robes : the scene was one which might have rivalled the beauty of Eden. So thought Mr. Dorset, as he looked around, and watched the boats returning from the ship, each bearing its group of exiles to their hopeless doom. And the cadenced songs of the rowers, answering from boat to boat, sounded mellow, melancholy, and wild, as the voice of music always does when it comes from the sea. By-and-by the gentlemen landed, and joined a group of planters, who stood on the beach, talking over the various incidents of the morning's sale, while the heavier craft were bringing up their respective loads of goods.

Mr. Cardon's purchases were the first to come, and the manager, who considered that his jurisdiction commenced from the moment the Negroes were consigned to his care, accordingly took the place of his master (though master he never acknowledged him), and issued his commands with lordly severity.

" *Párate, perro !*" he roughly called, trilling his *r*'s with wrath; "stop there, dog of a slave, and near to the right there, where the waggon stands, and make haste to drag out those niggers sprawling at the bottom of the boat."

" Berry well, Massa," stammered the sable boatman as he threw out one leg upon the sands; "but dem Eboe, me no sabey wharra for do wid 'em ; dem da sleep, me tink,—no lika for moob !"

" *Por Dios santo*, make them move, or I'll make you !" vociferated the manager.

Hereupon the boatmen, exercising on the wretched Eboes the same tyranny which the white men were wont to practise on themselves, snatched up the oars, and commenced bullying and tormenting the desponding exiles till they forced them to rise and follow their more lively companions, who were already filing off to dry land, glad perchance of any change that delivered them from the horrors of the ship.

CHAPTER IX.

WRATH AND RETALIATION.

WE may pass over our planter's return from the ship. Like other planters, he swore and bellowed at his slaves, and called them dogs and lazy "niggers;" and like other slaveholders, he carefully provided for the safety of his new slaves, ordering them to be rubbed down with citron-juice and rum to destroy the infection of the hold, and some spirituous drink to be given to revive them, well knowing how much his future wealth depended on their condition. As to the miscreant who had bearded him with such audacity at the sale, he had no hope of ever reducing him to submission and order; he therefore gave instructions for his capture and punishment, at the same time uttering execrations and threats of annihilation against the unhappy wretch, if ever he happened to come within reach of him : this done to his satisfaction, our coffee-planter mounted his horse, and in company with Mr. Dorset set off for the Palm Grove Estate.

A few words concerning Mr. Cardon. He was by no means what would generally be termed a hard master : he fed, clothed, and housed his Negroes well; he had a hospital for the sick, and a nursery to rear the little ones, with a *Mammy* to superintend it, and he took a pride in seeing his Negroes in good condition. He had also his fits of kindness and indulgence, and was often familiar with his slaves, mixing unreservedly with their conversation, and laughing at their re- marks; yet, even when in his gentlest mood, there was always something lordly and contemptuous in his manner, a sarcastic mockery in his merriest joke, which never failed to keep them down. He was a clever man, and wonderfully successful in the manage- ment of his Negroes; he had been known to strike at the root of their prejudices, when they affected his interests, with rare sagacity. Once, for example, he had speculated somewhat largely in a very unpromising set of Negroes of the Eboe nation. These Eboes are a desponding people, ahd frequently commit suicide at the first opportunity, from a belief that when dead they will immediately return to their own far coun- try. Contrary to our planter's orders, they had for some reason or other been stowed away for the night in a garret, and in the garret lay some old forgotten ropes. When the morning came, the greater number of the unhappy wretches were found hanging dead and stiff from the rafters. Mr. Cardon's tact was shown in the plan he adopted to save the remaining ones. He stalked in amongst them with an angry countenance, and addressing an Eboe interpreter, " Tell your accursed countrymen," he said in threatening tones, " that if I find one more of them hanged, I shall hang you all in a row, and myself at the head of you ; and if I don't follow you to your country with this whip, by —— ! " and he cracked it till the hills resounded again.   No Negro was ever found hanged on his estate after that.

It was with a view of applying a remedy to some such disorder in another form among his Negroes that he had induced Mr. Dorset to accompany him to the Palm Grove Estate.   This gentleman had gone through a regular course of study as surgeon in England, (a most rare qualification in the medical men of the Colonies,) and Mr. Cardon thought highly of his professional ability.

" I know very well what is thinning the ranks of my Negroes," he said, " still I would have your opinion upon it, and would stop it if possible by some new remedy, more efficient than the one hitherto applied."

For some time they journeyed on without much conversation, each occupied with his own thoughts. At last Mr. Cardon suddenly turned full on his companion.

" I am going to speak seriously to you," he said, " and to ask you a serious and important favour, Mr. Dorset.   You tell me you don't allow flogging on your estate ; well, that is as you like : but if I should find it necessary to use coercion on mine, I insist upon requesting you not to interfere, either by look, word, or gesture."

"What!" exclaimed the other, "may I not intercede for a culprit?"

"No! no! not on my estate, not on any sensible planter's estate: the Negroes must never dream their master's mercy could be greater."

Another interval of silence ensued, even longer than the first; to break through the awkwardness of which, and to divert his companion's thoughts into a pleasanter channel, the planter now inquired gaily, how he was getting on with his affairs. "The last time I saw you in town, you were just sending a dozen wheelbarrows to your estate: what were they for? how did they answer?"

"Hem!" replied Mr. Dorset slowly, and coughing lightly as he spoke, "I suppose I must confess to a failure. I got them to save the women: I couldn't bear to see them carrying such heavy loads on their heads."

Mr. Cardon burst into a fit of laughter.

"Well, in spite of all I could say," continued the Englishman, "they would persist in hoisting them on their heads; and whenever I expostulated, they only answered by twirling the wheel as it dangled over their faces, and calling it a ' cleber ting.'"

As may be supposed, this announcement in no degree abated the coffee-planter's merriment, the boistorousness of which somewhat wounded the *amour propre* of our novice; but he smiled placidly, and rode on.

" And what brought you," asked Mr. Cardon, stopping abruptly,—" you, a most tender-hearted, Negro-loving man, all the way from free, noble, moral England, to live among us cruel, miscreant slave-holders, to be a slaveholder yourself?"

" Simply this," replied the other quietly, " because I was left this little property which lies next to your estate, and as we were not rich, the obvious course was to come here and live upon it. I assure you, with the competition and ignorant prejudices of society in London, a young medical man must wait long for practice, and I had not capital enough to sustain me while waiting for the accidents of fortune. For the rest, I never entirely went with the public in running down the system of slavery, for I am inclined to consider it a means permitted by Providence to bring the inhabitants of a vast and unknown region into more immediate and direct communication with the children of enlightened Europe, and by this means to civilize the savages. It remains for me to do my part, by showing kindness, patience, and gentle teaching."

" And so you thought you would make your fortune by treating these Negroes of yours as you would your valet in your aristocratic country? Bravo! success to you! and tell me, how do you get them to work on your no-flogging system? Are you never treated with long rows of Negroes on a fine morning, when they have a mind for a holiday, their foreheads bandaged up, their eyes nearly closed, and their tongues all the colours of the rainbow, with complaints of 'head he da hut he; 'heart he da bong he;' 'kin he da burn all ober' ?"

Mr. Dorset stooped over his horse's head and coaxed it down with the whip, but made no reply.

"Were it not that I see you to be a single-hearted man, Dorset, I would leave you to your mistakes, and your fate. *Pardi*, I pity you!"

"Hem! thank you," observed the other drily.

"No offence!" cried Mr. Cardon, beating down the luxuriant boughs which obstructed his way; "every one is liable to mistakes, and the noise and fuss that are just now made in England concerning this slavery are enough to blind wiser heads than yours, *mon ami*. I grant you would be right if the Negro were a creature on an equal footing with the white man in point of common intellect; but he is not— he is far beneath us."

Mr. Dorset objected that he was in the habit of speaking with his own Negroes every day, and he had always discovered in their conversation proofs of the same powers of mind, the same reasoning faculties, the same feelings as those of white people, only not cultivated.

"Bah! bah!" cried the other impatiently, "you don't know what you are saying, *mon ami*. In the first place, did you never observe the form and style of the Negro's face, and did it never suggest a baboon to you? I can show you, on the very estate we are going to, some of the Moco nation so like the ourang-outang as to startle one: you would not have me consider those as equal to Europeans, would you? I tell you moreover the mind of the Negro is not the same as ours: it can't calculate, it can't combine the various faculties, it can't reflect; it has its will, its memory, its understanding, like the brutes, and little more. Now see here: yesterday morning I had a great many reasons for coming down to this slave-market, and I also had a great many reasons for staying away; I weighed the two,—the balance fell in favour of the market, and you beheld me there. But the mind of the Negro cannot admit of many motives at the same time: one is all he can entertain, and the impulse and action follow one another as the report of a pistol on the flash. What is that but brute-like? Therefore next to the brute I place the Negro, and his race must bow before the intelligent whites."

Mr. Dorset elevated his eyebrows. "And do you mean to aver," he said, "that the colour of the skin is a sign of the low condition of the brain?"

"I do!" exclaimed the other with a force of tone that betrayed his positive mind; "I do! no doubt about it! everywhere throughout the world you see it: look at the lazy Hindoos, the stupid Egyptians, the worthless Red Indians,—all!"

"Mr. Cardon, did you ever read the history of Egypt? We read even in the Bible that its people were the most civilized on the globe; and elsewhere we find that during one period the fair-haired race were subject and slaves to the Egyptians, and that the prejudice of caste was as strong in the Thebaid against the white people, as it is with us now against the Negroes. Remember that where the rod ruled once, it may rule again."

"Pooh! bah! tut, tut, tut!" cried the other, "*qu'est-ce que c'est que ça?* what old woman's story is that?—a parcel of nonsense propagated by the Jews. I tell you, *mon ami*, there are men in the world who burn to make their influence felt: their vanity is a thorn which goads them on to disturb society; so having nothing else at hand, they must rake up old women's stories, and set themselves up as saviours of a people. Now, supposing I admitted, for the sake of argument, that the Negro was on a level with us, still he has only a certain number of hours of labour, just sufficient to season his life and make him healthy: he is well clothed, well fed, well housed, well nursed in illness, well taken care of in old age; this is enough for him. But the poor in England, look at them; work, work, work, night and day without rest, upon starvation fare, and all for the aggrandisement of some mighty Nabob, manufacturer or middleman generally; was man made for this? I ask you. Have you ever visited the manufacturing towns in free, glorious England, Sir? I have,—*pardienne*, I have! I have travelled a good deal, and looked about me a good deal. Did you ever visit the courts and alleys of the greatest city in the world—immortal London? *Sacre!*"

"But, Sir! but, Sir!" interrupted Mr. Dorset, roused from his usual tranquil manner, "you forget they are free: a crust and freedom, surely!"

" They are slaves," cried the other with vehemence, as he pounded his saddle, " they are slaves, like my Negroes."

Mr. Dorset fairly wheeled himself round in his saddle, and gazed at his companion in amazement ; he began to doubt the soundness of the planter's mind.

" Slaves !" continued the other ; "what else are they ? what does it matter whether it is the whip of leather that drives one man to work for his brother man, or the whip of starvation ? the seat of pain is the same, the rest is all imagination. Did you ever go among the people who give you potatoes and pave your streets, who fight your battles and man your ships,—the Irish peasants ? I should be ashamed, Sir, to see the lowest dog in the Colonies housed and fed and treated like them. Did you ever visit the mines ? I should be ashamed, Sir, to treat my dog like some of those underground wretches. There is not a luxury you enjoy, I tell you, but is purchased by a thousand liberties, a thousand lives. And your legislators and aristocrats, and all your moneyed men ! We at least have our slaves always in our company, playing with our children, taking part in our joys ; but our brother slaveholders of England—' Faugh !' say they, ' keep those squalid beasts from our sublime presence : we like to take their life-blood, but we really must ignore the horrors of the slaughter-house.' Oh that I could write ! I sometimes think I shall write. I remember once, when travelling through England, I sat on the outside of a coach ; the man who sat next me was crying: at first I thought he had taken a drop too much, but a closer view satisfied me it was veritable, heartfelt sobbing. I felt for the man, and opened conversation with him: he was a servant to a baronet in the neighbourhood. *'The curse he gave me,'* said the man, *'just on account of a mistake, goes deep into me, till I feel like good for nothing. If I leave him, he will call me impudent, and hinder me from getting a place; and I can't talk, none of the poor can, we haven't words like those who are scholars, we can only feel, and be silent, and cry.'* Yes, I said, it would be like fighting with a little rusty wire against an enemy armed with a sharp-pointed sword. That's right, brother slave-holders of England, do as we do, *chers frères !* Whenever you educate the poor, they will cut your throats; when we educate our slaves, they will do the same. *Sacre Mulâtre !* to think of his insolence on board the ship today! to think of all I did for him,—sent him to France to attend on my own son! *Le chien !* he would cut my throat for it tomorrow; though I am —what was I going to say? *Sacre Mulâtre !"*

Mr. Cardon had it all his own way: it was useless for Mr. Dorset to oppose a remark, before the vehemence, the power, the eloquence of expression and gesture, which eminently belonged to the planter.

"Prejudice of caste ?—*parbleu !* they have none, —oh no! And pray what is that stand-off reserve which keeps so effectual a barrier between the moneyed man and the pauper,—the noble and the trader,—the master and the servant? Why you know right well that you would rather die than shake hands before company with the footman who waits at your table, though he may have saved your life in the morning."

" Sir ! Mr. Cardon !"

" Bah ! I am not speaking personally, I tell you ; I only say *you*, because I have no one else to say it to ; you stand for the English nation, and you must listen to me. How do you treat your servants ? Why, as if they had been created merely for your convenience and pleasure. You give them wages scarcely adequate to provide them with the decent clothing you require them to appear in. You take the health and the strength of their youth ; and how do you reward them in their old age ? Do you pension them and support them, as we do *our* old Negroes ? No ! you leave them to rot. What feeds the abominations of the English streets at night ? Servants out of place, sempstresses, and others who have no future before them. Who prey upon them ? Why, I tell you, the most licentious estate of the most licentious planter never presented one-hundredth of the nightly horrors of one street of your Babylon. Oh no ! there is no slave-hunting, nor slave-dealing, nor slave-buying, nor slave-murdering in dear moral England ! and that among not these half brute baboons, but just among God's loveliest creatures— women, sent among us to lead us to heaven. Pray where are your saints, your excessively virtuous saints, that they suffer these things to be ?"

Mr. Dorset laid his hand upon his arm to stop him, but it would not do, the planter's ire was up.

"Moral England!" continued he, "*pardienne!* Yes, the saints! they sent a ranting set of Methodist preachers down here: I kicked them off the estate, every one of them,—the murder-preaching set!"

"Oh! oh!"

"You may say 'oh!' but it is so. The boasted Christian spirit of the Protestant form! that is laughable too. In our Church, at least once a week the master and the slave kneel on a perfect equality before our God. Our priests are bound to ignore any difference between them, and they do so. How is it with the Protestants—eh? I will take a bishop going to the cathedral of his diocese on a holy sabbath. Will he imitate the humility of his divine Master only just a little? Will he go on foot only for this one day? Not he! on wheels he will drive, surrounded by the pomps and vanities of the very devil. And his wife and daughters, will they lay aside their silks and satins just for a few hours this one day, and join the poor in humility of garb and humility of prayer? No! behold them surrounded with rails, *noli me tangere* fashion, to keep them from contact with those loathsome bestialities, the poor. And the sermon, mind you, all the while runs on humility! yes, in fine, hard, grand words, which the poor are never taught to understand; but they understand the meaning of the pomp and the carriage, the silk and the satin, the rails and the stand-off looks, and they un-

derstand that humility is a Christian virtue intended
only for the poor, to teach them meekly to bend their
neck for the rich to set their foot upon them.   Let
me tell you that were I ever so much inclined to the
Reformed religion, I should be ashamed to bring my
Negroes to attend in your churches.   Such devotion
to pomps and vanities! such lack of devotion to
God!   Pah! disgusting humbug!—a word invented
by the English for the English, and befitting them
alone : you can't translate it into French nor German,
no, nor Italian nor Spanish, nor any other tongue.
Cursed be the day I put faith in their proclamations
and promises, and was fool enough to settle in any
Colony belonging to them.   At all events, we planters
are no humbugs.   Fate has placed the whip in our
hands,—a whip we call it, fearlessly and openly, and
as a whip we use it.   The moneyed men of England
have a whip too, and use it too ; but they sneak and
snuffle, and put on a sanctified face, and tell their
victims that the blows they give are so many blessed
proofs of freedom."

What more he would have added is not known, for
so intent upon his subject was he, that he had come
unwarily into too close contact with the overhanging
branches of the trees, and a bough laden with oranges
struck him full in the face.   "*Sacre !*" was of course
the word, as he beat and struck at the offending
branch, till the other, coming to the rescue, set him
free.

"There now !" observed the Englishman in his

good-humoured way, "you have annihilated all the branches of the trees, and all the aristocrats, to your heart's content, so let us take breath, and refresh ourselves with this delicious fruit. How luxuriant! how beautiful! I must pluck some," he said, filling his pockets and those of his companion. "There! while you were scolding head-quarters in England, my horses' hoofs have been trampling and squeezing the most luscious little oranges scattered about the road. Methinks that in the midst of such a glorious nature one could not well be very unhappy."

The planter took to whistling, and they continued on their way for some time without speaking.

Mr. Dorset was still in the fresh years of youth; he had tasted care, but not enough to dry up the sources of innocent enjoyment. In listening to the strictures of his companion, he was inclined to attribute much to acerbity of temper, probably produced by crosses and disappointments, and he felt disposed to bear with him good-naturedly on that account, trusting to time, opportunity, and well-timed argument, to bring him round to a milder *régime* with his slaves. The day was surpassingly bright and beautiful; and as he gazed on the wild and gorgeous banks on either side with delight and curiosity, he discovered that not a leaf on tree or shrub, not a blade of grass, was like anything that grew in his own England,—vegetation was on so large, so varied, so rich a scale. Sometimes it was difficult to tell which was bird and which was flower, so brightly and confusedly were they mingled. Now his eyes followed the blue bird till it was lost in a thousand mazes, or the oriole and perroquet perched on the tree-top like some brilliant flower; then they would rest on a tuft of blooming shrubs,—the macata, the red hibiscus, the oleander, and the African rose,—through whose closely twined branches the papaw shot up its silvery column, with its crown of leaves and pendent racemes of odoriferous lilies, and hundreds of humming-birds, all poised on their glittering wings, were sipping nectar from every cup; further on, the slim mimosa was seen hanging its delicate fringes among the thick and solid leaves of the aloe and cactus, and flowering lianas twined their wreaths from bough to bough, flinging odours to the wind, and grace over the wild confusion of the woods.

The sun had passed the zenith, and the heat, though oppressive in the towns, was here in the country tempered by a light breeze laden with perfume. Gradually the little birds grew silent in the woods, the wild beasts resorted to their lairs, and nothing was heard but the sighing of the wind among the leaves, and the faint bubbling of a woodland fountain, at which the horses stopped to drink. The sun shone with all the splendour of a southern mid-day, and the heat and stillness weighed on the senses with the quieting and dreamy influence of night. Even Mr. Cardon was content to smoke his cigar without offering to interrupt the contemplations of his more romantic friend. The horses, having satisfied their thirst, tossed their heads and snorted; the water dripped from their nostrils, and, after pawing the ground, they took the way unbidden towards the abode of their masters. The travellers proceeded beneath shady trees, fanned by mid-day breezes, and lulled to soothing reflections by the faint sweet sounds of reposing nature. By-and-by amidst all this stillness there arose, gently and sweetly at first, then swelling on the ear, the song of the Negroes, keeping time to their work. The Palm Grove Estate was in view. One voice seemed to lead in a sort of recitative, then the whole gang would join in chorus, and end the stanza : such is the true metre and spirit of African song.

Mr. Cardon seemed to lend a keen ear to the music, and once, when his companion addressed some question to him, he put up his finger in token of silence : " Hush !" he said, " listen."

> Oh! to beguile the labour of the day,
> And drown the sigh that struggles on its way,
> We'll cheat the white man as we creep along,
> *Chorus.*   With tune of merry song,
> Though plaintive of our wrong.
>
> Ah! little would he care like us to toil,
> For ever turning this detested soil :
> To us the harvest yields no joy or gain,
> *Chorus.*   But only brings us pain,
> The eating of our chain.
>
> The sea! that mirror of the heavenly vault—
> Is it the tears of slaves that make it salt,
> When vainly wishing they had early died,
> *Chorus.*   And o'er the vessel's side
> They lean, their tears to hide ?

K

When angry Heaven its airy cistern locks,
And with a drought the expectant planter mocks,
The whip's deep marks upon our shoulders grow,
Chorus.   And our tears like rivers flow,
            To enrich the soil below.

Our homes, our wives and children, what are they,
But the white man's mockery, victim, prey?
And how can we on such our love bestow?
Chorus.   A Negro's heart must know
            No feeling but of woe.

The white man's voice, 'tis angry, loud, and hoarse;
His frightful grasp, it has a hellish force;
And how can slaves escape his censuring eye,
Chorus.   But like the serpent sly,
            And with a coward's lie?

Yet, oh! when every fond emotion's still'd,
That ever once our own free bosoms fill'd,
And Slavery's breath has o'er our spirit pass'd,
Chorus.   Simoom from Obiah cast,
            With deadening poison blast.

Yet like the green Oasis in the waste,
One feeling still as fresh and rich and chaste,
Erect amid our soul's wide barren sand,
Chorus.   The love of fatherland,
            Will blooming take its stand.

Thus when a Negro stranger we shall meet,
And find in him a countryman to greet,
A bond all woven in deep mysteries,
Chorus.   By spirits in the skies,
            Will bind us in its ties.

"Some white man, I swear, has been teaching them that song : that is no Negro language nor Negro notion ; I have only caught the last words though," muttered Mr. Cardon.   "Fools! fools! fools! they have heard I am bringing home some fresh arrivals. *Les maudits!* they will sing anything but what I want them. See here, Dorset, here is something for you to learn."

The Englishman, who had somewhat lagged behind, now quickened his horse's pace, till he came to the planter's side.

"Here," continued the planter, "is some of the blessedness of slave-holding,—a confusion in the chaining, you will admit. Some years ago I took my family to live in the town, and of necessity left the management of the estate to my steward; but this did not quite please my Negroes: they liked their master better, they said: then how do you suppose they showed their love? Now, I am a man who likes to be absolute and have his way, but in this case the Negroes had theirs, *de par tous les diables!*—they instantly took to the poisoning work."

"Good God!" cried the other with a look of horror, "what is that?"

"They began with the mules; then the horses, cows, poultry, all went, till I began to fear worse; so I came down and listened to their songs, for the laws of society here forbid one white man to listen to any complaint against another. So, as I was telling you, I listened to their songs, found out what they wanted, and yielded."

"God bless me! but this is the most dreadful thing I have heard yet: I hope you found out the offender, and brought him to trial."

" Brought him to trial ! and suppose I did, and the wretch was condemned to be hanged, who would pay me for the loss, eh ? No, thank you ! when I want a Negro to be hanged, I hang him myself. But, *pardi !* in this case I knew them to be all concerned in it, every one of them, so I had nothing to do but to give in."

" What a horrible state of things !" exclaimed the other, drawing a long breath.

" Ay, but there is worse coming. This murdering work, or Obiah, as they call it, has been going on again upon my estate now for the last two years,—not only my cattle gone scores and scores of times over, but my best and choicest Negroes, till I am almost tired of renewing the gangs by fresh purchases. If I could only find out the sorcerer, or Obiah man, as they call him, I would hang him up on the very first tree ; but the Negroes are made to take such hellish, heathenish oaths, never to reveal how, when, where, and by whom the poison is administered, that it becomes hopeless to attempt finding out the criminals."

" Is there, then, no way of tracing it ? Methinks *I* could."

" No ; the poison is too subtle : neither taste, smell, nor appearance betrays its presence ; and when you consider that noxious herbs spring up everywhere beneath the Negroes' tread, you will begin to understand what a tremendous power they have in their hands."

" Well, well !" exclaimed the other with an expression of amazement, " at least for this there never was a parallel in England."

" You forget the Whiteboyism in Ireland, and the diabolical murders which could never be found out : can't you recognize something of the same sort here ? This is the only thing that makes me suspect Negro slavery to be a crime. Every system that sets might over right has everywhere the same result, and it often makes me dream that there really is some glimmering of humanity in the Negro. Dorset," he continued, " I once had three daughters and a son ; I loved them as all southerns love their children—better than my life. I accumulated wealth to establish them early according to their hearts' desire ; and, that I might see them happy, I travelled with them all over Europe, and brought them home, my three daughters first. Long as I had been gathering my wealth,—and God knows I have gone through hard trials enough to earn it,—I would have given it all to save my cherubs, and gladly have begun the world anew for their sakes. First went my girls,—my three beautiful girls : I saw them gradually and gently fading away before my eyes, and then in a few more months they were laid side by side in their quiet graves. My son ! my brave, bold boy ! I had left him behind me in France : that Mulatto dog was with him, or I should have laid the crime at his door. Well, my son returned, and married a poor but lovely girl : both gone, one after the other ! nothing left me now but their little infant to take care of. If I could save that one innocent head!—it is all I have left in the world to take care of or love. Sometimes I feel almost broken-hearted.

Mr. Dorset did not immediately address him. Whatever had been his opinion of his friend's hardness of character, he knew now that he had suffered; and a suffering creature, in Mr. Dorset's eye, had always a claim to sympathy.

"Can't you," he said after a considerable pause,—" can't you form any idea as to the cause of it?"

"Oh! how do I know? perhaps, if I were inclined to listen to the Overseer's gabble, I might suspect the woman Coraly."

"Upon what grounds?"

"He says he heard her swear on the dead body of her child to wreak vengeance on the family."

"But that is strange: what could it be for?—flogged perhaps?" said Mr. Dorset inquiringly.

"Flogged? *Pardi*, flogged indeed? she no more cares for a flogging than you would for the touch of a feather; I have seen the woman myself undergo a flogging that many a Negro man could never outlive. I have seen the blue welts rise like network upon her back, and when you thought she had fainted, she would suddenly jump upon her legs, and turning a pair of fiend's eyes upon you, would say, 'Tankee, Mas'r!' and walk unconcernedly away."

"God bless my soul!" devoutly exclaimed the Englishman, horrified at the tale, but too much interested in the issue to remark upon it yet; "but I can't help thinking, from what I know of the feudal submission of the Negro, that it must be some unusual wrong that has worked her up to vengeance: you ought to inquire into it."

"I tell you, you might do your very utmost with that woman, and she would not care. I have locked her up in the stocks myself, and she would scream all night, just to prevent the family from sleeping, and be none the worse for it next morning. But I'll tell you what seems to have been the cause: she was impudent to her mistress one day, and her infant was taken from her as a punishment, and locked up; the squalling brat took convulsions and died, and since that hour the very devil seems to have taken possession of the woman."

Our Englishman looked very grave. "Mr. Cardon," he said at length, "you are a man of intellect and feeling, and are reputed to be a man of honour and principle too: how can you reconcile to your feelings as a man,—excuse me, Sir,—to flog a helpless woman, to take away her infant from her, and lock it up? Oh, Sir! it is cruel work. You have talked a long time, with loud and bitter severity, on the social condition of England, but, thank God, at least we have not such cruelties as these to answer for: we don't carry barbarity quite so far as flogging a woman."

"Ho!" cried the planter with the least possible expression of levity, "chivalry! is it chivalry you are boasting of? English chivalry,—that's good! Now I acknowledge to considering the Negro but one degree removed from the brute, and I act accordingly. I should as soon think it a breach of the laws of chivalry to beat the mare I ride upon, as to flog an impudent Negress,—just the same. For the rest, where's the odds? You know the seat of pain is in the brain : well, what matters whether pain is excited on the back, when we call it flogging, or in the stomach, when we call it starving,—it is all imagination. But I tell you, Dorset, not to plume yourself quite so quick. We planters venerate the very name of woman,—mind, not a Negro woman,—but such as God has given her to us, fair, good, and beautiful,—an embodied angel, to refine our souls and lead us up to Heaven. We show it in our desire to establish our sons early, according to their hearts' desire, not for *money*, but for *love*. We are content, for this, to reduce our establishments as our children grow up, and give our sons sufficient to begin the world with, and to our daughters dowries to enable their lovers, if poor, to do the same. But what do your canting, moral parents in England? Would they reduce their establishments, to enable their sons to marry? No! but under the pretext of *prudence*, they grind their sons down to celibacy, till they are driven to profligacy. In the meantime, where has outraged nature taken refuge? In a boiling, seething lake of corruption."

"Sir !"

"*Oui, Monsieur*, a lake, into which is thrown

pêle-mêle the fair, the innocent, the trusting, the loving of God's holiest creatures. After that, talk to me of chivalry indeed! where is yours? Fallen like a needle into the sea of abomination which overflows the streets of your Babylon. Go, take a pitchfork, and rake it out if you can, and when you show it to me, I will give you my head."

"Mr. Cardon, these are grave accusations; there is scarcely anything more ungenerous than a sweeping censure. Just prove to me that the Negro is not a human being, has not a soul to answer for, has not a heart to feel, has not a claim to that salvation which our Saviour died to obtain; else I must deny your right to argue in this way."

"As for your women," interrupted the planter, perfectly unmindful of the remark, for he had got on his favourite subject again,—"as for your women, in spite of my respect for the sex, I don't know what to make of them. The mission of women from God is to sanctify our lives, and keep us brutes to what is right; but *your* women are so tainted with the hypocrisy of your Babylon, that to mention its corruption to them is an insult,—much more to expect them to correct it, poor innocent dears! Yes, they have suffered their work idly to pile up to such a height, that their souls may fly up to Heaven now, for any good they do; they are only in our way. *Fi donc! allez!* it is vain to speak; I see that you yourself, my friend, are so walled-in with a stone wall of prejudices, that you cannot even understand me. Well, no matter, for here is my domicile. *Mais que diable!*" he exclaimed, stooping low over his horse's head, and looking attentively on the ground, " what is all this?"

And in truth the road presented a strange appearance : it was strewn with broken eggshells, hair and feathers matted together with pitch and red powder and sulphur intermixed; further, from the overhanging boughs of the trees depended rows of eggs from a string, and, on rising suddenly to an upright position, Mr. Cardon's hat struck against one of them, which instantly burst, and covered his coat with a grey dry powder. The travellers both gazed at the strange accident; but in Mr. Dorset's face it was simple curiosity, while on the planter's brow there was care and anxiety. Neither of them spoke however till they reached the house, which they now approached at a smart space.

CHAPTER X.

THE MUSTER ROLL.

TROOPS of wild, half-naked domestics came out to welcome their master, with dips meant for curtseys, a wide display of white teeth, a rolling of white eyes, and a chattering of gibberish, to which the planter responded by a rap on the head of one, then of another, that stood in his way; while the pantomimic gestures of the sable youth and their sidelong glances at one another, as they discovered the powdered and stained coat of their master, may better be imagined than described.   There were some children among them too, young things eight or ten years old; but these kept behind,—not on account of their entire nakedness, for that gave no more offence than the nakedness of the cattle in the field, but in order to be out of the reach of their master's whip, for they read danger on his contracted brow.

The gentlemen dismounted before an open door leading through a veranda to the sitting-room of the house for, according to the hospitable custom of the Colonies, neither closed doors nor cautious porters ever impeded the entrance of strangers to any but a prison. The dwelling was low, formed entirely of wood, even to the walls, which were also shingled on the outside; and the naked beams and flooring of the garret formed the only ceiling to the rooms of the ground-floor. The partitions were neither painted nor papered, but wainscoted with fine cedar; and the uncarpeted floor, of narrow planks of the pitch-pine, just freshly scoured with sour oranges, was white as new wood, and fragrant as the forest grove. The windows had no curtains, but were guarded with frames of green gauze, instead of glass, to soften the midday glare; a huge crystal chandelier hung from the centre beam; and the furniture consisted of chairs, surcharged with heavy carving and broadly gilt, and an enormous looking-glass, hung obliquely from the wall, so as to reflect the floor and everything in the room at a falling angle. Between the windows, on one side of the room, was a stately sideboard, with all the glass furniture of the house laid out upon it; among which we must not forget to mention the sangaree-bowls, and several beautiful cylinders, used for shading the candles from the wind and night-moths, for the windows are never entirely closed. This was the saloon, or hall, as it is called in the Colonies.

Passing through this, the gentlemen entered an inner apartment, where a table in the middle, laid for dinner, at once showed the use of the room. The cloth was white as snow, the silver plentiful, the dishes and plates of the finest porcelain, from which a goodly row of female attendants, decked out with glittering necklaces, chintz skirts, and Madras coifs, were brushing away the flies with the aid of orange-branches and peacock-feathers. The mistress herself, a very fat, tall woman, with a languid look and sickly bilious complexion, was seated at the window, habited in a loose wrapper of white muslin, surmounted by a black silk scarf (she was in mourning); while on a cool Indian mat on the floor lay an infant asleep on a silken pillow, a Negro girl watching by its side. To this little object Mr. Cardon, after the usual salutations to his wife, directed his eyes on entering the room, and with affectionate pride he subdued his voice, and invited his friend to approach and take a peep. " Is he not the picture of peace?" he said, kneeling to look closer at him, and with fond solicitude fanning away the flies. " Look here, Dorset, he is the image of my poor son;" and further to show the expanse of its brow, he ventured to slip up the cap which had fallen over its cheek; but the huge fingers of the grandpapa were too awkward for so delicate a task, and several sounds of " hush!" from the other end of the room warned him to desist, just as a bunch of glossy curls burst from beneath the border, so black as to draw forth an exclamation of wonder from the Englishman. It was, upon the whole, a beautiful child,—not like the blonde and fair creations of northern fancy, but a little being in whose soft contour, though still marked with the helplessness of childhood, there dwelt many a promise of strength and stormy passion. He was about a year old.

" Whist! whist!" whispered the lady of the house, " leave the little creature to sleep, and do the honours of the house to your friend ; you must both of you be hungry, the dinner has been waiting for some time."

He was not long in obeying ; the infant was in the meantime removed to another apartment. After a short absence, to recompose their dress, the gentlemen took their places, and for awhile nothing was heard but the rattling of knives and plates. I scarcely know whether my readers expect a description of the dinner : it consisted, in the first place, like that of most planters, of a soup made from the *Arum maculatum*, and called calaloo ; there was also wild venison, stewed turtle, fricasseed iguana, and, to crown all, a dish of the famous grugru worm, for this is the grand dainty with old West Indians. Mr. Dorset shook his head when offered some, and looked away ; but Mr. Cardon assured him that his dislike arose from fancy and custom, nothing more, and that he himself was not less surprised and disgusted, when he first went to Europe, at the sight of stewed snakes (eels) and raw meat.

When the first demands of appetite were satisfied, conversation began ; at first in a general way, and afterwards on the more interesting particulars of home. Mr. Cardon inquired of his wife how the estate had gone on in his absence. She replied that things had gone on pretty well; that she had spent the day mostly in the hospital, attending to the sick, to the number of whom they would soon, by the overseer's report, have to add the Negro Anamoa.

"Well, that is no loss," observed the planter; "I was always sorry for that purchase. Dorset, I must show him to you; he is one of the Koromantyns, the only African nation, by the bye, for which I have a respect: they are brave, bold, and proud, and though I hate them for the trouble they give me, I am almost inclined to allow that there is something human in them," he added, smiling. Then, after a pause resuming, "As for this wretch, he was a prince in his own country, had his harem and his palace; he came to me just fresh after his capture, and, what do you think? at first he actually refused to work! I think I have cut that out of him though; and his countrymen in the field used to beg to do his task, but I have cut that out of them too, though I sometimes suspect they do his work by stealth. Well, how is Coraly?" he inquired, again addressing his wife.

"Oh!" cried the lady, "never speak to me about that woman, I am a martyr to her. I am the victim of my Negroes. You promised to sell her away to a distance : why don't you, St. Hilaire?"

"*Ma bonne amie*, I would give her for three stampees, if I could get any one to take her. I think I have struck bargains for that woman half-a-dozen times, if not more; but just as everything is concluded and she is delivered to her new master, she tells him she is good for nothing, can't work, can do nothing but spoil the Negroes and other wickedness; so of course I am obliged to take her back. However, Angélique, don't fret, I'll send her away over the sea, and get rid of her that way, for she is a curse upon me."

Madame Angélique Cardon sighed deeply, and Mr. Dorset, remembering all she must have suffered, felt compassion for her. Dessert was served, and showed the usual amount of delicious fruit — pine-apples, mangoes, bananas, balatas, sappodillas, etc., followed by confections and jellies, which Negro cooks so well understand. Dinner was about to conclude, when a sudden confusion arose at the upper end of the table, and half-uttered cries and sundry dips on the part of the Negro girls announced a domestic punishment; while the patient Madame Angélique, who had found a soiled plate set before her instead of a clean one, smashed it on the head of the sable attendant.

"Never fear!" exclaimed Mr. Cardon, observing the attention of his guest directed that way, "I assure you their heads are very hard."

A loud cracking of the whip put a stop to further remark: it was a signal for the muster-roll; and our planter invited his friend forth to an open lawn at the back of the house, where the Negroes were standing in a circle, each with a bundle of grass on the ground before him. The names were soon called, and they then commenced repeating the Vesper prayers in response to the Overseer, who stood a little apart, leaning against a mango-tree, his arms folded on his chest. Prayers opened with the salutation of the angel to Mary, which the Negroes repeated so unintelligibly as to call forth a remark from the Englishman expressive of regret that they were not taught to understand what they said.

"Hopeless, *mon ami !* quite hopeless !" replied the planter ; "you might as soon teach donkeys to speak. All that one can hope for is to inspire them with a religious awe once a day, and that is a great deal. Some of these Negroes were christened about a dozen years back ; I had just bought them, and my good wife, having very romantic ideas on the subject, took them in hand, and made a duty of teaching them."

"I am glad to hear that," exclaimed Mr. Dorset ; "so it was not she who took the woman's infant from her ?"

"My wife," continued the planter without attending to the question, "spent days in teaching those savages, and we had a priest here to perform the ceremony in a little pavilion attached to the house, which we always use for religious service ; I will show it to you. But the good Father neither spoke nor understood a word of the Negro patois ; perhaps he would have thought it desecration of his subject to give his sermon in it if he could ; be that as it may, he held forth in courtly French on the blessings of Christianity and the horrors of heathenism, and he

L

concluded with 'My friends, will you become the children of God?' Now my wife had taken particular pains to instruct them as to the way they should answer the priest whenever he put.a question to them; but the poor devils, addressed in a language they could not understand, had puzzled away their brains until startled by the question, and then they stood completely stupefied. 'Will you become the children of God?' again asked the priest kindly and encouragingly; when one fellow, that young black racoon you saw with me this morning—''

"Do you mean the one you called Quaco, who fell into the water?''

"The same; he was a lad of about sixteen or seventeen, apt and rash; he called out, at a venture, 'Non, mon Père!' Instantly the rest of the gang took it up, and the pavilion resounded with a round chorus of 'Non, mon Père!' The poor priest was taken aback: 'What!' he cried, 'do you wish to become the children of the Devil?' and Quaco, taking the lead, and thinking to correct the error, the pavilion again resounded with 'Oui, mon Père!' Out strided our impetuous pastor; he would have nothing more to do with such incorrigible heathens, he said; and it was with difficulty that, suppressing our laughter, we could pacify his anger and bring him back. So you see it is quite hopeless.''

During all this time the Englishman had full time and opportunity to note the groups before him. First of all there was Bretton, overseer of the Palm Grove

Estate,—a man with a small head and an immense visage, very sallow and much freckled; he had long bare jaws, and features in which a certain expression of low malice contended for mastery over the habitual indolent cast of his countenance. His dress differed from that of Mr. Cardon in being entirely of check-linen; it was very loose, in many places thin and much torn. He had no stockings to cover his slip-shod feet, and his large coarse straw hat hung slouching on his head, more from custom than with a view to ward it from the sun, for he stood in the shade. Mr. Dorset remarked that he did not remove it when the gentlemen approached, but merely nodded. This want of manners was partly owing to that footing of equality on which the meanest white person stands with the proudest and richest of his own colour in the Colonies, for it is to their interest that they should so uphold one another; but mostly perhaps this want of common civility belonged to the character and habits of the man himself, who had fallen too low to entertain any feeling of respect for a superior. He approximated closely to the savages whom he drove, without sharing one of their virtues; he was content to adopt the primitive habits of the African Negro, was equally destitute of the stimulus of am-bition, and equally forswore the trammels of decorum and self-respect.

For one thing however he was remarkable—no one had ever seen him under the influence of anger. Offences which often sent the master raving, only

L 2

made him laugh. His favourite pastime was first to provoke some unfortunate slave, and then, laughing at any impotent show of resentment, to punish the wretch with the wanton ingenuity of a mean nature: this formed the highest exercise of his intellect. Such was the individual who was leaning against the mango-tree. Having made his sign of recognition to Mr. Cardon, as related above, and gazed vacantly at the visitor, he turned away his head to speak to some of the Negroes assembled.

These were all barefooted,—not from poverty, so much as from a custom suited to the climate. The men were naked to the waist, and wore short trowsers; sometimes these were dispensed with, and a short apron adopted instead. Most of them bore on their shoulder their several implements of labour, viz. a bill, a hoe, and a spade, on which were hung a pair of wooden clogs, a gourd for holding water; a calabash to eat from, and a blue osnaburg mantle; a few carried a basketful of coffee-berries slung in front of them, as specimens for Mr. Cardon's inspection, as the full season of coffee-gathering was not yet come. The women were similarly laden; they also were barefooted and bare-shouldered, and distinguished from the men by having a kerchief twisted round their heads, and an ample skirt, whose folds, tucked up under their right arm, formed no ungraceful drapery about them. There was little to distinguish one nation from another, and whatever peculiarities had marked them in their childhood had now merged into one general character of care-less, hopeless apathy.

Some of the slaves, as in the case of Madelaine, had not a thought beyond that of following the orders they received; their covering fell literally in tatters from their bodies, and common decency, such as even Negroes understand it, was disregarded. Others again looked sickly, yellow in hue, and droop-ing in their gait, as, for example, a remarkably well-built Negroman, to whom the other slaves seemed to look up with respect;—very slight indeed were the tokens of it, sometimes only enough to raise a sus-picion, as, when bending under the load of his basket of coffee-berries, a young woman took it from him, and ran forward to show it to their master, asking his approval of the crop. He might have been forty-five, he looked sixty.

"Old crooked-backed thief!" said the Overseer with a drawling nasal twang as he pointed to him, and obliquely addressing the planter, " he pretends he is dying—it's all pretence; the lazy baboon, he does not like the work !"

"Won't work, eh ?" exclaimed the planter; " don't like it yet, eh ? maybe you will learn to like it when I take the whip to you myself."

The old man raised his head, and gave his master a look of defiance, while a smile of contempt and something like mournful resignation slowly crept about his shrivelled lips ; but this momentary feeling of courage, slight as it was, soon passed away, and he pointed appealingly to his legs : they were greatly swollen, and the skin all cracked.

Mr. Dorset, in his capacity of medical adviser, advanced to feel the old man's pulse : he examined his tongue, his eyes, his skin, and particularly his legs; one of the Negromen taking advantage of the opportunity to relieve him of his implements.

" Well ?" said Mr. Cardon inquiringly.

After a pause, and a renewal of the examination, the other replied, " Send him to the hospital immediately."

" Get along with you, you good-for-nothing old racoon," said his master roughly ; then added, " Go to your mistress." He always said this when he felt pity.

The Overseer began to laugh,—it was something between a sneer and a chuckle,—but he was too lazy to utter more till urged by Mr. Cardon. " Hey !" he then drawled forth, " he takes something to make them legs swell; he don't like the work."

" *He hab Obiah 'pon him*," answered some one in the assembly. The voice came from a woman resting sulkily against the wall of one of the outbuildings near. She was the healthiest-looking of the whole set, and seemed to have spirit and impudence enough for ten gangs; though standing apart, Mr. Dorset's examination of the Negroes seemed to interest her in no small degree, while with a keen, attentive eye, and an odd expression of contempt and curiosity, she watched every one of his movements.

"'Come, Coraly," said her master, "come here, you Negro-woman, we know one another of old; tell me now, and quickly, what you mean by Obiah."

The woman was erect in a moment, and with undaunted familiarity she spoke out.

"Me, Master! what nigger sabey (know), when white man not sabey?"

"I'll make you tell me."

"Me, Master!" she said, pointing to herself with emphasis.

"Or I'll take your grounds from you."

"Hey! hey!" she cried, stammering and stuttering her broken English with that childish accent which all, both white and black, adopt when speaking a foreign language they have never mastered; "hey! hey! well, me starve,—who lose nigger? not Coraly; who then care?"

"Coraly," said her master, fixing his eye significantly upon her, "I want to speak with you; come up to the house by-and-by."

"Master," continued the woman, "neber ask Coraly nothing, Coraly no sabey nothing; *no pick my mouth* (do not cross-question me), nothing there; but s'pose me sabey, s'pose me tell master, what good to Coraly? bring back a my piccaninny, hey? did master cry for Coraly piccaninny? Master, you 'member Mulatto Belfond's mammy? she loved master plenty, too much; she saved master's life two times: did that save her flog? no! dead saved her from flog."

She was interrupted by a nasal chuckle from the overseer, for which she darted upon him a look not entirely conscious of impotence.

Mr. Dorset was at this time busy examining a lad of about fourteen, whose countenance bespoke incurable imbecility. Coraly advanced close up to him.

" Fine slabe, Master," she observed ironically; "that oberseer good too much; cleber man ! he wanted to make this nigger-boy cleber too, so one time he flog him ebery morning 'fore he open his eye, 'nother time make him walk on four feet like a cat, then he tie him up like a dog, so maked him bark when people pass. So now Alibo, dis nigger-boy, is a fine cleber dog; put him under your bed, Master, a thief neber come to take your money again, he is a fine cleber nigger-boy."

The Overseer did not attempt to deny the account, but treating the story with that eternal laugh upon his lips which often rendered him so provoking, he asked Mr. Cardon whether it was not a good invention for punishing the boy who had poisoned the house-dog; upon which Coraly smiled contemptuously, perhaps because she knew it was a falsehood.

But now the eyes of the assembled Negroes turned in the direction of the road whence the noise of the great travelling waggon was heard creaking heavily on its wheels as it came slowly up the avenue, and Mr. Cardon, turning indoors, beckoned to his friend to follow. " We will look at them from the house," he whispered; "the meeting of the old and new Negroes is very amusing; but we must not stay here, or our presence will be a restraint, and then they are not half so comical."

The Negroes, considering themselves dismissed for the day, now left the grass-plot, and old and young, men and women, all started off to meet the new comers.

CHAPTER XI.

BLACK CATTLE BROKEN IN.——EFFECT OF THE COWSKIN.

THERE was one slave who had not joined the curious
throng,——Anamoa, the Koromantyn.   At first he stood
straining his eyes to see the inmates of the waggon;
then, as if seized with a sudden pang, he tottered away
in the opposite direction, till he came to a large stone,
when, overcome perhaps with exhaustion, he sat down
and covered his face with his hands.   And now the
rumbling waggon stops, the travellers alight, and immediately a clamour ensues which defies description.
The cry of joy, the warm greeting of love, the wail-
ing of grief, the deep murmur of disappointment on
the part of those who found none but strange faces,
and the muttered yearnings of childless mothers
anxious to adopt the young strangers, all offered a
scene of tumult perfectly bewildering.   Then a loud
voice was heard above the rest, and Quaco, his sable
face beaming with delight, led forth the savage beauty,
the young Talima, by the hand.   The noise subsided,

the crowd gave way as he passed, and with the whole assembly in his train he sought Anamoa, who was sitting upon the stone. The old Negro looked up, a scream rent the air, and Talima, throwing herself upon his neck, sank fainting at his feet. It was his child, his long-lost African child, whom he thought his old eyes were never again to behold. What were his feelings? Were they as keen, as bitter, as those of a white man placed under the same circumstances? Indeed I cannot say: the higher reasoning of the white man might render his feelings more continually tormenting, the deeper passions of the Negro might render his the keener,—perhaps yes, perhaps no; but this is certain—nature was there within him, degraded, injured nature, and the old man wept long and bitterly as he pressed his child to his breast. The other Negroes, who had gathered round, though all so noisy before, were now hushed, and spoke in whispers; even the little ones pressed closer to their mothers' side in silence, so sympathizing is the heart of the Negro.

The scene caused great merriment in the large house, the white people looking out through the jalousies and enjoying it each after his own fashion,—all but Madame Angélique Cardon, who was busy playing with the infant on the floor, while young Beneba, the nurse, though burning to join her companions, was kept dancing to amuse it. Mr. Cardon stood with his hands on his sides, contemplating the scene as one might a comedy. The Englishman, leaning forward on the window-sill, looked on with that interest which he might be supposed to take in the manifested emotions of beings whom he still considered human. Don Duro, the manager, who had come riding behind the waggon to see that the goods arrived safe, was sitting, nothing moved, and smoking, very comfortably on a chair, with his legs resting on the window-ledge; while the Overseer, with a low mocking laugh peculiar to himself, seemed unable to restrain his curiosity, for he soon left the company of the white people, to mix with the Negroes. Behold him now hovering round one group of women, then another, pulling their skirts, slapping their shoulders, or whipping off and flinging away their head-gear: he was very facetious at times. The young and good-looking girls shook him off with impatient disgust, the older and more prudent females moved out of his way, and the aged, who had learned something from experience, attempted a feeble response to his jokes. Thus disturbed, the Negroes, who hate the presence of white people in their leisure hours,—for, say they, "*white man's eye burns the Negro*,"—made a movement towards their huts, which were about half a mile distant, and visible from the great house, looking like a rustic village embowered in trees.

The Negroes on their way formed a circle round the old man and his daughter, as if to shield them from the white men's observation; but Bretton somehow managed to work his way into their midst, and as they passed, his playful humour prompted him to attack the young African with one of his lowest and most unfeeling tricks. Anamoa forgot himself: he had just recovered his child; his feelings had come back to him fresh and free, as when last he had parted from her; he, her natural friend and protector, forgot the loss of his rights, of his health, of his strength, when he saw her insulted; his ebbing spirit boiled up again, his feeble arm was nerved to vigour, and with one blow he felled the Overseer to the ground.

I have known a captain to be snoring in his hammock, wrapt in a sleep which not all the loud quarrelling of the passengers or the tramping of the cabin-boys could disturb: something went wrong on board, and in an instant the captain awoke, jumped from his hammock, and was upon the deck,—warned by what? some mysterious movement of the vessel, which he perceived as it were by instinct, even in his sleep. So it was with our planter: from the position in which he stood, and the manner in which the Negroes had crowded round old Anamoa, it was impossible he could see what had gone forward; but something warned him of danger, and before many seconds he stood in judgment on his recreant slave. A word had explained the blow, but no word was either asked or spoken concerning the provocation of this blow, though, if it had been, it would only have excited laughter; but the Overseer was not hurt, not he! there he sat on the ground, laughing with that low malicious laugh, most spiteful when least noisy.

At sight of their master the circle opened, and the

Negroes drew back terrified; and yet Mr. Cardon was merciful: he did not order the culprit's hand to be burnt, as was usually done for a similar offence in Martinique, St. Lucia, and elsewhere; he only ordered "the miserable brute" to be bound and flogged till not an atom of the flesh on his back remained whole. "*Sacre Dieu!* he would teach him to touch a white man: he would stand by to see it done himself!" The culprit was dragged forward, his body stripped, and bound to a ladder, in such a manner that the fore part of his person should be preserved from the action of the whip. While these preparations were going forward, Bretton, who liked nothing better than a scene of this kind, had seized the whip, and was diligently wetting it in a puddle near, to which he had crawled, —he was too lazy to stand up.

Mr. Dorset at first remained indoors, from a feeling of delicacy and reluctance to witness any domestic confusion; but when he saw them tie that tottering, feeble, sick old man to the whipping-ladder, the instinct of his benevolent nature induced him to join Mr. Cardon, though without any idea of interfering. His face contracted with nervous anxiety; he approached nearer and nearer, and then a remark from some bystander induced to look round at the Overseer. He well understood what the man was doing —wetting the whip, that it might carry off flesh with every stroke: impelled by indignation, he tore the whip from the wretch's hands.

"No interference!" whispered a voice in his ear,

" or you may witness scenes you won't like : believe me, let things be."

"I am not interfering," cried the young colonist; "but didn't you see what that—what the Overseer was doing? Don't you see plainly that the decrepit old Negro can't outlive it?"

"*Pardi !* he had strength to commit the sacrilege of touching a white man, so let him serve as an example."

Mr. Dorset yielded the whip into the planter's hand. But among the Negroes assembled a whisper began to circulate, which soon increased to an audible murmur, and those of the Koromantyn nation came forward and knelt in a suppliant attitude before Mr. Dorset. "You good heart, Massa ; *do beg for he,—he old ! he sick ! he shame !*"

"Back with you, you dogs !" thundered their master, leaving no time to his friend to reply to their request ; "*back with you !*" and before the uplifted whip, the sign of their degradation, the suppliants sprang upon their feet and took refuge timidly behind their companions. The whip has always a magical effect in taming men and reducing them to brutes.

But to the young Talima its power was yet unknown. During the foregoing scene she had remained completely bewildered. Her father, at whose word she had seen men fly, whose arm had felled lions in her own country,—her proud, fearless father,—she could not conceive why he had so unresistingly submitted

to be thus dealt with by those white men, unless perhaps it was part of some mystic ceremony; but when
she caught from the words of her companions some
idea of the truth, it was piteous to see how she seized
the cords with which they were binding her father,
and, her eyes streaming with tears, sobbed forth her
distress in her own unintelligible but earnest language.
Bretton dragged her away ; again and again she broke
loose from his brutal hold.

"Can't you hold her down?" asked the master,
grown impatient at the overseer's imbecility.   Bretton, in compliance, pinned the young slave to the
ground with his knee, laughing all the while at her
vain cries for assistance.

The whip was now handed to the driver.   The
driver is the Negro whose task is to flog the other
Negroes : he is always chosen for this honourable
post on account of his steadiness and obedience.   The
present driver belonged to the Mandingo nation, a
sly, cowardly, treacherous race, made ten times worse
by being reduced to slavery ; but this by the way, it
has nothing particular to do with my story.   The
cowskin was raised, and whistled as it fell, measuring
the old man's back.   He did not utter a word ; but
Talima's screams were fearful, to stop which Bretton
took off his shoe and stuffed it into her mouth.

"Lend a hand here," exclaimed Don Duro, "the
Negro is throwing back his head;" for the manager
had joined in by this time, and he was ever anxious
to show off to Mr. Cardon his knowledge of the

Negroes' ways. "Come, some one, light a piece of wood, and bring it here."

The temptation was too great for Bretton to resist, so giving up the charge of his prisoner to some of the slaves who stood nearest, he pressed forward to offer his services, for a new and more exciting pastime : and what was that? simply to raise the ladder, and place it resting against the tree, then to hold a burning torch before the victim's face, in order to divert him from suicidal intentions,—in short, from swallowing his tongue,—a practice often resorted to by African slaves when their lives become unbearable. In the midst of the confusion however Talima had again sprung forward, and, with her arms clinging fast about her father's neck, she endeavoured to shield him by interposing her person between him and the whip. Bretton tried to pull her away with one hand only, for he did not like to let go the torch with the other; but here the incensed planter stopped him.

"*Corbleu!* leave her alone," said he; "since she likes it, let her have it."

"Cardon! Cardon!" exclaimed Mr. Dorset, unable any longer to contain himself; "have you no flesh and blood in you, that you have so little mercy for those unfortunate beings ?"

"I'll double the number of stripes for that!" cried the planter, frowning.

"But the girl,—she has done nothing."

"Nothing? well! I tell you she likes the flogging,

M

or she would not put herself in the way of it. Strike away at her, driver, and let her have it well; when she has fainted, we'll go on with her daddy."

The cowskin descended again with a broad sweep, not upon the old man, but upon his unoffending child, and a blue welt rose high across the polished shoulders of the innocent victim.

" God of mercy !" exclaimed Mr. Dorset, horror-struck at the sight, " this place is cursed, let me hurry from it !" and he rushed precipitately from the scene,—he scarcely knew whither. He had strided into and through the house, up the palm-lined walk, and through the gate to the high-road, before he re-covered himself sufficiently to think where he was going. It was evening; the sun had just set, and earth for a moment was bathed in splendour, giving response to the departing glance of the light-giving god ; then twilight came, and already the curtains of darkness were drawing close around. It is thus that night comes on in those countries, with the rapid, pas-sionate character of all changes within the tropics. As Mr. Dorset slowly made his way along the road, many a sad and painful reflection came to his mind. The old fable of selling one's soul to Satan for wealth seemed to be realized before his view. He looked at the rich coffee-grounds which bordered the road, and in imagination he saw on each crimson fruit the warm droppings of human blood. His eye turned from them to the soil on which he trod; he thought he read there dire inscriptions of cruelty and wrong.

"O God!" he exclaimed aloud, "and is this the amusement of planters? are these the scenes which must in time become palatable even to me? England! my beloved country!"—but here he stopped, for a host of strange misgivings came crowding on his mind. The conversation he had had with Mr. Cardon in the morning—the things the planter had said—his retaliating accusations, could they be well founded?—were things so bad at home? Was the heart-rending misery so often witnessed there among the lower order, was it indeed inflicted on them by the upper classes? "Or," said he, "am I groping for truth in vain? Am I striving and vainly struggling against a wall of prejudice, as high as that which imprisons the feelings and reason of Cardon himself? Then, so is nature one universal working of cruelty, one echoing cry throughout the globe, of one creature preying upon another, man feeding on the vitals of his fellow-man. O Almighty God, show us thy mercy! make manifest thy providence!" He sighed deeply, and the sound of the evening breeze, passing lightly among the boughs of the forest, seemed to him an echo to the melancholy tenour of his thoughts.

CHAPTER XII.

THE OBIAH PRIEST.

THE mountains which rose at the back of the village were clothed, like all the Trinidad heights, with thick forests old as the flood. There was one however, not so high as the rest, on which the woods were somewhat thinner; its lower part was mainly covered with a comparatively scanty brushwood, but half-way up this gave place to a dense thicket of nux-vomica, palma-christi, the branched calaloo, poisonous shrubs of the cockroach-apple, and many other noxious bushes, all crowded so closely together as to be almost impenetrable. Nature, so beautiful and enchanting elsewhere on the mountains, here assumed a most repulsive aspect: dark, dismal blossoms, huge, misshapen fruits, and glossy leaves almost black with venomous sap, were mingled with thorns, long, pointed, and protruding, like spears of ugly gnomes; while a rank smell of unwholesome vegetation rendered the atmosphere around unpleasant and difficult to breathe.

The chance traveller, hewing his way in these unfrequented parts, would turn aside to seek more practicable subjects for his hatchet, and the wild animals, the free tenants of the forest, would avoid it, as by an instinct given them by nature; yet through the tangled bushes that formed these melancholy shades, ever and anon there peeped the shrivelled face of an old Negro, listening, spying, watching, as if for the approach of some one. Sometimes, in his eagerness, he would half expose himself to view, and then might be seen strange appendages—snakes hanging and coiling about him, caressing him.

At the foot of the mountain, just commencing the ascent, there was one who did not dream of such a spy. Belfond had taken this direction from sheer absence of mind: he knew it would be dangerous to loiter about the village, as he might soon be recognized; he therefore betook himself to the first opening or semblance of a path into the forest, thinking to return at night to the mimosa-tree for the rest of the money, and start with it to Guiria in any boat he could lay hold of.

Belfond had formed no particular plan for himself, but the world was all before him. Experience, it is true, had given him some hard lessons, but with youth, vigour, health, and that fillip to his spirits derived from having foiled the planter, how could he despond? Besides, his was a proud heart, which could not, would not bend before a disappointment, and he now sought to drown regret in the exciting dreams of ambition.

He would not allow his thoughts to revert to Laurine for a moment, but sought to keep them in check by amusing himself with anything hap-hazard. He drew a knife from his belt, and commenced trying his arm upon the strongest trees, and then pulled away by main force the tough lianas which looped and knotted them together. Then he climbed a tree, the tallest he could discover, and mounting from branch to branch with a dexterity which long experience alone can give, he stood on the very top, to watch the slave-ship from which he had been driven. His keen eye could even detect the movements of the people. He saw the Koromantyn girl taken down from the foremast, and recognizing his master's boats putting off immediately after, he judged by whom she had been bought. " But this is nothing to me," said he, " only I must get down now, unless I choose to be perched up here all day ; for should I get down but to eat a piece of bread while those people are walking about, they will catch me."

He quickly descended, and plunged into the thicket, going heedlessly on, until the pathway became fainter and fainter and was at last entirely obliterated, so that not even his practised eye could detect a trace among the impenetrable woods now thickening before him. Some confused recollection of the place kept him hesitating ere he turned back, when he was startled by the low snarling of a dog, and almost at the same time a wizen fiendish face peeped out from the thickest part of the copse. He knew it well ; it belonged to the being whom, after his master and Higgins, he disliked most in the world,—the Negro sorcerer, the Obiah man. It is true his dislike for them was not the same : his feeling towards the first was unmixed hatred, but here it was a loathing disgust. Fanty however had a claim upon him, for he was his mother's brother, and the only being upon earth to whom he could claim kindred.

Here, Reader, I find myself in some difficulty ; for in relating the conversation which took place, if I give it in the precise words and language in which it was uttered you could not understand it, or, if you could, the clipped and broken manner in which the Negroes connect the words of a language to them so foreign as their masters', would make that appear childish and ridiculous which was neither the one nor the other in its purport. So with your leave I will transcribe it into as fair English as my vocabulary permits.

Seconds passed, and minutes too, and still that fiendish visage and Belfond were eyeing one another. This seemed to amuse the wizard, for he laughed with a strange noise,—a sort of snarl, like that of his dog. Immediately after, and with the shrill quivering tones of fretful age, he said, using the similes and proverbs of Negro dialect, "*Flying deer hath lion near :* who pursues now ? And are the cayman's eyes sore, that the turtle has come out of the water ?—you are wet, I see. 'Tis well, dark sky looks out for the tardy sun, for it knows it must come at last : I have been watching for you ; come in."

Belfond obeyed, the bushes giving way as he pressed them.   An open space, with a sheltering mango-tree, was the sorcerer's parlour; his sleeping-room was a cave, from the roof-edge of which there hung numberless amulets, such as bags of all sizes, egg-shells, deer's horns, and parrots' beaks; his companions were an American dog bald of hair, and three snakes, which came hissing and rearing towards the stranger, when a growl from the sorcerer sent them back to their hiding-place.

"Sit down," said the Negro, bringing out a stool from the interior, and setting it down with force.

Belfond seated himself, and looked moodily on the ground, wondering how on earth he should get out of this malencontre.   The wizard went back to his cave, and remained there some time,—so long that Belfond began to look round him with a view to beat a retreat; but he was not quick enough—his kinsman was upon him before he could stir.

"Here," he said, "is something you are to do for me; you must go down yonder over the mountain, where your master lives."

"I have no call to the Palm Grove now, Daddy Fanty," which was the name this priest of dark science went by; for the Negroes number among their virtues a Spartan respect for old age: the old men go ever by the title of either Daddy or Uncle, as the old women by that of either Mammy or Aunty.

"You will have to call there for me; you must give this to Beneba."

Belfond looked at the old Negro's outstretched

hand; it held a tube of bamboo-cane, closed up at either end with a cork.

"This," continued the Obiah man, "is a soft paste, which Beneba must rub into the baby's clothes every morning, and down its back after it is washed."

Belfond recoiled with horror: "It is Obiah! it is Obiah!—take it away."

The sorcerer's arm stiffened as it fell to his side, his eyes glared, his jaws quivered with evil meaning.

"Don't give that to me," said Belfond hoarsely.

The Negro's eyes were still upon him, while a low, nasal, snarling murmur gradually and slowly shaped itself into words: "You mule! you fawn on the white man! you traitor, who would deny that your mother was a Negro—"

"Stop there!" cried Belfond, "you dare not say that in earnest; you know well how I have loved my mother's people, you know well what I have done for them. Who gathered the Maroons up in the mountain yonder? Who taught them to till the ground, to lay up stores, to do without white people and their markets? Who taught them songs, and order, and courage? Who would have raised the glorious standard of liberty for them,—liberty and freedom, like America, like France,—and have made them a people among the nations of the earth, had they but listened to me and gathered round me like men, brave, bold, generous? But no! they would not, could not believe me: they must be murderers like you, and go, like sneaking cowards at midnight, to set fire to the white man's house, and murder him as he escaped from the flames. I am not a man to do that; I wouldn't head such warfare, no, not to save a thousand lives if I had them; nor will I now be your minion, and bewitch infants with Obiah; go, send your snakes to do that work, not me."

"You, fawn on the white man!" continued the Negro, "you would save him, as your mother did."

"My mother!" said Belfond, "I know she loved my master, and I have not much to thank her for in that, and I know too what she got for it."

The Negro uttered a sharp snarl of exultation.

"Yes, I know she betrayed the secrets of her people when they were plotting an insurrection, and his would have been the first murder they had begun with: yes, and another time she spilled the poisoned coffee when he was about to drink it. Yes—"

"Your father!" growled the Negro, gnashing his teeth.

"Yes, my father! curse the word, I wish it stuck in my throat; I know all, and will tell you all, that you may know how deeply these things lie here," he said, pointing to his breast. "My father pampered her and brought her up to a gentle living, and I was scarcely born when he brought a wife home. Well, it was all in the regular course of things; but my mistress took a hatred to my mother, and, placing me with an old mammy to rear, sent my mother to work in the field, though she begged on her knees, crying and appealing for the sake of God to let her nurse her child just a little longer; and my mother could not dig fast enough, so they flogged her, and then she pined and died,—yes, by good luck for her."

"Not so Coraly," muttered the sorcerer, nodding.

"No, I know that; I know they met with tougher flesh in that woman; but I am not revengeful, and my mistress is subdued enough now: you ought to be content."

"But I am not content, and the little boy must go next."

"I will have nothing to do with murdering babes, I tell you," said Belfond, raising his voice.

"Then I will get some one else to do it for me soon enough," said the Negro, filling up with a low growl each pause as he spoke; "but for my dead sister, I would loathe you for a coward, a mule, a mongrel, a fawning lover of the cotton-face, a contemner of the true and the black. Look there," he said, pointing scornfully to the golden hue of Belfond's hand, "Koromantyns' blood has grown muddy there; and with a muddy heart, you mule, you love the whites that kick you; you writhe, and twist, and turn, and then you lick the foot that does it: the Obiah curse be on you and everything you love! I will get somebody else to do it."

Belfond did not resent the anger of his kinsman; his thoughts were busy on something else. "Poor little child!" he mentally exclaimed, "before God he stands as near to me as this murdering priest. Once, when by stealth I visited the Palm Grove, and met Beneba and her charge in the savannah, the innocent baby smiled on me, and opened its arms to come to me, as if I was its father. Poor little babe! I will not have it hurt: I will practise a deceit: God help me, that I cannot do the slightest good without treachery and cunning."

With this he turned upon the old Negro a calm, clear eye; but the tone of his voice was mournful, as he said aloud, "Daddy Fanty, I have thought better of it; I will take the Wanga oath; the old commands the young."

The Dagoman did not speak; he stood looking at him steadfastly.

"Yes," continued the youth, "give it to me; what am I to tell Beneba?"

The Obiah priest, still suspicious, squatted himself down on a log of wood opposite, and rested his chin upon his elbows to peer into the young man's face.

"Come, give it to me," said Belfond, stretching forth his hand, "you may trust me, I am half Koromantyn; I swear by the Obiah Wanga I am true; give it to me, I will drink the Wanga and obey."

The Negro, upon this, rose up and went into the cave.

"No matter," thought Belfond, "if I must, I must; and what if it is stuff to kill me and I die? an hour sooner or an hour later will matter to no one," he added with a sigh, "and life is but a curse to me; but if I can save the little child, he at least is a treasure to many, and his life will be precious to him by-and-by, since he can enjoy it. Yes, and the child *shall* live !"

The Negro now returned, holding a bottle, a small phial, and a mug. Into the mug he poured something from the bottle—it was rum; from the phial he scooped out with a slender stick some black stuff—it was the Obiah; and then he added water, and mixed them all: it was the drink of secresy, the Wanga, which should punish him who violated the promise given.

"Now," said he, "drink it off while I give you the words: now repeat with me:—

> Obiah's power, Obiah's spell,
> Pains of earth and pangs of hell,
> Alight on him who dares rebel
>   Against the Obiah's law !
>
> And toads' and serpents' tongues shall lick
> His flesh, which dead men's teeth shall pick,
> And worms shall creep in numbers thick
>   O'er him who breaks the law !
>
> And Obiah's secrets you shall keep,
> And in its magic you shall steep,
> Till comes your turn in death to sleep,
>   For such is Obiah's law !

Very well ! drink ! come, off with it !"

"Ugh !" said Belfond, draining the mug, "it is the most nauseous draught I ever took."

The old man's eyes twinkled: he had often before urged his nephew to take the Wanga without succeeding, but now he considered him his own, and in his withered heart there arose a sort of spurious affection for the young man. "There!" he said, "though I see you have spilt some, I am at ease now; *the dog is strong with his own.* Where were you going this morning?"

"I was simply waiting for the night, to go off to Guiria, but of course I will put aside that idea in favour of the Palm Grove ; give me the box."

"Belfond," said the Negro, "never can you try the sea without my leave, but I will speak of this anon. Here is the bamboo box : Beneba has her instructions from me already; here is her own antidote in this small bag, give it to her, she knows how to make ptisane of it : she must give it also to the mistress, according to my instructions, which she has already. And here is an Obiah bag for the master; it is to be sewed up in his pillow before tonight : when he puts his head down, the egg will burst within the pillow."

"And who," asked Belfond, looking up at the Negro with much curiosity,—"who of all these is to die first? Is it the child, or the master?"

"Master is not to die at all!" cried the sorcerer at the top of his cracked voice ; "he is to get blind, and then—by-and-by—go mad! mad! mad! And Mistress, she can't marry, and she shan't die ; and he shall go mad! mad! mad!" said the Negro, uttering a yell of exultation such as fiends send forth at thoughts of destruction.

"Whist! whist!" said Belfond; "prudence, Daddy Fanty! don't you know how many white men are near? *Mountains have ears as well as tongues.*"

" Ay," replied the other, recollecting himself, " *sleep should be light with him who eats the tiger's young one.* I forgot myself; but tell me, son of my dead sister, wherefore were you about to try the sea ? Why seek the water, when dry land has soft blossoms for your feet ? though, were it otherwise, a brave man's foot fears not even a thorn."

" I am no coward," repeated the young man proudly, " I fly no danger, I am ready to meet it now as ever."

" Then, O my son, have you tried the cutlass ? Know you how it cuts the cotton-skin flesh ? or do you love the white man too much to try ?"

" I have said before," returned the young man, rising angrily to his feet, " that I will fight the white man in a fair way,—man to man, and sword to sword, —as the brave do."

" Poor fool !" said the sorcerer quietly, fixing his eyes upon him : " know you the power which gives the white man sway over the Negroes ?"

" Certainly! undoubtedly! it is knowledge : I have been in their country, and I ought to know it."

" Knowledge ?" continued the other in the same calm tone, " yes, Obiah-knowledge ; and would you have the Negroes wield cutlass in the broad day against the white man's Obiah, which works in his head all night ? But let Negro cutlass cross white man's cutlass, and Negro Obiah cross white man's Obiah, and I will say for once it is fair ; but this they will not do, Belfond,—they steep their guns and cutlasses in their Obiah, and then they kill you. Poor

fool, Belfond! you won't believe old Fanty. My son,"
he added almost affectionately, "it is only Obiah and
cunning and sly ways that will enable the Negroes to
put their foot upon the high ground; use the Obiah,
my child; be wise, and then you will get to look the
white man in the face. The white man's Obiah is
weak before the Negro's Obiah, if all would only use
it: the Negro's Obiah commands life and death; fire,
water, birds, and brutes, all obey the Negro's Obiah.
Did you see such power as that with the white man?"

"Daddy Fanty, these things affect life, it is true,
and your fame the vales repeat to the mountains, but
let your power do good, not evil; your Obiah is no
real friend to the Negroes: he is no friend who kills
his friend."

"Yes, yes!" said the old man, with an emphatic
motion of the head and with slow and measured
words, "friend and true! For the Spirit of Death
that serves me, whither does it take the Negroes?—
through the Obiah power it takes them to Africa's
shores, free! free! free! where no slave-hunter nor
slave-chains can reach them. But hist!"

They both listened, the young man standing erect,
but grave and attentive; the crippled form and shrivelled face of the old man were bent anxiously forward,
looking down towards the valley.

"I hear shoes down the mountain," observed Belfond.

"Yes," said the old man with solicitude; "there,
son of my forefathers, they come; but stay a moment

yet," and he led him on a few yards, where the thorny
bushes seemed best to forbid approach : "stay behind
here, lest any one should come unawares." Then
leaving him for a little, he returned to his gloomy
cave, and brought back a string with an amulet de-
pending from it, and throwing it about the young
man's neck, he said—

"There ! not a Negro yonder, or anywhere, shall
dare betray you ; seek the white man ever so briskly,
ever so cunningly, for harm shuns this. Accompong,
the African Great Spirit, has looked upon it ; Assarci, the God of mercy, the Mediator, has blessed it ;
Obboney, the God of evil, fears it. The sun light thy
path, my son, and thy shadow fall upon him who seeks
thee ! for by the rising of my gall it is a white man
who comes."

So saying, the old Negro turned abruptly from the
bushes, leaving his nephew to thread his way through
the maze.

N

CHAPTER XIII.

THE VISIT OF AN ENEMY.

LEAVING our young traveller to make his way through the dense thicket with the usual ease of a forester, let us look in at the old Dagoman, to see whom he receives, and upon what errand. It was no unusual thing with him to receive a visit, but his visitors were rarely white people: his retreat, although the approaches to it were so dismal and forbidding, was sought by slaves from far and near; the discontented, the angry, the revengeful, the despairing, the wronged, all came to him for relief.

"The estate has been left in charge of a manager we dislike, give us a spell to bring back our master," said one; and the Dagoman would mix his dose, and mortality among the cattle would commence.

"Our master is going to Europe," would another complain; "I love him, and yet he leaves me behind, give me a spell to keep him with us;" and three horses would expire that night.

"Our master has understood, he has given in," would the party say on the next visit; "give us an antidote for the other animals we have commenced dosing;" and, true enough, no further mortality would be seen there.

"The situation of our grounds displeases us," declared a messenger from a distant estate, "they are on the side of a steep hill, and unpleasant for us to cultivate; give us something that will show our discontent to our master." This messenger came but once; the Negro songs at field-work revealed the cause which brought the odious visitor—the Obiah spell, or let me speak in plainer words, the poisoning work; the master wisely granted what was wanted, and it went away.

As may easily be supposed, our Negro sorcerer made a fair living by this work. He was one of the old and useless who had been turned off the Palm Grove Estate when Don Duro Harding took the management of it. This however was done without the knowledge or approval of Mr. Cardon: he had always been given to understand that these slaves had run away, and were not worth attempting to recapture. Old Fanty, driven abroad to shift for himself in his old age and crippled condition, turned sorcerer and poisoner to maintain himself. The trade he chose was a lucrative one; people said he had amassed an immense deal of money.

The old Negro adopted various contrivances for making himself feared: one of these was the choice

N 2

of strange pets.   The companions of his life were
three snakes, the largest of their kinds, and an American dog entirely destitute of hair.   Of the reptiles,
one was an aboma, or boa-constrictor, fourteen feet
long, which he called by the name of Mottle. Another
was a horse-whip snake, green, and tapering finely off
to the tail, not in reality a dangerous kind, but feared
by the Negroes from a superstitious belief that it
whips to death any stray Negro it can seize; this the
sorcerer named Cowskin. The third was a coral snake,
the most venomous reptile of the Colonies, figured
throughout its length with alternate rings of red and
deepest black; this he called Vixen.   These creatures
wound themselves about the wizard's neck and arms,
caressing him and obeying him, and guarding his
gloomy domicile with their various noises of alarm and
anger.   How he had tamed them no one knew; the
Negroes, over whose minds he had acquired an absolute
dominion, considered his control over them as part and
parcel of his divining power.   The native Spaniards,
however, or Spanish Indians I should rather say,
would hint at the wonderful properties of a pretty
little climbing plant, the *Mikania Guaco*, the juice of
which, taken internally as tea, and inoculated into various parts of the body, acts as an effectual antidote
to the bites of the most venomous serpents.   Its virtues, they will tell you, were discovered by a Spaniard
who accidently witnessed the fighting of two serpents.
The combat was deadly, and ended with the apparent
death of one of them; but no sooner had the victor

gone his way, than the wounded one crawled slowly and with difficulty to the bushes near, and choosing from among them the leaves of a climber, he recovered thereupon marvellously, and in a little time also went his way. The Spaniard with curiosity remarked and examined the plant, to which botanists have since given the name above mentioned. With the juice and leaves of this the sorcerer was supposed to have inoculated himself; or he may probably have extracted the reptiles' fangs by wrapping his hand in thick leather, presenting it to the serpent's mouth, and then dexterously withdrawing it, when the fangs, driven deep into the leather, would come away with it. Be that as it may, to the horror and awe of all who visited the sorcerer, there were the snakes, perfectly obedient to his word, and to him at least perfectly harmless. They knew him well, and came at his call, each according to its name—Mottle, Cowskin, and Vixen. As may be supposed, he was attached to them,—perhaps because he knew they were the only creatures on earth who cared for him.

With a considerable degree of agitation, the old Negro, just as he had parted from Belfond, and before he had had time to advance many steps, heard the loud yelping of his dog; then a confused noise of angry snarling and yells of pain, as if wild beasts were worrying his favourite to death; then a pistol-shot, and repeated blows as of a cutlass,—all within his domicile, and he but a few yards off! "Evil betide these limbs," he cried, "that I can't move quicker, and there is mischief at work in my home!" The first thought that came to his mind was that somebody had betrayed him, and that the bushrangers had come to catch him ; second thoughts convinced him he was wrong. Stupid as the Negroes are supposed to be, they are wonderfully quick at calculating motives and fathoming the interest which prompts to an action, and Fanty was a man of experience. " I should be a dead weight to any white man," thought he ; " they would have to feed me and house me, and I am too old and too deformed to work ; they don't want me ; they won't take me. But what can it be?"

He crept round amongst the bushes, peeped in slyly, very slyly ; then there burst from him a shriek which made the very woods to ring, and he leaped forward and threw himself on the ground,—a proceeding which astonished the visitor so much that he started back. It was Higgins. Luckily the dogs were too busy in finishing their work to notice the entrance of the Negro, and of course after their master had commenced conversation with him the sagacious creatures did not molest him.

" Holloa !" cried Higgins, on perceiving the Dagoman, " you old baboon, is this where you live ? Why I took it for the den of a runaway. Strike me dead, but this is luck ! But harkye, crooked ape, what made you go away just now and leave me to be bitten by your d—d snakes, hell-dragons I should say ? But I'm used to them, and I'll warrant I have laid them low ; had it not been for the Captain's dogs here, which by good luck I borrowed, I should have been a pretty sight by this time."

The Dagoman made no reply, but, with his hands clasped above his head, exclaimed, "Eh, my Gad! my Gad! my Gad!"

"Can't you get up from there, for a black deformity as you are?" exclaimed Higgins; "I have no time to lose in keeping watch over your wailings; I've got other fish to fry, I can tell you. But last time I saw you, and 'twas down in that there village, you told me you wanted a box of Obiah; so here it is, old cripple, I got it on the coast of Guinea. Come, have done with your —— swaying, and speak to me," he said, pushing him with his foot.

During all this speech the Dagoman had remained on his haunches, bending backwards and forwards, the very image of despair; but the contact of the white man's foot roused up all the spirit he had ever possessed. "Go off with you, cotton-face murderer!" cried he, striking back the proffered hand. "Obiah? me no Obiah. You have killed all I loved in the world: curse your hand!"

Higgins made a feint to laugh, though he felt more inclined to storm; but he wanted to see first how much money he could get out of the Negro by fair means.

"You and your snakes, old black Jumbee—! but I've got no time to be jawing about a madman's fancies; just you fork out the dollars. Come, just look now, there are all sorts of things there, and, by

Jericho and Neptune, the more Negroes you poison the better,—the better I'll be. I mean to turn trader myself, and bring contraband goods to the coast; so go on, ugly old shrivelled nigger, poison their sooty blood as quick as you can. Come, get up, and get me the dollars."

" I'll give you nothing," said the Negro, " devil yourself, and fiend !"

" You speak so to me, do you? my Jo, you won't find it much to your profit; but we'll see !" and he fairly lifted the old man from his sitting posture to his feet, adding, with a threat worded not in the holiest of terms, " If you don't now, this minute, fork out those doubloons,—and you shall give me three,— I will set the dogs upon you. Come, Bull ! Fangs !" chirping to the dogs, " just come here."

The old Negro, somewhat recalled to his senses, eyed the dogs and began to quake; particularly when he recollected how well trained to such work were the dogs kept by the white men, and how defenceless he stood, with his dead favourites strewn upon the ground before him. " I've got no money," he said doggedly.

" You have," said the sailor with a terrible oath ; " and if you don't make haste, I'll make you give out more than you like."

" And where is a wretched old Negro like me to get money ? Do you see me in the towns ? Do you see me working, or trafficking, or selling ? Would you squeeze blood out of a stone ?"

" I'll squeeze blood out of you in very quick time,

and teach you how to say 'Master' too, when you speak to me," said Higgins; and pulling forth a strong rope from the depths of his pocket, he proceeded to tie the old man in spite of his groans and remonstrances, while the two dogs kept snarling and showing their teeth, as if impatient to begin their proper task. But Higgins, entertaining some indistinct fear that the body of the Dagoman, if bitten, would bewitch the dogs, warned them off eagerly.

"Get away, Fangs, I tell you! Off, Bull, and keep your tusks for other game. Come! Whew!" and he enticed them away after him as he went into the cave to rummage; but what this cave contained daylight had never yet betrayed, and Higgins felt the want of a candle.

"Come, you ugly beast," he said, returning, "tell me quick, where is the tinder-box and candle?"

"A poor, miserable old man, a wretched, helpless Negro never has a candle, Master; he goes to bed by twilight, and he rises with the dawn."

Higgins entered the cave again, but soon returned with a roar of pain. "A scorpion! oh! sent by the devil to bite me!" he roared, as he came forth, holding out his hand to look at the place, and writhing with the pain.

Inwardly the Negro chuckled; outwardly he broke out into protestations of innocence, for he knew that the rencontre would be visited on him.

"Hold your foul tongue, will you!" cried the sailor, seating himself, the burning agony of his hand almost taking away his breath; "let me but get a little ease—oh, the pain!—and I'll serve you out."

His hand began to swell visibly; from the one puncture had oozed a drop of pink water, and around it, in a broad rim, was a livid purplish hue, which told how venomous had been the bite. Raging with pain he leaped up.

"I'll not bear this! Get me the money, you shrivelled bat, at once, if you wish to live another hour."

"How, Master," asked the Negro, in a meeker tone,—"how can I get what you want when I'm tied up in this way?"

"True! wait; but with this hand I can't manage," he said, as though thinking aloud; "I'll cut them!" So saying, he took the cutlass he had laid down, and without scruple cut flesh and rope together.

"Oh, Master!" yelled the Negro, "mercy! mercy! I'll get you some money! I have a little: I'll get it. Mercy!"

"Then get it, old vampire, and at once," growled the sailor, grappling the crippled form of the Negro and dashing him forwards; "give money, quick!" and approaching him again, he kicked him till he rolled over and over again; "get up, and bring me the money, and if it is not a handsome bagful, I will dash your brains out against the walls of this very cave, and leave the dogs to bury you."

The sorcerer knew he had no resource: his Obiah failed him here; it could do nothing against the sudden action of superior physical force upon a sickly,

feckless, powerless old man as he was. He was glad
enough therefore to get up, when, followed by the
white man, he crawled all trembling to the foot of a
mango-tree, and digging some little way down with a
spade which he took from the forking of the branches,
he uncovered to the astonished gaze of Higgins a
bag of considerable weight, which the sailor instantly
grasped with a hungry eagerness, forgetting for a
moment, in the joy of possession, the agony he en-
dured in his hand. It was heavier than he expected,
and he had to use main force to lift it, and still
greater efforts to heave it over his shoulder.

"Is this all you've got,—eh, black rascal?"

"Oh, Master, search all over here, I haven't a
stampee to buy myself a bit of cassava for supper."

The sailor did not deem it convenient to press further; the bag, he felt, was as much as he could con-
veniently carry or conceal; he allowed himself therefore to appear lenient, and made as much of it as he
could.

"You old ugly baboon devil, I know you have got
another hoard, but I'll let you off this time on one
condition. There's a runaway—"

The necromancer grinned dismally.

"Don't be showing me your ugly teeth, old bat, but
up, and help me to catch him."

"Me, Master? me?" exclaimed the Negro piteously, "with old legs like these? Turtle walks faster
much than old Fanty."

"Do you think I wanted you to run after him, you

drivelling old beast?   No; but use your Obiah, and
set a trap to catch him."

"Master, who do you want?"

"You know very well; it's the runaway Mulatto
they call Belfond: he's about here, I know, for the
dogs led me this way, and I daresay you know it too.
Come, set your Obiah quick, or by all the storms——"

"Yes, Master," he replied, his feeble limbs shivering with suppressed rage.   "Come tomorrow night to
the Palm Grove Estate, and there you shall meet me,
and have all that you want."

"You'll go there, you devil!   Now, if you don't,
I'll light a match between every finger and toe of your
body, and smear it with sulphur over a fire.   What
o'clock?"

"Cross down," replied the old man, pointing to the
southern sky, where that beautiful constellation is
known to sparkle.

The sailor then called away the dogs, who were
playing about the cave at French and English with
the mangled remains of the creatures they had killed,
and, shifting his bag of money with some difficulty
to an easy position for carrying, he went away, but
moaning with pain.   The sorcerer noted this: his
face brightened with savage joy, his teeth ground
with fierce pleasure; he followed him.

"Master," he said in a hoarse, eager whisper, "I've
got a bottle of cure for scorpion-bite."

Higgins turned round half-dubious, but did not refuse; and the Negro, hastening back as much as his

legs would permit him, in another minute returned with a phial of spirits and a dead scorpion soaking in it,—the most approved cure in the Colony for the bite of that reptile. Higgins was too well used to the fawning, crouching habit of slaves, who will too often best serve when most ill-used, and he did not suspect evil here. He did not withdraw his hand when the Negro anointed it; he did not even shrink when the warm blood dribbling from the wounds of the old man mingled with the liquor poured over his own; nor did he even recoil when the Negro, as he thus busied himself, displayed at the end of each bony finger, nails of a hideous length, containing inside them rolls of something like soiled wax. He suffered him to anoint, to rub, and to bind his hand with a strip of banana-leaf. This done, he walked off, threatening with a tremendous oath that failure at the Palm Grove the next evening would beget a flogging by no means comfortable to the bones of old Fanty.

The old Negro watched him from within the bushes for a long time; then, when he thought himself fairly released from the presence of the white man, he sat upon the ground to look at his wounds, which he bound up with what rags his den afforded. He longed to give vent to his rage, but he prudently looked out from the bushes first, then he listened well up and down, waiting to discover the direction his enemy took. At last, feeling satisfied with what he learned, then, and not till then, did he examine the ruin which Higgins had left behind.

"Oh, my Gad! my Gad! oh!" exclaimed the Negro; "Feto! my poor Feto! he can't hear me, he can't see me; never will he wake me in the morning again; never come with me to chase the game; never love me, never keep with me! All lonely Fanty! My money gone! but that is little. Oh, my poor little Feto, my faithful dog! My mottled beauty, even little Vixen here," he said, taking up the remains of the coral snake, "all gone! only friends I had. My poor little Feto, could you not bark, you brute, to tell me the enemy was coming? Obboney take you, cursed cotton-face! pain be your food! but you have got something: these nails—they smeared you, and you shall come to our feast,—yes, for a spectacle of death! Rack be your bed, Fetish horrors your dying dream, and shape of chained baboon your heaven to come! Achch!" he said, as he lifted his arms to Heaven, shivering with revenge, "Achch!"

CHAPTER XIV.

CHASING GAME.——NOT OVER-PLEASANT REFLECTIONS FOR THE GAME IN QUESTION.

WELL, was the fugitive caught? is our next question. We shall see. He heard the noise in his uncle's domicile as he stood a little way off amongst the bushes, and, in spite of the danger he incurred, he paused to listen; he heard the old man's cries, and instinctively made a movement to go and help him, but the voice of Higgins addressing his uncle, and the latter answering soon after, convinced him that the sorcerer had received no material bodily injury. He knew the voice of Higgins well, and he also knew what the man was capable of. Seeking a pitch-pine tree, on account of its strong smell, as most likely to prevent the dogs from scenting him, he quickly climbed up it to take a view of what was passing. He trembled with rage as he saw that conscienceless sailor bullying and kicking the defenceless old Negro, and he would have given worlds to have had a stone to hurl at his head;

or, as he thought to himself, if he could but rush in and settle all old accounts! but the dogs—they get scent so quickly, and fly at one's throat before one can see them or hear them : and prudence held him back. He remained in the tree long enough to see and to smile at what happened to the sailor in the cave ; but he felt it was best to take care of himself now, for Higgins, two dogs, pistols, a cutlass, and a rope, when all in company, boded no good to the runaway. Using a well-known Negro proverb, which singularly enough is found among the Negroes as well as the Spaniards, he said to himself, " *When I see my neighbour's beard on fire, let me water my own ; and when the storm rolls large stones down the mountain, let the calabash mind itself,* as Daddy Fanty says, so I had better be off."

His purpose was to travel quickly on till he came to a river, for he knew that if he could cross it the dogs would lose scent, and even if they were close upon him he might then climb a tree and be safe. But there was no stream in the neighbourhood. The pinguin, with its broad leaves formed to retain the water, was abundant here, as was also the " travellers' fountain," a climber well known in the Colonies as affording an abundant supply of crystal water from its stalk when cut, and both these plants grow only where springs are scarce. But Belfond, though no frequenter of this particular mountain, was nevertheless aware that some springs were to be found near the top ; he therefore directed his course thither instead of taking, as he at first intended, a direct course to the Palm Grove.

Higgins meanwhile had left the cave and its precincts, possessor of a bag of money much larger and heavier than he had ever dared to hope for. He at first felt a little bewildered, for the good reason that he did not know where to keep it. "Bring it to the ship?" he said, "that would never do! By all that's holy, I wouldn't trust one soul of them! Captain Hill himself would be the first to take it."

And even supposing it would be safe in the ship, still a difficulty arose, what account could he give of coming by such a hoard? His only plan would be to bury it somewhere in the woods, until he could decide what was best to be done. This moreover was an easy and a safe plan: he might bury it within three yards of the path, even while a wayfarer was passing, and provided he made no noise it would never be known, so dense is the underwood in the forests of Trinidad. But while he was yet cutting through the tangled network of grass and herbs to get at the ground, Bull and Fangs began barking like mad things, and making every possible sign to the sailor that there was game in the wind. Higgins understood in a moment, and covering his bag with herbage, not forgetting to mark well the place, he left it and sprang forward, cutting his way before him as he went.

Belfond was also cutting his way higher up the mountain; but as the trees and bushes were much thicker than towards the bottom, it was not to be ex-

o

pected he could go on very fast, and he had not nearly come to the mountain-top when he heard the dogs crying on his track. Now was the time when all his sagacity was needed! No one in Europe can form an idea of the difficulty of making way amid the pathless forests of the tropics: Belfond was accustomed to it, and in this lay his only safety. By the impatient yelping of the dogs, still far behind, he judged that Higgins was making no very great speed; but the dogs advanced, now bounding over the bushes, now creeping beneath; sometimes falling on a mass of branches solid as a wall, and being almost buried; sometimes getting nearly strangled by the interwoven creepers, through which they pushed; but still they gained fast upon him, and nothing remained for him but to get up into a tree and save himself from them.

Soon they came, clamouring furiously, while Higgins from afar was shouting with all his might to encourage them. Belfond, looking round from the high bough to which he had climbed, espied a considerable patch of the *Mauritia aculeata* growing thickly clustered, and mingled with smaller thorny bushes, which served to fill up the gaps. This plant is near akin, if I remember well, to the yucca, or Adam's needle, but much taller, and the spines at the end of the leaves are much stronger and longer; it covers miles in the centre of the island, where there is little rising ground, but is rarely seen on mountains; here however, by good fortune, it grew luxuriantly. Just in the centre of this thicket were rotten stumps of a group of palms, which had sprung originally, as they sometimes do, from an undivided bunch of nuts. These palms, growing all so close together, had been blasted by the lightning, and had gradually rotted to the ground. Upon this space Belfond fixed his eye; but the leap was hazardous, not only from the height at which he stood, but also from the difficulty of taking a spring, both on account of his narrow footing and of the crooked position he was obliged to maintain under so many overhanging boughs; but it was his only safety now.

Meantime Higgins was approaching, and the dogs, still barking with fury, made violent efforts to get at him. Moments grew precious; Belfond tried another bough, which, though more slender, yet promised better, from standing more apart. He had no sooner rested his weight upon it than it broke beneath him, and he slipped within five yards of the dogs: dexterously however he grasped a bough, climbed up like a monkey to his former perch, and recommenced searching for a convenient place to leap from. Unfortunately, in his rapid march, Belfond had made a sort of path for Higgins, who, having once discovered it, followed it up rapidly. He was now within a few yards of the tree, unable as yet to see the runaway by reason of the thickness of the foliage, but by the motion of a particular point he could guess very well where his game was hiding. Presently, as he drew near, he discovered, thirty feet up a tree, the figure of a man making his way to the end of a bough. As he approached the end, the leaves became less and less dense, and the figure stood out : Higgins recognized him, and the woods re-echoed with his shouts of triumph.

" Hem !" thought Belfond, " curse not the cayman's mother till you have crossed the river ;" and coolly and collectedly, amidst the looping lianas which threatened to entangle him in mid air, he took his aim, and leaped fairly into the middle of the thicket. Higgins, as he saw the feat, for a moment remained thunderstruck, but he took courage again.

" On, Fangs ! at him, Bull ! catch him, my boys!" and the dogs began to leap and bark furiously, but in vain ; the bushes were eight feet high, and four to ten thick all round : at every point, in every direction, long wicked spears crossed and recrossed one another, or the spaces were filled up with smaller bushes equally stinging. The dogs leaped up again and again, and each time they recoiled with shriller cries of pain ; then they snivelled at the ground, and at length one of them insinuated his body in beneath, dragging himself along on his stomach. At last he disappeared, and, to the oaths and shouts of Higgins, the other followed. Both were now out of sight.

Belfond, from within, was not unaware of his danger : his fine quick ear had detected the new movement, and with his eye fixed upon the place he perched himself upon the rotten trunk, which sank beneath his weight, all alive with wood-ants ; this however he did not mind. He held his knife ready, and just as the dog's head appeared from under the lowest leaves he struck it on the back,—it never barked again; the other dog followed,—it was harder to manage, and gave one dismal yell as it yielded its life.

Higgins now had some misgivings. "Bull! Fangs! at him! at him!" shouted he from without. All silence. "Dogs! devil! at him, I say!" Not a word anywhere. Then he fired his remaining pistol straight in the direction where he had seen the man leap; from hill to hill the sound reverberated, and then died away into perfect silence.

He now set about to reconnoitre; he hewed his way round and round the thicket, examined every side, but everywhere an impassable barrier was presented; he struck at the leaves, but they only blunted his knife. He attempted to reload his pistols, but even this he could not do now; he could not close his fingers, so huge and stiff had they become with the swelling. He tried to climb the tree: with great difficulty he managed the first bough, just high enough to catch sight of Belfond crouched down on the palm-stumps, safe, bold, and daring.

Their eyes met; they did not speak, the war between them was too deadly. Higgins took a long and close survey of the place, and having concluded, greatly to his satisfaction, that it was impossible for Belfond to get out,—in short, as he said afterwards, that he was as safely lodged as in the town gaol,—he descended and went away.

Belfond's acute ear detected the direction taken by

his enemy. He cleared a small space on the ground, put his ear down to listen, and discovered that he was gone towards the village, where he supposed he would try to get a reinforcement.

"Now is my time!" cried he, "now for dear life!" and leaping up he seized a whole bundle of lianas in his hand, dragged them to their utmost length, twisted them rapidly into a rope, and swung away, climbing the lianas like a squirrel, till he reached a bough; he caught hold, pulled himself up, and was again safe from the jaws of death.

No time was now to be lost. Belfond sped on his way briskly, nor did he stop till he got upon his proper track, which led across the valleys to the Palm Grove. Here he had to tarry awhile, to satisfy the cravings of hunger; and so many wild fruit-trees hung their offerings within his reach, that it were a marvel if he resisted. With his ear always on the alert, he sat down and enjoyed his repast. But soon, when the physique was easy, came reflection, none to him of the pleasantest. Then he got up again from sheer agitation, and, as he walked along, broke forth into mournful soliloquy.

"Pretty wretch, indeed, I am,—sneered at by my mother's people,— hunted like a wild cat by my father's! No Pariah was ever worse than I am. What business have I to do right, I should like to know? The Negroes would spit at me, and call me fool; the white people would kick me, and call me mule; and so they go on. Why should I care if that little child dies? If he lived, what then? he would grow up to hate me, because I, his uncle, would not be his slave; and he would catch me, and crush me, and chain me down to the hoe. And why should I care if my master goes mad? he would then give up hunting me down, and perhaps he would leave Laurine alone. Pah! what do I care about Laurine?

> Our homes, our wives and children, what are they,
> But the white man's mockery, victim, prey?
> And how can we on such our love bestow?
> The coloured race must know
> No feeling but of woe!

" Little did I think, when I taught them that song, how soon and bitterly it would apply to myself. Let me see,—hideous stuff! Ha! hellish fiend, I am not in your power yet: you did not see how cleverly I slipped the liquid down my clothes. Ay, there my master served me: in trying to drown me he got my clothes wet,—so well soaked that my trick was easy. Well, it almost deserves another good turn. I would prefer death to that horrid drink; I would rather have my master's hate than that old sorcerer's love. Hem! I am to give Beneba this bag to sew up in his pillow: it will make him blind, and then mad. And this paste is for the child: it loves Beneba very much; I saw it cling to her when it would not go to her mistress, and when they little dreamed I was so near, carrying messages backwards and forwards for Laurine. No matter! and in the midst the little thing smiles and frolics and caresses Beneba. She is to anoint it with this fatal Obiah paste, and the child will sicken, and pine away, and cling the closer to Beneba, crying to her to save its little life; and I am to be the medium of this behest!

"There!" he exclaimed, dashing it against a tree, "that is the way I obey your hellish law; and there goes the Obiah-bag along with it! and so you may keep your senses, proud Cardon, father and master to me! O God, what a lot is ours! debarred of the common ties which bind the offspring of the brute; and why? because I have had education enough to wish to be better and greater. What a curse is education to our race! Without it I might have sat down in my uncle's company, and enjoyed his clever tricks and evil witchcraft; I should have gained power among the Negroes from our relationship. Without education I should have settled down to slavery; my master mayhap would have loved me and treated me with confidence; how happy should I have been! Without education I should not have known how degraded is my existence; I should have had no ambitious dreams, no yearnings, no aspirations after good and great things; I should have been content. Education, then, is a crime with the slave; it condemns him to the penalty of an eternal rack. Where, then, is God's justice? where is his goodness, his providential care, since he awards such terrible punishment to the coloured man for those very aspirations which form part of his nature? There is no God,—no, this world is one mass of confusion upon confusion; no Providence; no reward for creatures here below, but the gratification of the tiger when he feeds on the life-blood of his victim."

With this he relapsed into silence, while nature around softly, whisperingly answered him, with her eternal hymn of harmony throughout all space. Gradually came the hour of sunset; the light departed, and night set in. Beautiful, wonderful is night, as it hangs over the tropics! The moon had not yet risen, but the stars shone full and clear with tropical lustre, while the larger planets cast a sensible shadow on the ground; and fire-flies by millions were dancing in and out through the trees and over the savannahs, and in every nook and corner, like young stars let loose to have a holiday upon the earth. Now, like telescopic star-dust, they converge and gather to a ball; then, like a bursting rocket, they fly away in all directions; here streaming to some point of attraction, or moving in and out in a maze of gambols. The air was alive and bright with them, and they seemed to go before our traveller like fairy guides, to cheer and light his path. Then came the moon—the bright, pure, majestic moon,—such a moon as a northern country never saw. Rising on her throne of light, she glided along her star-strewn path like a spirit of peace keeping watch over the slumbers of earth, hushing to rest all angry sounds, even in the heart of man. Her strong full light was not that of life, but of repose; so strong was it, that as the beams came pouring through the loop-holes of the trees, they seemed like solid bands; so still, that the patterned shadows of the leaves upon the ground seemed to move by enchantment; and the clouds, pillowy, fleecy, streaky, bore up the queen of night through ether of the deepest, clearest blue. The discord in Belfond's heart was resolving itself into the rich, grand tones of nature's eternal music. Gradually the impious theme died away from his thoughts; his feelings were lulled by the influence of the scene; and by the time he reached the Grove his mind had gained repose, disturbed only by the gentler and more generous emotions, like the undulations on still water produced by the soft evening breeze.

As he passed, he saw light in Mr. Cardon's house, but he did not approach; he bent his steps rather to the Negro-huts, to which he was readily guided by that peculiar distant murmur of voices, occasionally broken by a wild, startling exclamation, which characterizes the leisure moments of the Negroes.

The first hut he passed was Madelaine's: a pang shot across his heart, for here he had always hitherto stopped; however, it did not matter now, for it was dark; the door was open, but nobody was there. Next to that came Coraly's; that was dark and empty too, and so were all the others near; they looked deserted. He took a short cut across the gardens, to the Koromantyn side; here were crowds, and sentinels outside challenged him, but speaking the password, the crowd opened, and he entered the largest hut of the Negro village.

CHAPTER XV.

A PEEP AT THE HOSPITAL.

THERE was a low murmur of many voices at the door, and within a subdued whispering among a semicircle of Negroes, sitting crowded on the floor, round a sort of bed, in a corner of the room, where lay the Negro Prince of Fantyn, now slave on the Palm Grove Estate, ill, speechless, fainting unto death. I must tell how he came there.

St. Hilaire Cardon was cruel only by fits and starts, and upon extreme occasions like the present : now that he was left to himself, and no longer provoked by the resistance of the culprit, or the interference of an equal, he did not care to carry further a punishment which he probably considered had already reached the maximum of what was needed, when the girl first, and, some ten or fifteen minutes afterwards, the old man, were pronounced insensible. He ordered them both to the hospital immediately, with injunctions that they should be attended to properly.

Now it happened that Talima had fainted at the third stroke, less perhaps from physical pain than from fright and the shock her mind had received : but when, on her being removed, the cowskin was applied with double severity to the old man, broken, ill, and feeble as he was, yet was he a long time before nature entirely succumbed.   St. Hilaire himself had rarely seen a Negro endure so much, and his big heart was moved, as it was always moved when he saw any of the lower animals writhing with pain.

"Take him away!" he said, after looking at the old man awhile, " Bretton, leave him alone; Quaco!"

"'Es, Mas'r."

" I say, take him away!   *Sacre!* don't stand there rubbing your head, Sirrah : take him up very quietly, do you hear? and give him to the nurse."

" Señor," interrupted the Manager, " it's of no use wasting care upon him; in any case he could not live another week."

"Silence! and let me talk, will you?" said the Master impatiently; and addressing himself again to Quaco, he gave various directions for care to be taken of the patient, and then, like an autocrat, he betook himself from the field of slaughter to his own quiet abode, where, upon soft cushions, he sought, reclining, that repose of body and mind which he so much needed after the disagreeable commotions of the day.

Meanwhile Quaco and two or three others moved the Negro gently off the ladder to a sheet which they passed underneath, so as to enable them to carry him without altering his position; and in that guise, very gently and very carefully, they bore him to the hospital, where they as quietly laid him on the floor. For once Quaco did not speak, but looked intently at his burden when he laid it down; while the nurse, coming forward, looked as intently on the wretch she was to tend. "Eh, me Gad, oh!" she exclaimed, "where de use? dis no man's body—dis chopped fles. Eh, me Gad, oh!" and she put her hands to her face.

At this moment appeared at the door the sneering visage of the Overseer, with that semi-laugh upon it which only fiends can wear in the presence of cruelty. "Here, old baboon," said he, speaking to the nurse, "here's a citron and some salt and pepper; squeeze the juice in, and then rub the pepper and salt into him, it will soon revive him."

"Mas'r," said the nurse, "no use curin wid dat cure; de man neber go trouble nobody no more;" and she turned away, to busy herself in getting materials for a bed.

Bretton, nothing baulked, looked at the unfortunate patient, touched him with his foot, tried to turn him, then stooped down, and pulling away the strips of clothes which had been lashed deep into the flesh, he began powdering in the contents of his paper. A groan of agony from the wretched man told of awakening sensibility. The nurse turned round in an instant, and flew to the spot, jerking away the Overseer's hand with impatience: "Hey! Mas'r Bretton, what you meddle for ? Go mind you business; leave to nigger nurse de tings what belong to hospital; wha' for buckra (white man) meddle for ?"

Thus pushed away, the Overseer responded with a kick and a sneer even louder than before. He never cursed—his passions were not deep enough to require that—but he would sometimes call names, where he thought they would carry a sting most keenly; and so he did now, though I scorn to transcribe them.

"Mas'r," said the nurse, with tolerable unconcern, "jus look up dere."

He lifted his eyes; it was Coraly, looking in at the window, and fixing upon him a pair of eyes like those of a snake when it seeks to fascinate its prey. The Overseer quailed under that steady gaze. This Negro woman had the power of cowing him at all times, simply by addressing herself to that superstition which ever becomes the portion of those who give themselves up unrestrainedly to cruelty, even if originally brave,—how much more, if low beings like Bretton! With an effort to shake off what he still had sense enough to be ashamed of, he contracted his lips convulsively, and asked her with dogged assumption what she wanted.

"Mas'r Bretton," she replied, "let dat nigger 'lone; no touch 'em, me tell you."

"You nigger spice you, do you think I mind you?" he said, leaning backwards from his heels on to his hands; for when once down he never cared to rise immediately, but would pinch, and gall, and pull down the Negroes near him, even more effectually than if he were standing.

"Bery well, Mas'r," said Coraly, "no mind me; perhaps you no mind sleep tonight?"

"What should hinder me from sleeping, you black monkey?"

"Oh, notin 't all, notin 't all, notin; only jus don't touch dat nigger, dat's all. Me see Jumbee now at he head," said Coraly, fixing her dark glaring eyes upon the patient.

Involuntarily the Overseer started aside, and was on his feet quick enough this time; "I'm going for the cowskin for you," he said, with his finger up; and with this excuse he lazily dragged along his slip-shod feet, and disappeared in the gloom.

Any one who could have remained near the hospital unperceived would have been struck with the jeering laughter with which the two Negro women saw the Overseer departing, and the mocking, jibing tones of their remarks, as the nurse pulled bandage after bandage from her store-box; but she had something else to think about too. "Here, you piccaninny," she said to one of the children playing in front of the door, "go climb da banana-tree yonder, and bring me from de top dere dat nice young leaf for dis poor nigger,—quick!" and the girl ran. Then to another, "Here you, take dis here calabash, bring me water, clear—clear!" and this one was off as quickly. The nurse did not attempt to move her patient yet, but fixed a pillow under his head, and then sat on the floor beside him, looking at him with eyes full of sorrow and pity. She saw Don Duro Harding at a little distance, and called to him to come.

"Mas'r," said the nurse, as he drew near with a cigarillo in his mouth, "me no know wha' for do : so many niggers sick, dere no bed for dis here ; do go beg Missis come here, please mas'r, do, for God's sake !"

"*Perra maldita !*" exclaimed the Manager in his mother tongue, breaking into a fit of impatience, "where's the use of taking up the room with a thing like this? Send him to one of the Negro-huts, let him die there; don't you know very well that even if he got well of this, still he would never be any good? he can't work, he's diseased."

"But, Mas'r Duro," urged the nurse, "its our master self sent him here."

"Don Hilario does not manage his own affairs at all, it's my business to manage them for him, so do you do as I bid you;" and off went this hard man, very indignant at having been bored for such a nuisance.

"Me Gad, oh ! me Gad, oh!" exclaimed the nurse, in utter despair, "what me go do?"

"Come, sissy, never mind," said Coraly, coming round to the door; and then she called smartly to Quaco, who had retired some little distance to avoid the Overseer, whom he hated, as did every Negro on the estate.

Both Quaco and Coraly were for removing the patient, as the Manager had ordered; but the nurse, who understood the need of poor patients better than they did, persisted. in wanting her mistress,—she must have ointments and linen, and ever so many things besides; and then, she said, when she had made him "little comfortable," they might remove him when they liked.

Quaco was deputed as ambassador, and meanwhile, as the Negro lasses had returned with what they had been sent for, Coraly and the nurse moistened the lips of the sufferer, and, by degrees, got him to take water by spoonfuls. And then it was piteous to hear him moan,—not a loud moan, but a low, hollow, prolonged voice of pain,—and then again it died away, and the sufferer either slept or fainted.

Madame Angélique came at last, listlessly and slowly, and followed by a troop of black girls, whose duty it was to attend upon her footsteps, to pick up the briars from her path, and otherwise to watch lest her foot should strike against a stone.

It was her custom to visit the hospital once a day, generally in the morning, and she rarely refused a second visit when summoned by the nurse. In truth this was her good point: there are none so entirely given up to evil influences as not to have some little corner of refuge in their hearts, where the nature they received from above may abide in safety,—a bright spot, like a lonely star in the midst of darkness,— the soil for seed of future salvation,—the last hope of fallen man.

P

She approached languidly, put one foot upon the threshold of the door, handed the ointment and linen to the nurse, and then stopped, as if fatigued with the exertion.

"Tankee, Missis, tankee! do look here, Missis, do, please. All beds full: what for me do, for put dis poor nigger somewhere for rest? No bed 't all, nowhere. I give mine a'ready to one of dem sick niggers: I sleep 'pon de ground all night; so now there's no bed nowhere."

"Where's the Negro girl that was flogged this evening?" demanded the mistress.

"Oh, Missis! she's just down upon the floor inside there, fast asleep."

"I want to see her," said Angélique; "your master bought her expressly for me, and you must wake her up."

"Yes, Missis,—directly, Missis; but you see dis poor nigger wants a bed,—he bery bad, Missis, bery bad!" and the woman fidgeted about the patient, purposely uncovered the wounds she was dressing, commented on the difficulty of removing him, and went very near commiseration for the pain he must endure,—words in nowise pleasant to the lady, who knew very well what the man was punished for: so she cast a look of indifference upon him, and passed in the same slow way to the inner wards of the hospital. Coraly, I should have said, had gone away before she came up, for there existed between this slave and her mistress an instinctive dislike to meet;

it was more than hatred, it was the bitter recollection which the presence of each revived in the mind of the other, of injury inflicted, mingled with an indistinct sense of injuries yet pending.

The hospital on this estate was in good order: it was a well-appointed, well-arranged building, with everything provided that was necessary,—in short, such a one as a rich man might be supposed to have; while among the poorer class of planters the hospital was simply a larger Negro-hut. Here were three wards, for the women, the men, and the children; from the latter however, there being no sick children just now, the beds had been removed to the other wards, while the tables, chairs, and other necessary moveables were brought into this. Madame Angélique passed on, while the groans of the sick arose on every side as she appeared, not altogether from pain, but as much from a childish manœuvre to win attention and indulgence. To do the lady justice, she had a good deal to endure from them. Sometimes, from an obstinate indifference to their cure, proceeding probably from a lively sense of their value to their owner, they would throw away their medicine, or obtain from some of the stray Negroes lounging outside, some unwholesome fruit, which would entirely throw them back; or would act as did the head cooper, who was at this time lying ill at the furthest end of the room, and whose case I will relate.

He had exhibited symptoms of swelling in the legs and general emaciation for some time past, with a pain

P 2

in his left side, for which his mistress had that morning ordered a blister to be put on his back. She now inquired its success.

" Joloff, how is the blister ?"

" Bery bad, Missis ! bery bad !" he replied in a half-suffocated voice.

" Has Mammy dressed it yet ?"

" No, Missis."

" Has she looked at it ?"

" No, Missis."

She felt his pulse : he had a great deal of fever, and was really very ill.

" Hem ! Mammy, come here. Joloff, turn on your side."

The patient was lying rather upon his back. A groan, as if his soul were departing, accompanied the efforts he made to move; in short, he declared he could not stir, the pain was so great.

" Come, Mammy, help me ; what are you doing ? Leave what you are doing there, and come directly to me."

The nurse had been dressing the wounds of Anamoa, from which she now, with lingering reluctance, moved away at the summons of her mistress.

" Mammy, help me to turn this man."

Groans most dreadful, as if he were on the rack, ensued, and the whole of his weight met the efforts of the mistress and the nurse. They were obliged to give it up.

" But," said the lady, " his blister must be dressed,

and now I am here I will see it done. Call somebody
to help us; Quaco was here just now, call him."

The nurse went out, but not a soul was in the way:
everybody seemed to have disappeared like magic,
except the troop of young lasses outside, who would
only giggle and fuss, and do nothing if called upon to
help.   One of them was sent to call the Manager to
assist, and, as by an afterthought, the lady rose to
follow : perhaps she suspected some trick, as with a
step very different in speed from her slow progress
before, she tripped after her messenger, delivered her
own behest, and returned, bringing the Manager with
her, in no very good humour at having been disturbed
from his evening lounge in a well-swung hammock.
In his powerful grasp the patient was effectually
turned; his groans went for nothing now, and he was
made to lie on his face, to allow of examination.   The
bandage was raised a little, then a great deal, then
loosened entirely.

"*Juste ciel!*" exclaimed the mistress, "there's no
blister here at all ! Light a candle, and bring it here ;"
for it was rapidly growing dark.

The nurse searched up and down, here and there,
through the bed and through the room, the man groaning piteously all the time ; but not till the Manager
happened to put his head out of the nearest window
was the plaister found,—on the ground, where it had
been thrown by the patient.

Madame Angélique, so faint and ill and feeble before, now acquired energy all at once. Her rage burst

uncontrolled upon the unfortunate nurse, and shrilly, snappishly, overpoweringly, she reproached her with neglect. Why did she not watch him? why did she not tie his hands, or fasten him down on his back? It must be done now forthwith, as soon as the blister had been replaced, and the bandages properly fixed; to witness which Angélique sat down, fanning herself the while with her lace-bordered scented handkerchief, quite overcome with her manifold exertions of muscle, nerve, and voice.

Meanwhile Don Duro's keen eyes were wandering about the room for something to vent his spleen upon. Mammy however had been careful: she was a capital nurse, and had often detected and cured disease in the absence of the doctor; not always, however.

"I sent in some of the new niggers, where are they?" gruffly demanded the Manager.

"Down yander, Mas'r, a toder room; dey no bad enough for want bed, so me put 'em in de piccaninny ward. One of dem hab guinea-worm."

The lady being still too much exhausted to move, the Manager took a candle, and went alone to see this guinea-worm;—a thing somewhat like the first string of a violin, which inserts itself between the skin and flesh of the patient, in which it occasionally perforates a hole, and peeps out to take a view of the world without. Mammy had done her duty: she had pertinaciously watched from the moment she first detected it, had caught the head, fastened it gently to a card, and then awaited a further protrusion, to wind off its length; for if this be not carefully done, and the worm break, the leg will mortify, and the Negro be lost. There was clearly no fault to find here.

Further on, among the sore cripples gathered gibbering on the floor, was one with hideous sores all over his body. By means of black ointment and plaisters these had been covered and concealed by the Captain at the sale; but when rubbed and cleaned by Mammy and her assistants, the hideous truth revealed itself, as the Manager held the candle near, and started back with horror.

"Nigger-wench!" he hoarsely called, as he retreated backwards into the first ward, heaping upon her head every curse and every oath that fumed from hell, "the clabba-yaws are in there!"

This disease is an aggravated species of small-pox, which occasionally rages within the tropics in Africa, and for which a species of inoculation is sometimes practised on children.

"*Perra!*" he roared, "how is it you never told me of that?"

"Hey, Mas'r," said the nurse with undaunted effrontery, "da's wha' me tell you over and over, and beg you so hard for call Missis."

"You didn't, you nigger! it was for the old black beast that lies stretched on the floor there."

"I never said notin 't all 'bout 'em," said the woman doggedly; "me beg you call Missis 'count of dem clabba-yaws."

"Don't let me hear you say that again!" growled

the Manager, gracing his commands with a kick, as she stood sulkily with her back to him ; it was a spiteful, strong kick, which made the woman stagger, and maybe hurt her too, for she turned round quick upon him. A year before she would have borne it all patiently as needs be, but she had heard reports from town which had worked her up to courage ; besides which, she was conscious of tripping on the score of truth, and was put upon her mettle to defend herself ; she retorted accordingly.

"Wha' binness you hab for come here meddle for ? I go tell Mas'r 'pon you ! I go ask Mas'r wha' binness you have for cuss me."

"*Qu'est-ce que c'est ?*" shrilly drawled Madame Angélique ; "do you talk of appealing to your master, and I here ? what new thing is this, you impudent woman-monkey ?"

"Me no monkey !" replied the nurse in the same angry tone ; "me take care your niggers ; me no sleep night and day, mindin sick nigger : monkey never do dat ; and you let da man tand dere for cuss me,— you tink me love cuss ?"

The Manager, blazing with wrath, was about to seize her, but Madame Angélique stayed him with a gesture ; and while he made his retreat by the door, as he always prudently did when punishment was taken out of his hands, the lady, taking off her slipper, then and there, in the ward, with the sick groaning around her, belaboured the nurse to her heart's content, about the head, from right to left, upon the ears, upon the face, upon the forehead. There really was nothing very extraordinary in this,—it is a thing of daily and hourly occurrence : slavery begets a host of petty vices in the slaves, which are ever provoking the slaveholder; and he gets into the habit of recklessly using his irresponsible power in punishing the provocation. But this woman had latterly grown impudent. "Tankee, Missis!" she cried at every blow, "da wha' you give me? tankee, Missis!" till Madame Angélique's arm was fairly tired, and then she gave the woman one last hard blow, pushed her violently forward, saying, "There!" and hurried away all fussed and heated and angry, stumbling over the wretched Anamoa, who still lay senseless on the floor at the entrance. And so the bed was forgotten.

Madame Angélique, followed by her sable attendants, panted and puffed on her way home, longing to throw herself on her bed to rest, and feeling ready to fling a chair at the first unlucky wight who should disturb her.

CHAPTER XVI.

THE YOUNG AFRICAN'S STORY.—QUACO ALSO RELATES
HIS ADVENTURES.

RETURN we to the hospital. The bed of course
never came; Mammy gathered up her coif, blubbered
awhile longer, and at length grumbled herself into
something like composure, and then, as if by magic,
the Negroes who had disappeared now came crowding
again about the windows and the door, commiserating and commenting in rapid and vehement language.
Mammy's kind heart however was with the poor Negro who still lay upon the floor untended. She set
to earnestly now; " Neber mind de buckra," she said
to Quaco, who came in to volunteer assistance, " we
do bery well widout 'em;" and when the patient's
broad wounds were all dressed and " made tidy," as
she said, the strongest of the Negroes raised him between them on a sheet, and gently bore him away to
a hut, which the former occupant had vacated for him
because it stood by the sacred cotton-tree—the Fetish

tree of the estate. The Negro-women made a collection of petticoats amongst themselves, and formed a bed of tolerable softness in a corner, and then they laid him gently down. Life was fast ebbing away, but they did not know it yet; they thought he only slept, exhausted from loss of blood.

"Now," said Mammy, when everything was arranged to her satisfaction, "da gal Talima, wha' dem call 'em, must come for watch 'em daddy: me must tand in da hospital for watch dem clabba-yaws." So adjusting her coif anew, and rubbing herself into order, she approached the place where the young girl lay fast asleep, unconscious of what had been passing around her. "Poor gal!" said Mammy, holding the candle close to her face, "da boddersome Missis been want for wake 'em up, jus for see wha' kind o' gal she be; now Mammy must wake 'em up for she see wha' kind a daddy she hab. Poor ting! sorry for wake 'em." After a considerable amount of shaking, the girl awoke, with the motion of the ship still in her head, bewildered enough, but not overcome, and she was soon made to understand where she was to go, and for what purpose. Mammy then helped her up, and with her strong arm fairly carried her into her new abode, where a couch of fresh-gathered, well-picked cocoa-nut leaves, spread by the side of her father's bed, awaited her.

It is a custom among the Negroes, and to some extent even among the Creole white people too, when a person is sick, for friends to gather round him in proportion as he is liked and respected. It never occurs to them that the unfortunate patient requires rest and quiet; all they think of is the pleasure it must give him to receive so many testimonies of solicitude. Accordingly the hut was crowded, and conversation, prompted by curiosity concerning the various events of the day, became eager and earnest. The whispering increased, and, in subdued tones, questions, comments, narratives, and exclamations passed rapidly from one to another among the company. There was no subject however in which they felt deeper interest than in the fate of the Negro-girl Talima, and therefore, while the sick Anamoa slept, she was called upon to relate the events which had brought her among them. She consented. The listeners quickly arranged themselves in a semicircle, and then, in the strange, sweet, rolling utterance and emphatic idiom of the Koromantyn language, she commenced; her audience, like a company of story-telling Arabs, greeting every new incident with appropriate expressions of sympathy,—moaning, sighing, barbarous exclamations of surprise, or words of dislike and execration. Her story has been thus interpreted to me by one of her companions.

"That old man, who lies there so defenceless," began the maiden, waving her hand with dignity towards him,—"he, so lately trampled underfoot and degraded before you,—he, whose tottering form would have obtained mercy from the worst cannibals of Africa,—that broken defenceless old man but a few years ago was strong, his form was erect, his brow was high, his arms made the tigers tremble in their lairs, his voice called thousands of men before him, for he was Lord of Fantyn, the most powerful kingdom of the Koromantyn district."

The narrator paused, when, by a simultaneous movement, every hand in the company was raised, and every head was bent low, in token of reverence and honour.

"Most of you here have heard," continued the young girl, "how vast was his palace and his household; his children numbered by tens and tens, but I was the loved one of all, because the orphaned image of his favourite wife, and I loved my father with the strength and the warmth of an African heart. Our town, Anamaboe, was not then, as it is now, crowded with white men, residing there in tall and handsome houses; it was a simple African village, with low houses shaded by thick trees; at the head was an extensive court, and scented groves concealed the place where I spent my happy childhood."

Here again she was interrupted with words of commiseration and pity. She scarcely paused, but continued:

"I divided my day thus: from sunrise till noon, while my father was with his men, I strayed with my handmaids over the savannahs near the harem, where we gathered flowers, or sat quietly in the fragrant groves, fashioning ornaments with parrot-feathers for the warriors of my father's band; from the height of the day till the cool evening I watched for my father's voice, for he would often call me to him to give him counsel in times of trouble; or, in peace, I would mount the steed by his side, and scour the forest after the lion, the quagga, the zebra, and the antelope."

A murmur of applause ran through the assembly, while some few sobbed aloud at the recollection of pleasures they were never more to enjoy.

"Years rolled on, and the time came when suitors presented themselves to woo. A young warrior, son of a chief whose domains bordered on those of my father, proposed an alliance, and, according to the custom of our country, he brought spices, gold-dust, elephants' teeth, and that which you know is the most valued amongst us, heaps of salt, as gifts corresponding to the boon required. The affair, my friends, was nearly adjusted; we were allowed to meet, we were betrothed. Oh, groves of Fantyn, showering down blossoms upon our heads! oh, perfume of flowers, filling the air with bliss as we breathed!—gone, like the smiles of happy dreams! Friends, this prospect was soon destroyed. By whom? Listen!—the white man!"

"Obboney!" (evil spirit,) cried the assembly, waving mournfully from side to side.

"The white man who dwelt in the large settlement down by the beach was my father's friend. I hated him from the beginning, for I saw treachery in his cold cotton-face; but he spoke so sweet that my father would not suffer any one to say a word against him.

The white man heard of the projected union with a frown; he was indignant: 'What!' said he, 'are those the gifts they bring for the most beautiful daughter of the great Anamoa,—so few and so mean? It proves the rumour true, that Anamoa is mocked and despised by the young man's sire.' My father repelled the charge, but he remembered the words, and they sank festering in his heart.

" It was at the chase of the zebra that he and Liguena quarrelled. My father by right aimed first; but his horse stumbling at the moment, he failed; Liguena, close by his side, brought the animal down, and, unconscious of any feeling save respect, he shouted as he gained the prize, and laughingly seized it. My father conceived it was in mockery,—the mockery which the white man had so repeatedly and strongly warned him of: words of defiance, provocation, and insult roused Liguena to reply, and then he was told to go, never to return. Rage and passion consumed his heart; he did not even seek an interview with me, but gathered up his presents and called his attendants at once. The white man was on the watch, and, as he set forth homewards, sent him a secret message of condolence. 'Make war,' he said; ' we will furnish you with arms and powder, and all we ask in return is that you give us the prisoners you take : let us have them as slaves.' Liguena listened to the white man's whispers, promised all that was asked, received the necessary arms, and war commenced. Anamoa flew to the white man; ' Liguena,' he said, 'is crossing my borders; I have no arms, you are my friend, help me.' And now was the crocodile made manifest. The white man wept at the treatment of my father: it was injuring himself, he said, to injure his friend. 'Make war, make war; we will furnish arms and powder, and all we ask in return is the prisoners you shall make; give us slaves.'"

The speaker was here forced to pause, such was the prolonged and oft-repeated hiss of disgust that ran through the assembly. She resumed:

"At first my father worsted the intruders, and Liguena showed some inclination for an amicable understanding; but the white man would still come about my father by night as well as by day, far into the heart of his kingdom, as well as near the seacoast; he advised him to push forward into the enemy's country. Friends, behold the horrible success of war! for we are strong-feeling, earnest people, our hearts are not the stones that fill the white people's bosoms; our rage, like our love, is a burning fire, either to warm and foster, or to consume; and my father was as brave as he was skilful in the art of war. And now see the happy villages, with the smoke curling from every roof; hear the sweet voices of the mothers calling to their children at play;—that is in the morning. Look there again by-and-by: the cottages are empty, people fly in terror, flames enwrap the towns till the clouds seem red-hot, blood flows like rivers in the streets. The fair fields are spoiled, the corn is gone, and then follow famine and despair, pestilence and death. Those were the tracks of my father's footsteps; and in the mellow evening, when the slaughter was over and the hour invited to pastime and rest, there, where the young mothers sang and the children played, my father's band would collect skulls by thousands, and under the shade of the palm-tree select the best for throwing the ball, or drinking palm-wine.

"My father would have returned now, but the white man had sent him messages to urge him on with false hopes and promises; but he had ventured too far already; he was betrayed by the very messenger who brought him advice: he was taken, not to meet the brave man's death, but to be sold to the very white man who had pretended to be his friend— who had encouraged the quarrel—who had furnished arms for the contest. I never saw him again in Fantyn, and the dark treason was only revealed to me this day, when, after moons and moons of separation, we have met."

"Ay!" cried the assembled Negroes, in deep pity for the girl, "a story most sad! it makes our hearts ache, it brings the tears to our eyes."

"Meanwhile these transactions were carefully concealed from the black Court of Anamaboe; village after village had been taken on the frontiers. The towns were occupied by the enemy, and each day brought fresh news of his approach. I had a brother at the Court, but scarcely old enough to undertake

Q

the defence of the place.   I did my best; I rallied
the men, I kept them for a time steadily at their
posts.   The enemy came at last—the attack commenced.   Hemmed in on all sides, I sent to the white
man in my father's name for aid; it was promised to
us, and given to the invaders outside.   Then came
horrors and carnage!   Friends, I saw the flames hissing on the blood as it ran; screams of women, cries
of children, moans of the old, rose on all sides; it
was a fine harvest for the slave-dealing white man,
and ships were just in port to take away those who
were captured."

"Oh! yah!" again sighed the Negroes, "the treason is great with the white man! why should we be
more just?"

"I had now done all that a woman could do, and
I knew there was nothing left me but to escape.   I
threw a cotton veil about me, and, amidst the wide-
spread confusion, fled to the gate.   At one and the
same moment I stumbled on the dead body of my
brother and fell into the arms of—Liguena!   Softened
in a moment was his eye, subdued was that hoarse
and passionate voice, and he clasped me in an agony
of shame and remorse.   'Come with me, O maiden!
I little thought to find you so near the groves of
Anamaboe: they told me you had long, long ago
gone far away with another.   Yet, O Talima, I will
save you yet; I will bring you where, for my sake,
they will shelter you and take care of you.'   Liguena
led me rapidly through the fitfully glaring night, and

I found myself entering the settlement of my father's friend, the white man. Instantly I saw the treason; I clung to Liguena, I wept, I begged him to take me away, but he was blind—blind like my poor father. He soothed me, rallied me, coaxed me; he promised me on the Fetish tree they were sincere, and he tore himself from me but for a little while, to stay the slaughter of the harem. I mounted on the window to see him go: I waved my veil by the light of the fires, I knew I should never see him more. Oh, Liguena! he who trusts to the fidelity of the white man is a fool, and I was the cause of the misfortune by which you learned it. Before I well knew where I was, the manacles were about my wrists and ankles; for the wind was fair, and the tide served, so was I borne to the ship directly, and the groves of Fantyn faded from my view for ever."

Talima ended; and unheeding the sympathy which each and all lavishly bestowed, she drooped her head mournfully upon her hands to weep; then she rose and looked at her father, but he still slept, and, reluctant to disturb him, she finally settled herself, reclining on her bed of leaves.

"Poor, poor Talima!" murmured the whole assembly compassionately, "God help thee! Hands that never worked must dig the ground now; no rest, no safety, no comfort for any; and her eyes will have to ache yet for what she will see her father suffer."

"I remember well," quoth Quaco, "seeing him mounted on his favourite animal, a beautiful zebra:

Q 2

these creatures are hard to tame, and fierce, and white men and Negroes crowded to see him. Oh, brave sight! All dressed in gold and scarlet mountings, a crown of long parrot-feathers on his brow, and mounted on a zebra which none but he dared to touch! brave, grand king! I was young then, quite a boy."

"Oh, hey!" exclaimed the company, now excited to a story-telling mood, "Quaco, you tell us all about Koromantyn land, and how you came here."

"Me!" said the lad with ready gesture, "nothing much about me; but if all you can hear, Quaco can talk." Then placing himself beside Talima, the better to engage the attention of his hearers, he addressed them, in language which I thus translate.

"Countrymen, we can't go back to Koromantyn-land, but we can call Koromantyn-land to us, and times back and things done; for these belong to us—. Master can't touch them, never! for *thought has no master*. We can love them, and tell them over, and share them, countrymen; and though Quaco's tale is nothing beside poor Talima's, yet he can cut up his little crust, and, like all good niggers, share what he has got.

"My daddy belonged to King Anamoa; he was one of the guards about the Court. Brave man he was, but very old. War came,—not the war that sent Talima here, but another one long before,—and slaves must be sold to buy arms; war pressed very hard, and the white man pressed very hard too for slaves.

Then my daddy, who loved the king, said, 'I am too old now to hold the sword or fire the gun, my hand trembles; sell me, O Anamoa, and get arms, or all Fantyn will fall into the enemy's hands: see, they are already at the borders.' King Anamoa was troubled at the thought, but the old guardsman would have it so, and he joined the gang of slaves and put the chain himself about his foot. I followed to the beach, for my mother's tears had sorely moved me, and I went to see what would become of my daddy.

" The white man examined the slaves, and it came to my daddy's turn to be looked at. 'This man is old,' said the slave-dealer, ' he can't work, he is not worth feeding;' and then it came into my head how they would starve my daddy because he could not work, and my mother's cries went to my heart. I went to the white man; ' Take Quaco,' I said, ' he can work well, so let my poor daddy go home.' The white men laughed at me; then they said, ' Come in the boat, to speak to the captain about it.' So Quaco jumped in, and sat by the side of daddy, comforting him. But when I came to the ship, the captain said, ' You fine young nigger devil, you must stay to keep your daddy company.' So they put chains upon my legs, and drove me below into the hold with the others. Then I shed a few tears for my poor mother's sorrow; but, thinking I could help my daddy when they put him to hard work, I said to him, ' Never mind, some day we shall run away and go back to Fantyn.' But my daddy's heart was full;

he held up his hand, and showed me the big sea, and the ship going very fast. By-and-by we began to feel very hot, and to look about for a cool place to sit. Oh, it was like the *fourmis chasseurs* in a rat-hole,—Negroes, Negroes, Negroes, piled here, piled there, standing on one another's feet, pushing for place to lie, unable to breathe, unable to sleep, the place smelt so bad; we longed to die.

"After seven days, the captain made us all come up to dance. We could not dance,—there was no music, and we were sick and sad; so then they brought the big whip to make the music, and they lashed us till the sickness was forgotten, and we danced sadly for an hour—many had fainted in try-ing. When we went down again, the place had been cleaned of the great dirt, and scoured, for it was wet still; but we lay down one at top of another, not caring, and we slept heavily and long. After that, a storm came—a great storm—and we all laughed and shouted to the wind, because we thought it would take us away; but it stopped. Then it happened that the ship did not move at all for a long, long time.

"They used to give us horse-beans and lamp-oil, but by-and-by we had not much of even this; and though the sick died by tens, still our meals got smaller and smaller—there was not enough provision for us; we used to scramble for it, and fight, and often the weak got none. One day the captain came down, and looked about him, choosing the old, the sickly, and the weak: my poor daddy was one, and I never saw him again, only by-and-by one of the Negroes looked through the one little window, and the sharks were playing about, opening their big mouths for more. Ohe me! that's the way my daddy went. I thought of my mother, and my heart was full."

Here a pause ensued for some minutes, to permit of the usual comments and expressions of sympathy, and then Quaco with his natural briskness plucked up again cheerfully and resumed.

"I have not told you how I came here; listen to this : all white men are not brave like Koromantyns, as you shall hear. When the ship came to land, I was sold; my first master was old Mr. Lamarre, who lived down at the wharf there in Port Spain; he wanted to make money, so he got a lot of cottons very cheap, and filled a little ship to go and sell them down in Angostura yonder, and goes on board with them, taking me. The captain was a Peon, with heavy looks; he set his dark eye upon master, and just when we came into the big waters of the Orinoco, what does the captain do, but he and the mate take me and fling me flop into the river. Quaco was not going to die so soon if he could help it, so I swam about the ship while they were fastening down master: but one of the men caught sight of me, so he shoved me off as I was catching hold; 'You nigger devil,' says he, 'I will chop your hand off, if you come here again.' So I swam another way, and climbed up the banks of the biggest island. The ship had gone off out of sight by this time, and hey! my friends, when I looked

about me, there was master all naked, tied to a cocoa-
nut tree hand and foot, trembling, and crying, and
begging to Quaco,"—and here the narrator mimicked
to the life the beseeching tones of the white man,
while the audience gave lively testimony of their enjoyment.

" 'Oh, Quaco! dear, good Quaco! pity me; you so
kind heart, Quaco! untie these cords, and as soon as
I get to Trinidad I will make you free.'

" Hey, Master, said I, buckra never keeps promise
to poor nigger.

" ' May the lightning of heaven strike me dead if
I don't,' says my master.

" So I pitied the white man, and when I had done
laughing, I untied the cords and let him go.

" ' Now,' says master, ' dear Quaco, I am very
hungry; get me something to eat.'

" Hey, Master! nothing here for nobody.

" ' Quaco, let's look for something.' So we went
about to look. But in a minute master again calls,
and says, ' Quaco! oh dear, Quaco! a wild beast has
been here; look at its foot-marks.'

" No, Master; no wild beast, that's a man's foot.

" ' Quaco! Quaco! that's worse; Indians here eat
people; let us run !'

" We were going along a wood of cocoanut-trees,
I following my master, and he trembling and running.
Somebody called to us; we looked about everywhere;
nobody to be seen, though the voice was quite near.
Something made me look up : what do I see but a

lot of naked Indians they call *Warahoons*, all on the tree-tops, in little houses like, and eating their dinner. '*Comer?*' said they, holding out a piece of raw fish. I knew they meant the Spanish word for *eat*, and that they wanted to give us something; but my master understood *come here*, so he catches hold of me all shivering. 'Oh, Quaco! dear, good Quaco! they are calling me, to kill me and eat me!' Hey, countrymen! I could have pushed him, I was so ashamed of him for a mean coward; but he was my master, so I was obliged only to look up at the Indians and laugh. I ate the fish they threw me, and my master, seeing me talk with them so free, was soon glad to take what they gave—raw and dried fish, and fern-roots,—which he ate faster than I did. Soon the Warahoons began to talk to him too. 'Come and live with us,' they said, 'and be free, like us; not slaves to clothes and to money, as you are. We are free,—we never work, we live as we like; we bask in the sun, we swim in the water, we sleep in the shade, we are happy.' But master shook his head; he wanted to go back to Trinidad, he said, so he asked them to sell him a boat, and row it to Port Spain, which, against their inclination and with much grumbling, they did, and Quaco went in it of course: master could not do without 'dear, good Quaco!' When we got to Port Spain, and master had done paying those Warahoons with a few bad cutlasses, Quaco said, 'Now, Master, there's lightning in the clouds you swore by; won't you make me free?'

'You black devil!' said he, 'after all my losses, to want such a thing! go and do your work, till I make money out of you,' and the next day he sold me to the Palm Grove. Hey! I am not sorry,—Master Cardon is a master, and not a coward: Koromantyn would like to fight with him; Koromantyn don't mind his chain so much; but for that other—whew! hi! hey! yah!" and Quaco's concluding interjections were repeated in chorus by the whole assembly.

Admonished of their too energetic voices by the watchful Talima, who feared they would wake her father, they instantly subdued their tones, calling nevertheless for another story, for, like a toast, it must go round. Madelaine was squatting loungingly in a corner, and they cast their eyes upon her.

"You are oldest here now," said they, "we begin to call you Mammy Madelaine for respect; give us lessons from your experience; tell us your adventures with the white man, and how, when a girl, you managed your rags. Where were you then, Mammy Madelaine? How were you when Laurine was born? —tell us."

Thus challenged, the automaton woman sat up, and uttering one of her wild heedless laughs, she drew her coif tighter about her head, gathered her rags closer about her, and, after much pressing, related her history.

CHAPTER XVII.

MADELAINE SHOWS THAT SHE HAS HAD MUCH TO EMBITTER HER LIFE.

"NIGGERS all!" cried old Madelaine in tolerable English, "you want to know, and maybe I shall tell you. No! I was not always this way : when I was a young girl, I was a hard-working, loving thing, what the white people call a good girl—what, in truth, is *a fool*. Ants befooled me ; death made me wise."

"Hey! hey! yah!" laughed the whole assembly ; but Quaco, wag as he sometimes was, possessed the African virtues, and leaning across from his seat, he rapped the young ones on the head, reminding them of Madelaine's age, and enjoining them to hold a respectful tongue in their heads before her.

"Now, Mammy Madelaine," he said, "tell now, please, was that *fourmis chasseurs*, or *blessing of God*, what white people call, swarming your cabin, eating up all centipedes, scorpions, and ugly creatures that come for hurt you?"

The old woman shook her head; it was not those, she said.

"Was that parasol-ants, every one with a tribute-leaf in 'em mouth, marching to give 'em to two-headed snake in 'em nest?"

"No, nor that; it was the small red ant*, that some of you may remember in Africa; the slave-ships brought them over to this side of the sea: they were the things that made a fool of me. You shall hear," said old Madelaine, speaking in her native tongue; "where shall I begin? When I was a little child I belonged to the Congo nation,—honest, fine people, as the world knows. I used to see the white men come ashore; our people mistrusted them, would not speak to them, and kept away. Then the white men laid their goods down, and went away. So by-and-by our people came and looked at the goods, and as they liked them, they took them, and laid money down instead, and went away again: so you see how the white men trusted us. By-and-by these same white men found me playing in a field, so caught me up, put me in a bag, and ran away with me; that's all I know about it. The ship brought me to Granada, to old Mr. Perrin, father of the one who came here and laid out the Palm Grove Estate. I was brought up in the house, to play with the young ladies. Missis was always pleased with me, and as I grew up, she would give me the care of many things. I had the care of the cows, the sheep, and the fowls;

* *Formica omnivora.*

I took care of everything then, it gave me pleasure. I liked the creatures; they all knew me, and each of them had a name which it answered to. I kept them clean and well fed; they were never troubled with toads or snakes, and they were very thriving. Sometimes the insects would get into the coops, but then I soon drove them out with burning green wood. Once upon a time the ants got in, and I was obliged to burn shavings on the ground for two or three days together, and I thought then there would be no more; but you shall hear how they made us leave Granada.

" One morning I went to the fowl-house, to see after some chickens just hatched. As I walked, I felt my poor bare feet stung all over—the ground was covered with ants; I could not go on, so I went to the carpenter's workshop to get a plank to walk upon, and I set it down from the door of the fowl-house to the coops; but the hens were off their nests, dancing and screaming as hens will do when they are stung, and the little chickens, when I looked at them, were all dead; the nests were covered with ants. I called to one of the women to come and help me, and between us we took out all the hens, picked off the ants, and got tobacco-plants, which we left burning on the ground. It was late now: I took my pail and went to milk the cows for breakfast. On my way I looked in at the sheep, there had been a sick one among them I wanted to see. Hey ho! my friends, it was dead! covered with ants thick upon it, so that you could not make out what the living heap could be till you brushed them off like a piece of thick crust. I did not stay then: I called to the cowboy to take away the sheep, and I went to get the milk. As soon as I had done, I made all haste to take it to the house, for by this time breakfast should be ready. I found Missis very cross: the breakfast was spoiled with the ants, the coffee was full of them, so were the cassava-cakes; and the syrup, which the white people use instead of sugar, was a mess of them. I had my tale to tell, and the family had nothing to drink but the milk I brought in. But the worst of all was the bread: wherever you cut it, there were ants inside; when you put a piece in your mouth, ants stuck to your tongue and stung it. We spent the whole of that day, we house-servants, pouring boiling water over the boards of every room and into every hole; and I stole out in the afternoon to look at the fowl-house, which I cleaned and smoked, and then strewed the ground with chopped tobacco-leaves. I felt so tired that night with having worked hard allday, that I had only time to throw myself on my mat and 1 was instantly asleep.

"Next morning I woke early, and then I went to the fowl-house again. Oh, it was worse now! the hens were all dying, the bigger chickens were dead already, and the new-laid eggs were bored through and swarming inside. As to the ground, I could not find a spot to walk upon, and no sooner had I put the plank down than I had to sweep it again, it swarmed so. I heard Missis's voice calling already, though it was so early; she was very cross,—everybody was cross,—ants were everywhere. The nurse of the hospital was at one door, crying out that ants were swarming in the beds of the sick; the cook was at another door, grumbling that the kitchen was all swarming with ants in every corner; and before any of us had a bit of breakfast, there we were, busy, busy, all busy,—some scraping the meat, some sweeping the shelves, some scalding the vegetables, some straining the syrup, some trying to clean the flour; but no use, no, not a bit ! The dinner was ant-soup, ant-stew, ant-fricassee, and ant-pudding,—ants everywhere, ants in everything. After dinner the same business over again, and we were obliged besides to put every pot and kettle down, even to the frying-pan, to boil water in, for flooding the kitchen flags and walls; and the vessels not being enough for this, some of the Negroes were sent to borrow more pots from the estates near us. No sooner were these gone, than messengers arrived on the same errand from the very places Missis had sent to. We stared, I can tell you, when we heard those estates were just like ours, overrun with ants. By-and-by our Negroes came back with stories still worse : in one place the cattle were eaten up alive in the night; in another place a sick mule was found eaten in spots to the bone, though he was not yet dead; and we soon fared no better ourselves,—the next day nothing could be got for the Master's dinner but some fried plantains and omelettes ; and some of the field niggers were kept about the house, to sweep the paths and pour hot water wherever they appeared.   There was now something to see : such running here and there from the house to the kitchen and back again ! such talking ! such work !

"When night came we were all of us troubled to think how we should keep the bread fit to eat.   Some of us thought to place jugs standing in basins or tubs of water, and on the top of the jugs to put dishes and plates with the bread and anything else that wanted keeping.   Then we placed all these in a row, and giving a last scald to the floors of the different rooms, we thought we might go to bed, for it was very late ; and I laid myself down as usual at the foot of the young ladies' bed on the floor, and soon fell asleep.   This did not last long : I soon started up out of my sleep with the stings of ants, they were all over me.   I got up, and went to the lamp to pick them off me,—a hard thing to do, as I found, for no matter how you brushed them off, the heads always remained behind stuck in your skin.   But just when I had begun this work, there I heard one of the young ladies calling to me that her bed had ants in it, and the next minute both young ladies were on the floor, crying out for help.   Soon after, the whole family was up,—Missis and all the servants, for the same cause : nobody could sleep, and we were obliged to bring large calabashes, into which we lifted the bed-posts, and then filled the vessels with water.   Of course we brushed and picked the beds until they were cleared. Missis allowed me to take the old hammock, and hang it up for me to sleep in, and I felt nothing more till daybreak.

"It was now the fourth morning since the ant-swarming began, and everything had been tried to stop it; but no sooner was I up than I found them in more plenty than ever. The fowl-house was a great moving mass of them. The cattle were covered with them, and dying; and when dead their bones were laid quite bare and white in one hour after. In the fields, the coffee-berries, at that time nearly ripe, were all eaten dry on the bush. The Negroes could no longer dig without shoes; Master had to get a pair for every one of them. Everybody now began to be frightened,—white people, Mulatto people, niggers : all Granada was running with ants, no house was free; no window, no door, no box or keyhole, but they went in and out like a stream. The paths were thick with them, in some places they were stopped up with hills of living ants. There were more and more every day. They took to eating something more than people's victuals : they ate silk, Master's black coats, Missis's stuff table-covers, then glue, then the horsehair from off the sofa and chairs, and all the shoes, and the saddles and leather. When these were all gone, what did they do but begin to eat the young ladies' linen, the cotton petticoats, the muslin frocks, paper, wood,—yes, and brass !

"Green vegetables now got very dear ; soon there

R

were none. The leaves of the trees were eaten up, the grass was eaten up; the sugar-canes had all disappeared long before, because they were sweet; every one said we should die of hunger. The ants grew bold and impudent : they got to the sick, we could not help them, for, if we did, we soon got covered ourselves; they told me that the eyes of one infant were eaten out while it lay asleep. People slept in hammocks now, some one always sitting up to watch in every house, daubing the ropes with castor-oil every now and then. Master took it into his head to draw a thick ring of chalk round the pegs which held his hammock, but it had to be done over and over again so often, because of the ants running over it so fast, that castor-oil on the ropes was found to be the best plan after all. It was so hard to get enough of it; we had to work now all day at getting the oil out of the castor-bush seeds, or we should not have had enough, for everybody was wanting it. .

"The field niggers were all called from their regular labours, and all day you might see them pounding the ants on the roads and about the houses, or pouring boiling water over them. But no sooner had the scalding water made heaps of dead ants, than heaps of living ants came crawling over them, just as if no scalding had been. Poisoned meat was thrown amongst them : then it was a sight to see how the ants got mad and ate one another up ! but this was of no use either, there were only more of them instead of less ! Another thing was done now : great fires were lit up to burn them ; all night these fires were kept burning, and you might have thought the whole of Granada was in a blaze. But not a bit of use was it ; the ants would come pouring over the burned heaps and put out the fires. The rivers did not stop them ; you might see them making bridges over one another's bodies, and passing over the widest rivers. At last you could not even sit down and rest for any time, and my work all day was sweep, sweep, sweep, sweep, round the chairs wherever Missis or the young ladies were sitting.

" You might now see plantations left without master or nigger : the masters had run away to other countries, and the poor slaves roamed about looking for food, and for some place where they might sleep. You might now see fields all moving with ants, only here and there were the whitened bones of the cattle they had eaten ; or at the doors of the houses you might hear the groans of the sick being devoured by the ants, which it was dangerous to disturb. No work now ! no buying or selling ! no dancing ! no singing ! no one in the markets, no one in the streets.

" Well, niggers, the Governor made a proclamation, offering a reward of twenty thousand dollars to any one who should find out a way of stopping the plague : it did not make much talk, people were too downhearted to think much about it, for everything had been tried already, and the cleverest people had all left Granada before the plague got to the worst.

But for me, a poor little Negro girl, I found out something—I found out that though these ants would crawl over the sweet potatoes, still they would pass them by, and not eat them; and for some time I had been supporting Master's family with gathering sweet potatoes. I did not think anything about it at first, till the poor niggers who were left without a master would come begging at the door. I used to get up early in the morning and pick the sweet potatoes, and heap them into one of the little nigger-huts to give away when any poor hungry creature came. The storehouse I had already filled for the family, I and some of the other niggers, and we were still keeping it full; but at last so many of the begging niggers came to us, that I got afraid I should have no more to give them soon, and something put it into my head to go and tell the Governor about the sweet potatoes I had found out. I could not go myself, but I sent a young nigger, Paul, that I loved, and in a few days the Governor sent for Master and for me, and he and some of the gentlemen there talked to Master to sign a paper to give me free,—so said I, curtseying, let me marry Paul, and I will stay and work for Master till he dies,—and this they put in the paper. I asked to let me marry Paul, because I always saw that, when white people got married, no one ever took them from one another; and I thought if I married Paul nobody would take me from my husband, nor my husband from me. So we were married that day.

"Niggers! now all of you listen," continued the

old woman, "for I have something more to say. The plague, as the Governor called these ants, was worse than ever; we could not plant sweet potatoes fast enough, and we began to look down, and to think we must die of starvation at last, when, one day, the sky darkened all at once, and before we had time to stop up the windows and stop up the crevices, crash went the trees, roar went the thunder, whiz came the lightning, and the houses rocked like mad! My mistress called us all to prayers, and there we were, huddling together, and praying to God, not knowing but we were just about to die; but the storm passed, and when we looked out, oh! to hear us shout, and cry, and laugh!—for the plague was gone. Nothing was to be seen of it but a few wet heaps of dead ants, here and there, up against the houses or on the roads,— the rain had carried all the rest away. Now the church-bells rang with thanks, and Granada looked glad and hoped for better times*.

"But my poor master had suffered too much; the plantation was destroyed,—the ants had not left a leaf of tree or grass, the storm had not left a field level; he had to borrow money to plant it all afresh, and to feed the Negroes and the family till the coffee should grow. Poor old master! we worked hard for him, for we pitied him, he looked so ill and heartbroken; and he had always been good to us,—he did not beat much, and when he spoke to us it was more fatherlike. But those coffee-walks he worked so hard upon

* The plague here described took place in 1780.

—for he worked with us himself—he did not live to see them come into bloom ; before the buds came out, he was in his grave.

"I haven't spoken to you yet about young master, —he was not in Granada all this time, and he came from over the sea to take the estate.   He was a sickly sort of man, very yellow, and he brought a wife with him. I should have told you, the young ladies had married, one gone one way, and one another; and for me, I still lived with my old missis, because of Paul.

"I had two children, Felix and Anne ; now, nig- gers, all of you, put all your hearts together, and all the love you have for one thing and another, and it would not come up to the one big love I had for my two children ; they were free, you know, because I, their mother, was free,—that is the law in Granada. Well, niggers ! all at once, young master said we must leave Granada and go to Trinidad, where people were rolling in gold, that's what he said ; and says he to me, 'You may come too, for I must bring with me all my niggers, and Paul too.'   I did not half like the thought, for my old missis had just died, and somehow I did not like the young ones : young master was cross, and was for working the niggers hard, and the missis made me work in the house after old missis was dead, just as if I was a slave.   But Paul was going, so I swallowed the thought, and I packed up my little box and went, Master paying the passage.   Then Master bought all this land covered with big bushes and old trees, and he wanted to clear it, so says he to me, 'Madelaine, you must work in the field now, and help to clear the land.' 'Master,' I answered, 'I can't cut down your trees, I have got my children to mind at home;' so up with his fist and he knocks me to the ground; 'that will teach you,' he says, 'to talk to me that way: when you married a slave you made yourself a slave, and we are in another country here, and that old d——d Governor in Granada can't meddle.'

"Well, it is of no use talking much about those times: I was obliged to leave my little hut, and go with the other niggers to fell the trees: Paul of course used to keep near me, and that kept up my heart a bit. But the very first week, my little Anne tumbled down the sawpit and broke her leg; Master would not let me stay at home to nurse her, and the little thing, so used to my love and care, she died. It was very hard for me; I used to put my head on Paul's shoulder and cry myself to sleep every night, for I could not lie down.

"One day Master went to town and took Paul with him,—he told me he must make a coachman of Paul, he was such a fine young fellow; he said this to throw dust in my eyes, so that I should not make a noise—and they went. Paul never came back, and the niggers that pitied me got news that Master wanted money, and had sold him. Oh! oh! I did not cry—I could not cry, I got sick, my heart turned within me; I did not eat for days and days, and then I began to want to eat earth; I used to take it up by little bits at first, after that I used to stuff my mouth with it all day.   My master was not long before he found it out, because my look was bloated, my face grew yellow, and he had other ways of knowing besides.   He set the overseer to watch me; but he could not watch me so close, but that I would fill my mouth the moment he turned his head.   He put me in the stocks, and kept me there on the sitting bench for one whole day without even drink, and then they brought me dinner,—pah ! I could not touch a bit. So they tied my hands behind my back, and let me out so: well, in a little time the overseer found me lying on the ground on my face, licking up the earth with my tongue.   The next thing they did, was to get an iron mask, and put it on me : they thought they would cure me now ; but they soon caught me putting the earth up between the mask and my chin,— ho ! did not they rage ?

"But it is of no use for niggers to kick against the white people—I found that.   Listen to what they did : they took my dear little boy Felix ; they brought him to the field, where I was with the other niggers clearing bushes ; they stripped me, made me lie down on the ground on my face, and, giving one great lash to the child just for a taste, they put the cowskin into his hand, and made him flog me ! I did not look at the child myself when I stood up, but I knew that the niggers looked dark upon him, and he had run away to hide himself.   The child did not come home for his supper, he did not come home to sleep, nor all night; next morning they found him drowned in the pond. Well, oh, niggers! this gave me another turn. Paul was gone, my two children were gone, freedom was gone: what should I care for more? The sickness left me, and from that day I became the Madelaine that I am now. What should I care about Laurine for?——she is not Paul's child. Hey! and they will soon make a slave of her too. What am I?——I am not my my own slave, I am my master's slave; then let him take care of me, let him feed me, let him clothe me, let him watch me,——that is his business, his look-out. I don't care at all, *for notin' nor nobody.*" And, relapsing into the wild half-idiocy usual to her, poor old Madelaine flung herself back against the wall, and gave a wide gaping laugh at her own folly in youth, to have ever cared for anything.

CHAPTER XVIII.

BELFOND'S STORY.

THE loud expressions of sympathy which Madelaine's recital called forth were interrupted by the entrance of a new comer. The Negroes all looked up, smiled, opened their arms, and uttered exclamations of welcome; for who better loved, trusted, and respected, than Belfond, the coloured man? It was now, who should make room for him?—who should find him a place?—who should get him supper and make him comfortable?—and that one felt proud who could do anything for him. While he was eating, they entertained him with accounts of all that had passed, and when he had finished, he in turn had much to recount,—not about his visit to his uncle, that he kept to himself,—but about his escape from the ship and from Higgins. This amused the company so well that they one and all pressed him to tell them his history.

In relating his adventures, however, unlike his

darker comrades, he did not tell all that had passed in his mind. He knew that their understandings, unawakened to anything above the little affairs of their brute condition, could never comprehend the tumults of his own struggling heart, or the strange feelings which had grown up in him. He was silent, therefore, on many things, and only told such as would interest them, and such as, he hoped, would give them new ideas, and tend to raise them to know themselves, and the masters before whom they crouched. He loved sympathy too, and in his gloomiest moods the warm friendship of the Negroes had often acted beneficially upon him,—had taken him out of himself, and, for a time at least, would make him forget the gnawing doubts which preyed upon his very vitals. To fill up the blanks of his tale, it will be necessary that I should take up the recital, and tell for him those facts connected with his early life which will serve to throw light on the workings of a mind fortunately not entirely bent by his condition to evil.

Born on his master's estate, and called upon from early childhood to pander to the caprices and submit to the tyranny of the white children, he became early an adept in all those vices which slavery burns into the soul of man; and if, in the practice of falsehood, flattery, and theft, he showed himself a greater adept than his fellow-slaves on the estate, it was not that nature had found him more inclined to those vices, but simply because he was more clever than they.

With the same amount of talent, on a freer, happier soil, he might have been morally, and perhaps, too, intellectually great; but under the evil influence of his condition, his best and highest faculties only served to give strength to the vices he contracted.

Thus he throve, till the time arrived when his master considered it necessary to think of education for his children. It was the custom, and a beneficial one, among the planters, to send their children to Europe for two, or five, or more years, to complete their studies. Up to that time the children were much indulged; and in those days of colonial pride and ostentation, it was considered as a thing of course to send a slave to wait upon the young student during the toilsome period of his learning; and we may easily imagine the pomp with which the young West Indian paraded the streets with his slave behind him, like an autocrat with his one subject.

On Belfond, the visit to Europe had a great effect. It was ruinous to him as a slave, for it awakened within him feelings suitable only to a free man: it raised his mind above the level of the brutes, roused his energies, elevated his thoughts, and taught him self-respect,—all which only sowed the seeds of discontent and unhappiness.

It would have been a curious study for the philosopher, to follow the mind of this young slave, as his faculties gradually emerged from the prison in which they had hitherto been bound. At first, he could not comprehend why he was not despised and kicked on account of his complexion, and how it was that white servants admitted him among them. It puzzled him still more to detect and understand the differences which the white race mark out among themselves. He was shocked at their avarice, their hardness of heart, their inhospitality, and he would say to his brother slaves, "These white people, in their own country, have no kindness for their stricken brothers. When did the poor African leave the storm-driven traveller without a shelter, or without a share of what little he may have? We make the wanderer welcome, we are proud of such a guest; but the white man shuts his door to the hungry, and gives the leavings of his meal to his dogs sooner than to the wretch who has no bed but the wet stones of that cold country—no food but the refuse he may pick up in the gutter. Oh, comrades! their hearts are like their land,—cold, hard, and barren; they have no virtues, not even respect for old age." But that which most excited his curiosity was the power of reading; in speaking of it to the Negroes, he described the print as a white ground with black patterns laid thick upon it, which patterns spoke to the eye as the voice to the ear; he explained a book as the bridge of ideas from one man's mind to another,—the permanent stamp of passing thought,—the indelible footsteps of speech.

In a few years St. Hilaire Cardon paid a visit to Europe, and, with his children, travelled over its various countries, Belfond of course accompanying them;

and when his master returned to the Colonies, he was left with the son and heir, who had now entered one of the French colleges, to complete his education. This gave still greater facilities to the young slave for improving his intellect. Now, for the first time, he heard of Toussaint L'Ouverture, and the unfortunate Ogé of St. Domingo. Revolutions of kingdoms, the march of freedom, and the equality of men, were subjects that soon became familiar to him. He awoke, as from a dream, to find himself one of the great human race—a creature endowed with a soul, animated by the breath of the Almighty; and it was with a mingled feeling of awe and astonishment that at last he took in the eternal truth, that the black man and the white man stand before God equal in his love, equal in his care, equal in his promise of a heavenly home; for before that time he had never thought of an after-life, save in some low condition, far, far behind the meanest white men. By stealth he learned to read and to write, and he extended his knowledge wherever books or conversation came in his way to favour it. Often, indeed, while his young master spent the night in pleasure-hunting, Belfond stole out to hear lectures, or remained within to study, till of the two—the young master and his slave—the poor Mulatto was in reality the cleverer, and by far the better educated.

At length, by dint of search and reflection, Belfond thought he had succeeded in solving the mystery of that tremendous power which the white man holds over the black race. "It is knowledge," he said, ad-

dressing his comrades,—"knowledge gives wings to
man ; it carries him in mind above all grovelling things
of earth ; he looks down upon them, moves them, rules
them, destroys them, or saves them, just at his own will
and pleasure. Poor creeping, crawling things like us,
he pounces down upon, like the condor of the Andes
on the unprotected sheep. The only resource left us
is to get the wings ourselves, and the way to grow
them is at learn to read,—in short, the book-magic—
the white man's secret—that which he so much
dreads we should obtain." But it was an ill-omened
state to which he had arrived : every day he was
losing more and more of that apathy which makes
slavery tolerable, while at the same time his condition as a slave necessarily prevented him from ac-
quiring the virtues of the free. He had, it is true,
floating notions of nobler aims ; but those alone
who have once been subject to bondage, can tell
how blighting is its influence upon the soul, and
how the constantly-repeated words of scorn and contempt wither up the best and dearest feelings of
man. Even religion,—for, like all those of his race,
he was inclined to devotion,—even religion was in
its doctrine a dim, confused, incomprehensible page.
He read the Ten Commandments :—Thou shalt love
thy God : Thou shalt have no other gods but
me, thou shalt not adore them nor serve them :
Thou shalt keep holy the Sabbath-day : Honour thy
father and thy mother : Thou shall not kill : Thou
shalt not commit adultery : Thou shalt not steal, etc.

And as he read, and strove to understand, it came upon him as a new thing, that profession and violation of the sacred word are too often one and the same with the haughty master, and that (as he graphically expressed himself afterwards) while the minister read one set of commandments from the altar, the whip cut another table upon his back :—Thou shalt love thy lawful master : Thou shalt yield submissively to his will, thou shalt not question his justice, thou shalt obey him in preference to thy Heavenly Father : Thou shalt keep holy every day by working for him : Thou shalt honour no father, thou hast no right to know of one ; thou shalt honour no mother, for she has no care or training of thee : Thou shalt not steal thyself from thy master by flying from him, for thou belongest to him—thou, and thy soul with its highest faculties, and thy heart with its dearest treasures. What wonder, then, if his mind was confused between right and wrong—between his duties as a slave and his duties as a Christian—between the rights of his master and the rights of himself as a man? His mind was like the image of an Apollo defaced and broken up : the casual observer would pronounce it a worthless heap of misshapen stones ; the student of Art alone would judge how beautiful the statue had originally been, and how cruel and wanton must have been the blows which deformed it.

The time came at length when the young master was recalled to his Colonial home, and the slave must return also.   What ! must he waste the remainder of his days in disgusting slave-work?—be compelled to labour in the field, and grovel with his fellow-brutes? Twice ten Christmas seasons and four more, as the Negroes are wont to say, had been counted since his birth; nine of them had been spent in the white man's country. He had remained too long; he had tasted freedom, and learned its value but too well. The bird born in imprisonment pecks the grain and sips the drink unconscious of the existence of any higher joy; but once let it use its wings, how soon will the bars which lately sheltered it, and the hand which fed it, become odious!—new feelings are aroused within it, its wild nature is awake and throbbing; it may see starvation before it in freedom, but even this is a paradise compared with what it must undergo amid the luxuries of a prison.

Belfond could no longer brook the idea of slavery; he loathed the very thought. He spent his nights in groans and tears, and his days in kneeling to his master's friends, frantically entreating that they would intercede for him, that he might stay. He would work, he said; he would send his earnings to his master, every sous; he would exercise his talent; he should rise in the world, he was certain, and all should be for his master's glory, his master's profit, from his faithful, grateful slave. But in vain he pleaded. A few pitied him, but could do nothing; others treated his words as the ravings of a maniac; and he was desired to pack up his young master's things, and be ready to sail next morning. It was then that the demon tempted him,—the slave-nature worked within him, and despair framed an excuse : he rose in the night, took money, jewels, plate, all that he could lay hands upon, and stole away to the south, to the sea-port of Marseilles.

It was not then in France, as it was already in England, ordained that every slave on touching its soil should become free. Captain Hill was just then taking in a cargo of olive-oil and figs, and having seen young Cardon in Paris with his valet, he recognized Belfond on the wharf, and watched him. The mate, Higgins, enticed him on board, seized upon him unawares, and threw him headlong into the hold, where he was instantly secured in chains. After a long and stormy passage, the vessel at length came in sight of Tobago, when the captain, having for some reason sailed into port there, went on shore to spend the night. The sailors of course made merry, rum circulated freely, and its fumes broke forth in song and revel. In a moment of inspiration, Higgins proposed to have up the slave, and make him dance for their amusement.

Belfond was no sooner brought upon deck than he saw at a glance the opportunity that presented itself; he did his best to please them, exposed his shrunken limbs for their jesting, and rattled his chains in a dismal dance to their hallooing. At length, one by one, they sank upon the deck, where they lay stretched like swine, and the general snoring warned Belfond that his time was come. He gathered his irons about him, seized the boat, and launched forth, without knowing whither his course would lead him. For more than two days he was upon the open sea; on the third day however he drew near land, and it proved to be his own beautiful island, the land of his birth, fair Trinidad. The Indians on the coast were ready to help him strike off his fetters, and for awhile to afford him shelter. He remained a time with these good people, but, afraid of being discovered by the missionary of the district, he left them, and went forth to wander in the pathless forest, taking care to avoid the habitations of the white man; he afterwards assembled such of the Maroons as were inclined to a peaceful life, and they dwelt together in a forest village of their own building.

His tale of love is soon told. Laurine was as superior among the girls, as he among the young men, of the coloured class. He saw her—loved her,—it was a thing of course: his was a southern's passion, and with southern vehemence he wooed and won her heart. They were to have been married as soon as the maiden had earned sufficient to buy the freedom of her mother. But even here the evils of his condition pursued him: jealous of the girl he adored, and suspicious of all who approached her, precisely because he knew the extent of the danger to which she was exposed, he had too hastily taken umbrage at a refusal which, had his mind been only free from prejudice, would have won his admiration.

" For the rest," he said, in conclusion, while relating his adventures to the Negroes, " I have learned this, that I have a right to my own free-will, and to the exercise of my own free judgment, and I will use them while I have a leg to carry me and a head to guide me.   So, hurrah for the woods ! hurrah for justice—for life—for liberty !"

CHAPTER XIX.

THE SLAVE'S BURIAL.——LIGHTS AND SHADOWS OF SAVAGE FEELING.

AT the sound of Belfond's last word,——a word so dear to every human heart,——the dying Negro woke. The vital flame, which had sunk even to the socket, flamed up once more with a clear, bright, full light, ere it died away again for ever. Even before he spoke, the young Talima was on the alert to aid him in his efforts to rise : this he found very difficult, for he could not lie on his back, nor on either side ; but, by the united assistance of the other Negroes, he was at length placed in a sitting posture, with his head resting on the shoulder of his child. Eagerly his sable friends crowded round him. They gave him water, bathed his temples, moistened his hands, and spoke words of comfort, such as poor slaves can utter who know what suffering is, and have nothing to give but the deep sympathy of their own hearts. Mammy of the hospital was then sent for : she came, with the fussy and important air which she was wont to assume amongst her fellow-slaves; but she had hardly looked at the sick man when her voice lowered.

"I knowed it," she said in a subdued tone; "I telled ye all da same. Now, niggers, get all you want ready, for you'll have to bury him 'fore cross-down; he face tell dat; no comin' back from dat 'ere, no ways."

Anamoa looked up brightly on hearing these words, —to him as tidings of near relief. "Liberty!" he murmured, repeating to himself the word which had waked him, and which was one of the few he could pronounce in English, and a smile of joy came over his face. Talima, who had eagerly inquired the meaning of what the nurse had said, pressed her arms about her father with wild, uncontrollable distress. The pitying Negroes comforted her. "Courage!" cried they; "think, poor Talima, of the triumph that will soon be his! think of the freedom he will gain, and shed no tear, lest you spoil the glory of this hour."

But hush, Reader! give me a moment's patience before you breathe a word of doubt. It was not the triumph of Christ they spoke of, nor the glory of the coming kingdom of Heaven. They had never received tidings of the holy Gospel, to bring comfort to their souls, to give hope to their grieving hearts, —they were heathens. The unexplained prayers at muster-roll were as Latin to them; the word Jesus —that charm which lifts the veil of Heaven to the

Christian soul—that tie which binds man, trembling, yet hopeful and joyful, to his God—was to these poor Negroes simply a hard word which they could scarcely pronounce. Yet God forsakes not even his lowliest creatures in the season of their trouble and pain, and truly hath he spoken, "Come all ye that are heavy laden, and I will give you rest;" and so it was even here. Over the dark untaught soul of the dying Negro hovered the pitying angel of mercy; and, wrapped in the African superstition that death bears the exile to his native place, came the dim foreshadowing of a better world—the promise of rest, of peace, of happiness for ever. There was no mourning, but encouraging words and cheering expressions; and many a message of love to their far-distant friends did these creatures whisper to the exile returning to his home. Sometimes they were interrupted by the sobs of Talima, which their chiding could not subdue, and here and there a hand was seen raised to a moistened eye; and the dying man sighed, grieving that he could not bear away his child with him.

Belfond was deeply moved by this touching scene. He was foremost in supporting the dying man, and it was chiefly on his arms that the burden rested, leaving as little weight as possible on Talima. But, even thus, her strength began to fail her, and the sympathizing Quaco gently shifted himself into her place. Anamoa's eyes grew brighter; the expression of his face was almost radiant. He seemed to gaze for awhile at something above the earth—at some joy beyond, which he was about to grasp; then looking round upon his friends, he made signs to them to draw near.

"Children," said he, "the Great Spirit calls me to him; he whose eye is the light-giving sun has ordained that, at the first ray of tomorrow's light, my spirit shall ride away to the region of my birth. Children, my last word—be true to one another! Truth, honesty, goodness to the tyrant, remember, O children, is treachery to yourselves. Children, may Assarci, the spirit of mercy, spread his golden wings over you! I am going." And all perceived the unmistakeable signs that the hour was come.

In the midst of the varied activity of this strange busy world, what a sublime event is death! what a mysterious transformation! Revealed in its awful significance to the Christian, it is still to the heathen a bewildering change. Sometimes his instinct leads him close upon the truth; then away he wanders, his fancy peopling the unknown world with the strangest forms. The awful moment was now nigh; not a sound disturbed the stillness of the room. The women stayed their breathing; the men, as noiseless, stood up with instinctive respect in presence of the dread mystery. Anamoa breathed harder, then the sound grew fainter; a slight convulsive movement of the face, a shudder, a sigh, and all was over. The bands of life were rent asunder, and that poor Negro's soul, upon which the light had never shone, now stood trembling and heavy-laden before the great God who had created it, seeking the promised refuge of the weary and the oppressed.

No sooner had his head dropped lifeless upon the shoulder of Belfond, than the Negroes in wild excitement simultaneously shouted in triumph; they tossed their arms aloft, and sang a sort of pæan,—wild, gladsome notes pealing in alternate measure through the still night; for that which brings deepest grief to the free, is the signal of joy to the slave.

Then gradually the women stole away, and after them the men, to make preparations for crowning the festival, the final deposit of earth within its mother earth. They wrapped the body in linen white as snow, and placed it on a table; then upon the head they put a gorgeous crown of parrot-feathers, such as the chief was wont to wear in Fantyn, and, as they came in, each addressed his spirit, believing it would hear them: "His spirit still remains with us," said they; "he will not leave us until sunrise, for so he said."

"The great Accompong," said one, in African dialect, as he approached with an armful of palm-leaves, which he placed one by one round the table, "has looked down from his high place. Assarci, in his mercy, has taken our fallen chief to a place where he will never suffer again."

"Thou wast brave," said another, bringing a branch of the sacred cotton-tree, which he placed between the hands of the dead; "thou wast mighty as the storm; but there are caves where the storm has no power, and the mighty chief of kingdoms has fallen into the pit of the traitor."

" Thou wast generous, O good Anamoa; thy kingly palace had room for the needy, shelter for the houseless, and food for the hungry."

" Thy people were happy under a sway gentle as the dew; thou wast kind to them as a father."

" Rest, O fallen king! exiles like thee, we shall remember thy dying words; we have gathered them up like golden treasure, and placed them deep within our hearts."

" Thy child's heart will we keep warm. The stumbling-stones will we roll away; the thorns will we pick up which encumber her path,—where we can, O Anamoa, for the promises of slaves are as barren land, and yield only briars."

" Hear us, O Anamoa, while yet thy spirit tarries; bear our messages to distant homes; say how we weep, and how we hope to join the loved ones again."

And a few wailings, but not many, closed the songs of those who brought offerings to the dead.

The room was decorated with savage yet graceful taste. Gigantic leaves of the cocoa-nut and tree-fern, set upright upon their stalks, formed a canopy above, from which garlands of the blue and pink convolvulus, and long chaplets of scarlet berries, were looped and festooned in various lengths, while the choicest flowers covered the table, and fragrant leaves carpeted the ground. Bouquets too, tastefully arranged, were placed within the hands, upon the chest, and about the face of the dead.

Mammy of the hospital had left the hut, for the head cooper was very ill. He had been a clever, use-

ful man, she knew therefore that it was of consequence she should be at her post. He groaned very
much, and was always calling for water ; Mammy had
given him diluted lemon-juice for about the twelfth
time, and was debating within herself whether she
should risk another castigation for disturbing the
slumbers of her mistress, by sending to the big house
for a composing draught—when some one entered.
Satan himself, with hoofs and horns, would have been
to her a much more welcome guest, for it was Fanty,
the Obiah priest. Mammy, whose kind heart found
pleasure in her task, made it· a boast that she had
often carried Negroes through the most dangerous
attacks without doctor or instructions ; but she knew
too well that Fanty, wherever he came, was the har-
binger of sickness, decline, and death. But, for wealth
or life, she would never have breathed a word to betray
him, or have done aught against his will.

For a minute he stood still ; he did not speak, nor
did Mammy speak to him. He then went to the
candle, and stretching out his bony, witchcraft-work-
ing fingers, with their long nails, he stooped as if to
examine them minutely. Then he went close to the
bed of each of the patients, looking at them and feeling them, and passed on till he came to the cooper.
" You're thirsty," he said : " drink this ;" and he held
up a gourd, and supported the patient's head while he
drank. Strange as it may appear, although the sick
cooper knew that the draught was poison, and it is to
be supposed he was born with as much inherent love

of life as other human beings, yet not a sign of hesi-
tation did he manifest in taking it.   Then the sorcerer
smoothed his forehead, stroked his eyelids with his
horrid claws, and forming circles of incantation round
the bed with the right hand, as he muttered strange
cabalistic words of some unknown language, he laid
his left hand upon the patient's heart; Mammy, with
her eyes fixed upon him in silence, standing motion-
less all the time like one entranced.   He went out as
quickly and as noiselessly as he had entered.

Meantime the preparations for the burial were still
going on in the hut.   Up to this time Belfond had
been chief actor in the various decorations of the
room; for, with his warm imagination and the keen
poetic sensibility of his particular colour, he took
pleasure in seizing the spirit of the strange festival.
When everything had been arranged, he called Quaco
aside, to fix with him on some spot where they might
be certain the body would remain undisturbed.

"Dunno no such place," said the Negro lad; "sabannah hab rat, tree hab snake, and, worse nor all,
white man's spade break da ground eberywhere: cutlass and rest neber live together."

"How do you mean, Quaco?" asked Belfond,
rather puzzled to know what his friend alluded to.

"Eh hey!" exclaimed the other, with the sharp,
quick utterance peculiar to Negroes; "just hearee,
you Belfond: you know dat tall bamboo-tree by the
great sabannah, dere de grass is soft, de shade wide
and cool, birds sing in de leaves, and at sundown

we love to sit dere and talk. Time out o' mind poor Anamoa sit down dere when he weary, and talk 'bout far Africa to young people like me. Well, s'pose we bury him dere,—tomorrow-day massa Manager come past wid big dog, debil dog smells ground, scratches up, so whines, den massa Manager calls out, 'Niggers, come yere! somefin here! come, dig away, let me see;' so poor nigger 'bliged to dig till de spade dig up body, den massa Manager flog all round. Hey, Belfond, da neber do!"

Belfond listened to his companion and mused. He looked at the calm, streaming moonlight, which traced fantastic forms in the deep shadows of the woods, and he wondered perhaps how far they would have to go to obtain rest, in a landscape which, at that hour at least, appeared all so peaceful. Unconsciously he looked in the direction of a small field in which it was customary to bury the slaves; Quaco, perceiving this, seized his arm eagerly.

"Mustn't go dere, no ways," said he; "bodies now'days tumbled in dere anyhow; too many niggers die now for hab quiet dat place. Last week, two buried together one sundown,—next morning all de ground scratched up, and two niggers gone!"

"Gone where, Quaco?"

"Gone back to Africa, don't you know?—and it is a weary long walk."

Belfond laughed outright,—which nettled the other greatly, for, habitually good-humoured as the youth was, touch only ever so slightly on his superstitions, and directly he became irritable and impatient. It was in vain that Belfond suggested the interference of tiger-cats or vultures : the more said, the more angry the Negro became, for the love of the marvellous brooks no meddling of reason.

"Well," observed Belfond at last, after vainly trying to talk Quaco into common sense and equanimity, "this won't tell us where to bury the body. What shall we do?"

"I no speak no more : come here to dem new Koromantyns, and maybe dey'll someways tell what people do in Fantyn."

The group in question were sitting on the ground within the hut, talking and laughing in exceeding glee, like spectators at a *fête*. When questioned by Quaco, they all stood up, and instantly went to the Fetish cotton-tree outside, and pointed· to the sod beneath ·it.

Quaco, with a gesture of impatience, struck his forehead. "Fool!" he muttered to himself, "where Quaco head gone to—didn't tink o' dat afore?" then gaily resuming, "Come, you comrades, eberybody, come, let us dig. Now, Belfond," he said, looking at his friend, "dis 'ere cotton-tree belong to nigger, neber no white man disturb 'em here." Strange as it may appear, he spoke what he believed; for planters who violate the first rights of their fellow-creatures are usually found to respect the trees—often fruit-trees —of their slaves ;—one anomaly among a thousand to be found in slave-holding society.

They proceeded to prepare for the burial; for, in tropical climates, a body may not be left more than three or four hours above ground.. As the preparations were going on, Belfond said slyly in Quaco's ear, "Are you sure now that Anamoa would not rather be left above ground, to walk freely away to his own country?"

"He too sick!" roared the incorrigible Negro, frowning at what he considered his friend's stupidity, "and de way too long! we must bury him deep, so make him stay dere softly."

"But, my friend, how then can he ever get back to Africa?" persisted the other, laughing.

"Ah! you! cho!" exclaimed Quaco, nudging him impatiently with his elbows, as if he almost despaired of enlightening such idiocy; then turning again, "Don't you see?" he said, "when spirit finds he body 'bove ground, he takes body wid 'em. Now, what could spirit do wid body all cut up like dis 'ere? Go 'way!" and he went and fetched his spade, and, like a good sexton, commenced his work of digging the grave. "Eh, me Gad!" he went on, grunting to himself as the company left him one by one, "somebody must come for help me here,—neber dig deep enough dis way."

A cold hand touched his shoulder: he turned, and lo! before him stood a figure dressed in white. Instantly the mind of the imaginative African beheld in it the form of the departed risen again. He staggered back with affright; "Eh, you!" he gasped with a quick utterance and an odd mixture of terror and solicitude; "go lie down again! you no fit for walk all dat way, me tell you."

"Hist, idiot! hold tight tongue in your head, will you? *Toad's cry betrays toad. Screams go through walls*: do you hear?"

Quaco instinctively clutched hold of his amulet, for he knew the voice of Fanty. "Me Gad, oh!" he whispered to himself, but he said not a word more. Fanty beckoned to him, and he followed into the hut.

As the sorcerer entered, the cheerful murmur of merry voices from those who were busy with the various arrangements for the burial dropped in a moment, as if under the influence of a spell. An undefined awe seized upon them, which was greatly increased by the old man's unusual appearance.. His body, arms, and ankles were thickly bandaged round with linen all soiled with recent bleeding; "besides," said each to himself as he looked, "where are the snakes and the dog?" for never before, since he had assumed the priestly office, had he appeared without them.

"You fools!" exclaimed he, frowning, as he eyed them all round; "what noise! Far in the woods, a mile away, I heard you. Are walls deaf? Is the Master mad? Fools! keep your voice down: *lions should never roar near the hunter's tent*, do you hear?" then, perceiving the dead laid out, "And is that what you were going to bury under the Fetish tree?" he asked, turning slowly to Quaco, as he pointed to the body.

" Yes, Ta Fanty," meekly replied the youth.

" Not there! for if the tree belongs to niggers, don't you know the ground belongs to white man, you fools?——no, not there, but under here!" cried Fanty, stamping upon the floor, "under here! And you, Talima," he added, as he drew her forward from the company, "you shall live here and watch the sacred dead, lest the white man's dog may come and smell it out."

Then the priest called for drink, and a large gourd, full of the refreshing mawbee, prepared from the seed of the *Mammea Sapota*, was officiously presented him by Coraly; and, as this circulated, libations were poured on the ground in honour of Assarci, who, as well as being the God of mercy, was also the God of regeneration.

" And now for an oath! a new oath!" cried the man of darkness, raising the fresh-filled bowl high in the air, "to a new oath! Mark that Belfond!" he said, pointing to the Mulatto, who was leaning against the door apart from the rest; " there is the son of my dead sister! the blood-thirsty cotton-faced tigers are seeking him. Let one of you dare betray him, dare neglect to shelter him, and, by the dread mysteries of Obi, he shall spin out eternity as the slave of the slave of the white baboon! Augh!" he hoarsely and vengefully drawled, "pass the bowl for the new oath!" and, amid stamps and violent gestures and imprecations of horrible import, the Negroes promised to lay down their lives before they would see one hair hurt which

T

had ever grown on Belfond's head. Whereupon the old man opened his mouth again, and, as if to reward their ready obedience, with inspired looks and fiery eye he prophesied a visit from Higgins the night after the following, when he, the bushranger, he who hunted and hacked about the African worse than if he were a dog, " Here," he cried, " shall fall before the whole gang of you, a blackened corpse! Ach!" and the old man shook and gnashed his teeth in anticipation of his revenge. In breathless silence the Negroes listened and received their instructions, and when Fanty took a low stool and buried his face in his hands, they silently commenced digging; for while Fanty was present, they considered themselves under a leader whose will, not their own, should direct them.

The grave being dug, Fanty rose: this was the signal for burial. The women strewed the bottom of the pit with sweet-smelling flowers, and Fanty, with the help of Belfond and Quaco, lowered the body, wrapped in its swathing linen, and gently laid it on the perfumed bed.

" Now," said Fanty, " where are drums? where is the music?"

The instruments were procured: a portion of the hollow trunk of a tree covered over tight with calf-skin was the drum, on which they struck with amazing celerity; a couple of African trumpets and short horns, and a rude sort of guitar, on which Fanty himself performed, completed the band; and they struck up

triumphantly a hymn, composed long before by Belfond for some similar occasion. Belfond sang the
recitative; the assembly joining in the chorus, accompanied by their savage music.

Sleep, roy - al Fa - ther, sleep, To thee at length a

long re - pose is giv'n, Thy woes are o'er, thy

chains are riv'n, And earth for thee now melts in - to a Heav'n of

Peace, deep mys- tic peace! . . Peace, favoured brother, peace!

> No more thou'lt watch the morning sun arise,
> With heavy heart and swimming eyes,
> Nor send to Heaven thy unavailing cries
> *Chorus.* For one little moment's rest.
> Rest, Father! calmly rest.

> Thou'rt now secure within thy quiet grave,
> So, let thy tyrant Master rave!
> He cannot blast the hope which cheers the slave,
> *Chorus.* When Death rings his solemn call,
> All hail! joy! brothers all.

> For where's the wretch would for his fetters grieve?
> A life in chains, who'd weep to leave?
> No! Death is ever but a kind reprieve
> *Chorus.* To each poor degraded slave!
> But oh, thou! no longer slave!

Behold, aloft, in yon mysterious height,
The glorious host of sparkling light!
Spirits they are who wait thy heavenward flight,
Chorus.   Where all men, all, are free,—
Free! happy brother, free!

They'll bear thee where the wild palm waves
Its plumes above thy fathers' graves,
Abodes where haply soon thy fellow-slaves
Chorus.   Will meet in the breezy air,—
There in the breezy air.

Where all day long our mothers sit forlorn
By the rude huts where we were born,
We'll fan, with perfumes of the rising morn,
Chorus.   Our own loved native groves—
Own loved native groves.

The women pressed round with their aprons laden with flowers. Talima came first, to fling in her offering; then others followed, and showers of blossoms soon hid the body from sight. Old Fanty then came forward, and was about to cast in the first clod, when . . . .

Nay, but to make my narrative clear, I must crave permission to look back a little, and note what passed at the Master's house, where they supped and chatted and slept, unconscious and unmindful how in the slave-huts death was welcomed with that strange wild scene of revelry and music.

CHAPTER XX.

CONVERSATION IN THE GREAT HOUSE.——A DISCOVERY
AND A CAPTURE.

ON a downy couch, his head resting on cushions, and
protected from the flies by smart young Negro lasses,
who fanned them away with branches of lemon and
cinnamon,——his feet rubbed by Beneba, because she
had soft hands,——reclined the proud owner of the Palm
Grove Estate. Sometimes Beneba, lulled by the
silence and by the monotony of her task, would let
her eyelids droop, and her head would nod : then her
master would give her a kick, and, awakened to a
sense of her transgression, the unlucky girl would re-
commence rubbing with renewed zeal and activity,
to the suppressed giggles of the Negro girls at the
upper end of the sofa. But neither the scented air,
nor the cushions, nor the soft hands of Beneba could
charm away the gloom which had settled on the
planter's mind. Turn his thoughts whichever way he
might, there would still arise before him that day's

scene at the muster-roll,—Mr. Dorset, his looks of
horror at the scourging, his words of pity for the
rebel crew, and, to crown all, his words of disapproval
openly and unreservedly spoken before the whole
gang.   In vain he pshawed and poohed and uttered a
hundred Gallic *bahs !* expressive of his contempt for
the whole affair : it would not do—he knew too well
the danger of incurring the disapproval of a single individual of his own class and colour, while in
the governing country public opinion against slavery
was becoming every day more embittered. . In sooth
he found himself just now in no very easy position,
and certainly in no very bland mood.

The scene of the young Negro girl striving to shield
her father by the intervention of her own person,—
which was ever recurring to his mind,—excited his
sympathy, and something akin to regret came over
him, when he thought of the stern necessity of crushing all self-respect in a stock so closely resembling—
he did not exactly add *human beings*—but white people.
While he was pondering these things, Don Duro
entered.   It was the custom of that worthy individual
to come in about this hour to talk over the affairs of
the estate, and smoke a cigarillo by way of company.
St. Hilaire suffered him to sit down, and dismissed the
girls in attendance, who hurried away in great delight,
making sly grimaces to one another at the manager
as they passed out.

Don Duro jerked his small person into a chair, and
bending his quick, watchful, little black eyes upon the

planter, as if seeking some point by which he might lay firm hold of his mind and steer it his own way, he commenced, in his usual ceremonious wording and unceremonious manner. "The Señor is tired?"

"What have you done with that old Negro?" asked St. Hilaire abruptly.

"Señor, I have left him to his fate," rejoined the Manager; "it would never do for any of us to appear anxious about such a dog."

"Where is the girl?"

"In some of the Negro-houses, I daresay; but if the Señor wishes it, I can inquire: shall I send, and have her brought up here?"

"No! no!" replied the planter, turning away with evident ill-humour; "*Pardi!* can't I inquire after my own Negroes, without raising your officious suspicions?"

Don Duro was silent for a space. He was not a very good-tempered man himself, yet not altogether deficient in the power of self-control where his interests were concerned. He had long made up his mind to humour the impetuous planter, and so to exhibit devotion to the welfare of the family as to win his patron's confidence and gratitude; for he knew that if he could only once obtain these, it was by no means unlikely that the generous planter would make him a present of a share in the estate. These were his general plans; but he had a particular design in view this evening. He therefore allowed St. Hilaire's ill-humour to subside a little, and then very gently drew

his attention to the affairs of the estate—how the crop
was gathering in—the labour done during the day—the
diminished numbers of the Negroes—the increasing
mortality—all the pains he had himself taken to preserve the black stock in health.   Next he spoke of the
hospital—told the story of the cooper and the mammy
—of the new slaves and the clabba-yaws, and, without
much respect for truth, he boasted of his care of them
and how much he had done for the prevention of further
infection.   Nor did he omit the usual protestations of
his extreme devotion to the interests of the family in
general, and the happiness of his patron in particular.

At length, when he judged that he had brought the
planter into tolerable good-humour, he drew a long
breath and started the subject he had come upon,
by asking his patron whether he had ever examined
Laurine's papers, stating that he had reason to believe
they were not drawn up in legal form, and therefore
that the girl was as safely the property of St. Hilaire
as Madelaine her mother.   The bait did not take,—
not even when he reminded him of what the girl was
saving money for; nor when he related how he had
seen her, early on the morning of the sale, in close
and intimate conversation with the Mulatto, and was
therefore amenable to the law for harbouring a runaway; nor even when he insinuated his belief that
the girl had something to do with the Obiah.   He
read only silent contempt in his patron's face, and in
his eye a slightly satirical, suspicious expression, as
though doubtful of what all this tended to.   But St.

Hilaire, however lofty his mind, was not proof against the continuous attacks of this designing man, whose scheme was now to bring the planter gradually to recall to mind his recreant slave,—how he had defied him on board the slave ship, how he had escaped, and the probability that he had been the sole author of the poisoning. He hoped, by this means, to induce a sort of collateral wrath against Laurine, as abettor to those evil-doings, and thence to obtain his consent for arresting the girl and holding her prisoner on the estate.

Don Duro had already roused the proud planter into the desired state of anger and indignation, and was proposing the old plan of slashing the tendon-Achilles, whenever the fellow was caught; by which means he would be crippled for life, and effectually rendered unable ever again to escape. But in the midst of these tokens of gradual success, the manager was interrupted by a very unusual visit at this time of night; for in rushed the Overseer, the image of horror, his hair standing fairly on end, while his goggle eyes threatened to fall from their sockets.

"What—what—what is the matter?" cried the planter and manager with one voice. But the Overseer only chattered with his teeth, and made a mumbling noise, which died away in his throat.

"Can't you answer me?" cried Mr. Cardon, taking him by the collar and shaking him, to call back his senses.

"I—I—I—" stammered he, staring deliriously

round; "don't you hear them? Don't stop me! Run for your lives! They are coming to cut our throats!"

"Who? who?" demanded the planter with the greatest impatience.

"The Negroes! they're all up in rebellion!"

St. Hilaire listened; truly enough there were trumpets and horns, sounding notes of warlike triumph through the still night. Mr. Cardon was not a man to waste time in moments of emergency: he dashed away the Overseer, and in another moment he was equipped with arms,—musket, belt, knife, and cutlass, —and giving arms to Don Duro, who received them somewhat trembling, though taking good care not to express any objection, he ordered the two to follow him. "Pooh! you infernal coward!" he cried to the Overseer, who was shivering and lagging behind, "come along! and if they but dare to touch a hair of your head, I'll soon settle them. Here, take your whip and these ropes, and come along: 'twould be dangerous to give you a gun;" which orders the chattering, trembling Overseer was fain to obey, for fear the Negroes might otherwise discover him alone and murder him.

Prudence suggested that they should gain on the Negroes by stealth, and reconnoitre. The noise in the Koromantyn hut was at its height, and to this point they directed their steps, selecting a path behind a thick mass of bushes. The warlike instruments and triumphant voices sounded loud and clear, and the party crept round to a place whence, through a badly closed window, they could see what was passing within, and St. Hilaire, imposing silence on his companions, looked on with curiosity and amazement. They were just lowering the dead body into a hole dug in the centre of the hut-floor. Strangers too were present. One tall young man stood with his back to the aperture through which the white men were watching: who could it be? The planter instinctively concentrated his attention upon him. The hymn commenced: he led, singing the recitative: at the very first sound of that voice Mr. Cardon started. Yet he waited till the song was over; then the party stole round, step by step, the Overseer getting ready his ropes, the Manager his whip; St. Hilaire himself was ready with his weapons, should he find it necessary to use them.

The doorway was so thickly crowded without and within, that it appeared impossible to enter without being seen; but with one push St. Hilaire stood in the middle of the hut. Before one of them had detected his presence, Belfond was on the ground, stunned with a blow from his master. "I say, you there, bring the ropes quick, before he comes to!" At this Don Duro came up, with the scared-looking Overseer holding fast to his coat, and the process of tying and securing the prisoner was soon got through.

St. Hilaire was still stooping down, fastening the last end of the rope, the Negroes standing off to the furthest distance, dropping off one by one through the door and window, when an apparition approached,

at sight of which the Overseer roared for his life.
A bent, dwarfish, demon-like figure, with glaring eyes,
had fastened on the planter, and sent his vampire
claws up through his hair; and when, with an oath of
annihilation, the planter turned and caught hold of
the arm, it was gone as soon as touched : so well was
it smeared with oil and grease, that it slipped like an
eel through his hands, and the figure disappeared.
Troubled at a vision he could not account for, and
although his reason was too sound to believe in su-
pernatural visitations, still St. Hilaire felt uneasy,
and unconsciously hurried over what yet remained to
be done.

It was necessary to remove the prisoner, who was
still senseless ; on the Manager devolved the task of
locking him up in the stocks.   Then the place was
well examined, and secured for the night; the watch-
dog was chained near the door, and the Manager
himself lay down ready dressed, to be on the alert at
the least noise.   The Overseer was charged to have
the dead body taken up ; and his fright having by this
time evaporated, he could enjoy the delight of cracking his long terrible whip, and driving before him the
sullen gangs, who were made to carry their dead chief
to the appointed burial-hole of the estate.   Mr. Cardon
himself, leaving these several tasks to his employés,
retired,—not to rest, but to pace up and down his
room in trouble and restlessness until morning.

CHAPTER XXI.

TWO TRAVELLERS OF A DIFFERENT STAMP.

NOTHING could be quieter that the village of Sant' Iago on the morning after the slave-sale; the merchants and planters had returned to their several homes, and the empty ship, leaving Higgins behind, had sailed away up the Orinoco, to take in a cargo of turtle and lamp-oil, for the grand port of Trinidad. Laurine was up with the grey light, and more alert than was her wont in getting through the little affairs of the morning. By-and-by she went towards the woods, to gather choice blossoms to make up into bouquets for the Port Spain market, a grand festal day being near at hand. The hedges, banks, and roadsides were covered with the gay adornings of the season, and all things seemed to smile; but the beauty of Nature only increased the sadness of her thoughts, and, sobbing and choking with grief, she was fain to turn back to her little home, and seek comfort in the society of her simple friend. Their little table was already laid : she sat down and tried to eat, but every morsel stuck half-way down, and she could only answer her friend's remarks with monosyllables, which it cost her a painful effort to utter without permitting her tears to start afresh. When the meal was ended, and everything neatly put away, she took up some needlework, and, seating herself at her little window, began to sing; Catalina, good soul, took a chair too, and amused herself with reckoning the gains of the morning over and over again. Suddenly Laurine's voice dropped : Catalina looked round, and saw the tears fast streaming down her face. The child is tired, thought she; and then immediately added aloud, " Laurine, you don't look as if you had slept last night, what is the matter? I am sure that work will kill you, you are for ever at it."

Laurine, with an effort to check her grief, answered briskly that she was " well, quite well," and standing up, she displayed her work to her companion. " Look here, good Catalina,—have I not managed this work nicely? It is a festal dress for La St. Jean : look at these sleeves plaited in cross-barred patterns, and at these pockets edged with gay ribbon,—do you see how I have filled them with little pink cowries from the shore, to jingle like money while the dancer moves. And I have gummed down the wings of the small gold-beetle and of gay butterflies, and what pretty patterns they make ! I have been a long time collecting them in this little cedar box, because the wood preserves them ; and I expect a good price for this dress. I ought, I am sure, to be thankful to God for the number of good customers he bestows upon me."

"And above all, my child," said the dame, in a warning but affectionate tone, "never be proud or vain; always bear in mind the fate of the crabs on the day of creation."

"Oh, Catalina, pray tell me about it, it will do me good to listen to you."

"Well, my child," answered the aged spinster with a solemn face, "it is a deep lesson for youth. When creation began, it took four, five, six, seven days, and then God called all the animals together, to receive their heads: they assembled on a wide savannah, and the heads were handed to them by angels. All the animals stood there quiet, one here, another there, all modest and respectful, save the little crab, and she kept walking here and marching there, and showing off her pretty steps sideways and every way, for people to see, till, when she thought to ask for her head, the heap was gone—there was not one left. So you see what pride brings people to! The Holy Virgin protect you from such a sin, my child!"

"One could almost fancy," observed Laurine, "that some animal had taken up a head more than his share: was it the two-headed snake, I wonder?" she added innocently.

"I suppose it was, my child; and I have heard tell of another thing,—that the monkey, full of tricks, jumped in front, just as the crowd reached the savannah, and with one spring he whipped up a human head, and skipped to the top of a palm-tree with it. The angels said, ' Come down, rascal!' He would not come, but threw down the head : it was then so dirty and bruised that man would not have it, and the angels were obliged to make him an entire new one; so monkeys have human heads, and remain thieves and vagabonds, to this day."

" Very true, good Catalina; and I just remember I have heard another story about those wonderful beginnings of all things : I heard it from Fanty, who is learned in African magic, he says——"

" Likely, likely," said the spinster, shaking her head, " and Fanty knows a great deal; but oh, my child, keep clear of that man : remember that religion forbids us to commune with evil-doers, lest we become so ourselves. Padre Martino says that Obiah is a crime, and everybody says that Fanty is an Obiah man. But, *Ave Maria ! Santísimos Santos !*" she exclaimed, crossing herself with great rapidity, and looking with horror towards the back door, " here is the man himself ! I hope he didn't hear me."

Despite the good dame's advice, Laurine rose to bid him welcome; for was he not aged and infirm, she said to herself, and poor?——he was also near akin to her loved though too hasty and impetuous Belfond. As she opened the door however, she uttered a faint exclamation of terror. His face was bound up in blood-stained cloths, and one of his arms was in a sling. Before she had time to say a word he addressed her.

" Sorrow is on my old head," he exclaimed with a harsh and tremulous voice, " and Fanty will soon be laid far down under the grass. See!" he cried, holding up his wounded arm, " this is what poor old Fanty gets for helping others; but body-pain is nothing,—heart-pain! that's worse. Better had Belfond drunk the death-giving Obiah, and Fanty had laid his old head under the grass beside him, than that he should die by bits in the white man's dungeon."

Laurine did not utter a word: with her hands crossed upon her bosom, and the big drops standing on her brow, she gazed at the Negro, awaiting in terror the explanation of his words."

" *Ahí!*" continued he, raising his voice to a shriller key, " *sorrow comes easy; trouble is cheap to get; years and money cannot send it away;*" saying which, he turned to go.

Laurine sprang after him: " Speak to me, Fanty!" she cried; " oh, tell me what has happened to him—to Belfond!"

The Negro eyed her for a moment keenly; then, as if moved by her entreaties, he edged himself to a low stool, and, squatting down upon it, related the facts which are already known to the reader.

During the colloquy, Catalina had joined them with eyes and mouth open to listen. As soon as she had heard enough to understand what was the matter, she suggested a remedy after her own fashion. " My child, we will speak to Padre Martino," she said; " he is a holy, pious man."

U

The Negro's wounded and disfigured visage became contorted into a hideous sneer, which so terrified the spinster as to prevent her from finishing her speech. "Away!" he cried, raising his bony hand; "away with white men's sorcerers (meaning priests)! *does not right hand wash left hand?* who ever heard one white man say another white man did wrong?"

"Fanty," said Laurine eagerly, "and you, good Catalina, leave it all to me; I will do it if I die. I will go to the Palm Grove, and beg mercy for him myself. It is but a few days ago that Madame Angélique herself wanted to coax me away from my shop to nurse the little child, because it loves me, and I play with it so merrily. I will say, Take life, take freedom, only let Belfond live."

"*Santísima Virgen!*" broke forth the pious spinster, throwing up her eyes and fingering her beads; "is it among the tempters you would go? Oh, my child, never go where the wicked are! stay here, and God will put it into our hearts to think of some way of saving him yet."

"Don't stop me!" said Laurine passionately, "for do something I will,—though I scarcely know what yet. I think I'll go to the Fountain Estate. Yes, that is it! Lead the way, Fanty; bring me to Mrs. Dorset's, she is kind and sweet, she will listen to me, she will pity my sorrow."

"My child," whispered La Catalina close to her ear, "will you go alone with that man?"

"God is with me," said the young girl, "he will

take care of me;" and throwing her arms about her friend's neck, she wept long and bitterly.

"She is right for once," said Fanty. "Young girl, they are looking for you, to catch you and make a slave of you, and on the high road you must not go; but across the woods, to where those good people live, you are safer, so come at once,—old bones like mine have no business in the place of danger: come!" then, tearing herself from Catalina's embrace, she fled in haste with her companion. As she sped beside him, her spirits began to rise; her young heart prophesied success, and already she saw her lover at her feet, safe, free, grateful, and devoted for ever. Unconsciously she quickened her pace, and glided on, unchecked by bush or thorn, till warned by the voice of her companion to stop.

"Old legs may fall and break," said the old man crossly, "who minds them?"

Laurine felt her error, and though her heart and wishes were bounding before her, she nevertheless stopped to help him, made him lean upon her, and talked kindly to him; and before her sweet influence his ill-humour soon vanished. The road they took was a shorter and much less frequented way than that taken by the two planters the day before. As they advanced, the country became wilder and more lonely, the hedges grew thicker and higher, till at length none but forest-trees flanked their path, their branches entwining so closely above as to obstruct the light of day, while the dark woodlands beyond resounded with the howlings of monkeys, and the screaming of parrots, as they fled at the approach of man. Amid scenes like these, and with such a companion, we cannot wonder that the young girl's spirits in some degree reflected the gloom around her; but she was a hopeful creature, active, contented, looking always to the bright side of things, and finding cause for cheerfulness even under the darkest cloud.

They ascended a gentle slope, where the thick woods opened suddenly into a pleasant glade, and from the top the sea came in full view before them. The sun was just touching the western horizon; the rolling masses of purple and gold, which seemed to bear the fiery orb, were surmounted with streaks of delicate green, like glimpses of a distant fairy-land, and these again shaded softly away to the pure azure of the zenith. A crimson splendour clothed the valleys, and the outlines of the hills were softened by a transparent veil of delicate lilac. The sea, like a resplendent mirror of gold, reflected the tints of the sky above, and its burnished waves, laden with the glow, pressed on impatiently to the shore, as if unwilling to keep such treasures to themselves. Laurine clasped her hands, her knees touched the ground, and she prayed. Fanty looked at her, and drew aside, for there is a guardian spirit ever near the innocent and the earnest, which warns the wicked to keep aloof, and even the fiendish Obiah priest respected her devotions.

When she rose, the glory of the scene was already fading, and twilight was approaching. The change to darkness was rendered more sudden by those masses of clouds lately so bright and gorgeous; they were now moving heavily across the sky, which soon became quite overcast, and, in a few minutes more, rain descended in overwhelming torrents, like those which must have fallen when the great Flood began. Laurine clung to the nearest tree, lest she should be forced down the hill; she was of course soaked to the skin, but she thought more of the old, feeble, and wounded Negro than of herself, and tried to persuade him to keep under shelter with her. But he shook his head, and beckoned her onwards: "I knew of this," he said, "that is why old Fanty came this way. Just behind these trees, quite near us, is an Indian's hut. Forward! quick! and remember old Fanty's tongue can't twist to their Spanish words; young girl must talk for him."

The twanging sound of an old guitar, and the nasal, drawling, monotonous song of a Peon—*i. e.* half Indian, half Spaniard—was now heard above the roar of the descending rain, and by dint of strong efforts Laurine and her companion came to a good-sized low-roofed hut, the inmates of which seemed particularly busy and cheerful. There were a great many women and children, but only one man,—the Peon, who seemed to be the head of the family. There was no need of introduction: our travellers were strangers, and caught in the rain,—this was enough. The women wiped the best stools, set the pot to boil, and slung the hammock on the peg; by-and-by a small table was set in the middle, and a meal offered to the travellers, of which, according to savage etiquette, they must partake, or be considered enemies. When the repast was finished, Old Fanty, grunting with satisfaction, for it was a long time since he had eaten anything so savoury, ensconced himself on a low stool in a dark corner, took out his pipe, and began to smoke. Laurine joined the women at their work; they were busy in preparing cassava from the poisonous root of the far-famed manihot, in a shed adjoining the dwelling-room.

It was late in the evening when the women finished their work, and Laurine, fatigued with her long journey and her late vigils, slept soundly until morning, when the merry voices of the Indian children waked her. The rain had passed away, and nature awoke with renewed loveliness, giving forth fragrance with double profusion. The air was cool and invigorating; and a thousand birds were on the wing, chirping and warbling with gladness at the revival of daylight and serenity. The children were out too, laughing and shouting at one another, for they were earning their breakfast in true Indian fashion, by shooting at pieces of dried fish and tassa, hung upon the tree-tops, as rewards for their skill.

Some chocolate was then prepared, and with this, together with large tempting cassava-cakes, Laurine and her guide made a comfortable breakfast. They had scarcely finished, when Old Fanty grumbled out his hurry to move, and in truth Laurine required no pressing. The ·Indians would fain have detained them, but the old Negro waved his hand in token of refusal, " For," said he to Laurine, whom he beckoned to interpret, " we must be away now ; old feet such as mine, and soft-footed like you, are both slow. " Then I will go with you a little way for company," said the Indian ; " I am going towards Bande de l'Est, to my brothers and friends, bound for the Orinoco tomorrow morning at three by the bright moonlight : we are off on a hunting expedition along the banks, and *acuerdate bien,*" he added, addressing Laurine, " if anything should happen to make a boat welcome, meet us by the Tamana river, on the sea-shore."

This piece of intelligence seemed to afford pleasure to the Negro ; he grunted, and nodded, and looked as pleased as with such features he · could look. Then Laurine received the good wishes of the women, calmly, quietly expressed, in the manner of all Indians. The Peon called to Emanuel, his eldest son ; and these two heaving on their shoulders a bundle of nets, cutlasses, guns, and poles, the little party set off.

Old Fanty however did not seem to like the path which the Indian took, and after awhile they parted, the Negro and the damsel continuing their journey alone. The late oppressive heat had been tempered by the last night's torrents, while the few hours' sunshine of that morning had been sufficient to suck up the sopping wet, leaving only enough moisture to make the ground cool and comfortable. They had not proceeded far, when the woods began to thin, the

country grew more open, and a prospect soft and
beautiful as any in those sunny climes presented itself
to their view: the colours of the landscape grew
richer; the verdure of the hill-sides and savannahs was
lost in the overspreading hues of azure, scarlet, yellow, white, and purple; while in the cultivated hollow
before them, the planter's house was seen peeping
from amidst groves of palm and bowers of passion-
flower, peaceful, happy, and beautiful, as a spot stolen
from the gardens of Paradise. Here Fanty took his
leave of the maiden. "Assarci look upon you!" said
he; "Assarci guide you and bless you! For you
never feared poor old Fanty, though everybody hates
him and shuns him. Go! no harm shall come to
you; though Fanty dies to get it, you and Belfond
shall have happiness and freedom soon. Go tonight
to Madelaine's hut; Fanty will be there too: white
man will give no ear to Laurine's prayers, but Fanty
will. Away! go!"

They parted, and Laurine sped on hopefully, and
never once turned her eyes to look at the blooming
temptations of the country, which at other times
would have made her linger for hours on the road to
cull them. She was already amidst plantain-walks,
where the fruit hung in large and heavy bunches,
and in another moment she was skirting the cacao-
walks of the Fountain Estate, where the songs of the
Negroes proclaimed them at work. Anxious to avoid
them, lest they should detain her with their conversation, she crept along in concealment behind the trees.

The harvest had begun : companies of men, women, and children were dispersed among the trees, some stripping the boughs of their purple fruit, and dropping it into baskets beneath ; others were seated in the shade, extracting the beans or nibs, which were cast into a large receiving basket, while song, joke, and laughter went round, to cheer them at their labour.

Leaving these on her right hand, Laurine soon approached the rude dwelling of the Fountain Estate. But rude as was the building,—no better indeed than a log-house in the backwoods of America,—it looked pretty, with its little garden, fenced all round with blossoming pomegranates, and its trellised bower of granadilla dropping bright-tinted flowers and ponderous fruit; and close by, on the edge of an abrupt descent, a natural fountain gushed forth, beneath the shade of huge native fruit-trees. It was from this pretty fountain that the estate took its name.

Laurine approached the house, and requested a girl to beg of her mistress that she would allow her to speak with her. In a few moments she was ushered into a room in which Mrs. Dorset was sitting, surrounded by half-a-dozen little sable attendants, whom she was teaching to sew. Laurine, as she entered, dropped a curtsey.

" Well," said Mrs. Dorset, " I am glad to see you, Laurine ; what news ?"

The poor girl attempted to reply, but her courage failed ; and when her lips moved, her voice died away in upheaving sobs, as though her heart would burst its bonds.

Mrs. Dorset laid down her work, and in sweetest and most encouraging tones addressed her: "Tell me, my poor girl, what is the matter with you, and what can I do for you?"

Poor Laurine was quite at a loss how to tell her story; she had been dwelling, all the way she came, on the certain happy result of her petition, never once reflecting on the difficulty she might have in presenting it; but the kind words of the lady reassured her, and the recollection of the dungeon, and the captive within it, doomed to starvation, gave new energy to her mind.

"Please your mercy," she said, adopting the form of speech which the coloured people are taught to use in Spanish colonies, "there is a fellow-slave of my mother's on the Palm Grove Estate, who is in disgrace."

"On Mr. Cardon's estate, is it? What, the old man? or is it his daughter?"

"Please your mercy, it is neither of them; it is a runaway slave, who was caught the other night, and they are going to do something terrible with him."

"Is it your brother, Laurine?"

The young girl hung down her head, and her heart began to throb, while tears,—big, silent, burning tears,—fell upon her apron as she grasped it in her trembling hands. With the quick instinct of a woman's heart, Mrs. Dorset guessed the truth at once, and, with equal delicacy, she refrained from asking any further questions, beyond the culprit's name.

"Please your mercy," replied Laurine, looking up through her tears, "it is a Mulatto slave, who years ago went to France to wait upon Mr. Cardon's son, who is now dead.   He ran away, the evil spirit tempted him; please your mercy, I know it was a very wicked thing to do; but, if you will beg for him, please your mercy, he will be steady now.   At all events, he is in the dungeon starving!"

"Starving!" exclaimed Mrs. Dorset, with a look of incredulity and surprise.

"He has been there since last night, your mercy; and Mr. Cardon declares he will make an example of him to all the runaways in the Colony, for he is spoiled and ruined for ever, he says.   Yet I think, if your mercy would only beg for him this once—"

"Starved!   Heaven preserve us!   starved!—that must not be : and yet what is to be done?   Shall I call my husband?—he left Mr. Cardon's last evening in anger for some other such demonstration of severity,—he won't go there again, I am sure.   But why can't I go myself?   Laurine, do you think your master would listen to me?"

"Surely, your mercy; he never refuses a lady."

"Then I will go;" and, tying on her bonnet in haste, she left the house, followed by Laurine, and set off for the Palm Grove Estate.

CHAPTER XXII.

REPRIEVE.

WHEN Mrs. Dorset and Laurine reached the Palm Grove, not a soul was to be seen : the place seemed deserted. Laurine proposed that, as the sitting-room was much exposed to the sun, the lady should rest awhile in Madame Angélique's room, while she went to reconnoitre. Mrs. Dorset entered, and took a chair. It was a long and somewhat narrow room, the floor of which was waxed and polished. A low French bed stood in a recess at the upper end ; there were also a prie-dieu and a couch covered with fine linen white as snow, a white marble table in the centre, a marble lavatoire, a marble toilet-table, a large swing glass, and a magnificent pillared wardrobe,——all of rich and costly materials, giving an air of refinement and luxury to the room, which contrasted strongly with its homely construction. A door, which was now locked, formed a communication between this room and another.

Soon a sound reached the ear of the visitor, which at first she had not noticed,—that of a heavy footstep in the room adjoining, pacing up and down, backwards and forwards, without cessation. "At all events," thought she, "there is somebody within, and I had better look for Laurine." She rose, and moved towards the window, when she saw the young girl returning in company with Beneba, whom, after a good deal of searching, she had at last discovered, walking with the child in her arms under the trees. Beneba informed the lady that Madame Angélique was out making calls, and that the step in the next room must be that of her master, who had shut himself in his study since breakfast.

"Can't you tell him I wish to speak with him?" asked the lady.

Beneba looked scared at such a proposition: the whites of her eyes glistened, and her fat African mouth was puckered up like the drawn opening of a sack, while the baby, little amused by her dulness, threw itself, crowing and laughing, into the arms of Laurine.

"Do let your Master know I wish to speak with him!" reiterated Mrs. Dorset.

"Madame says you are to go and call Master," repeated Laurine, with an imploring expression. "Do go, dear Beneba!"

The girl muttered something between her teeth, then answered aloud that she would go to the kitchen, to tell Clora to look for Rosaly to send Quaco to speak to her master. Mrs. Dorset was obliged to submit to this roundabout arrangement, and composed herself to wait, while Laurine, her heart throbbing with anxiety, took the little laughing babe to her heart, and smiled through her gathering tears as the little hands gaily loosened her long tresses from the comb which confined them.

Their attention however was soon drawn to one of the remotest of the out-buildings, whence proceeded the sound of many voices, apparently in angry contention; and presently three or four Negroes, surrounding a taller man, came forth, the Manager and Overseer following close: they approached the house, and made for Mr. Cardon's study. Laurine looked as if her eyes would start from their sockets, and she put her hand to her heart to still its beating, for she recognized her lover, and saw by the Manager's look that his fate was sealed. The group entered Mr. Cardon's room by a side-door which opened into the courtyard. Laurine strove hard to catch a sound of what was passing within, but a stillness as of death ensued. Presently a stir was perceptible, and faintly, yet distinctly, there fell upon the ear the clank of chains and the ringing of iron instruments. Forgetting everything save her lover, Laurine dragged Mrs. Dorset to the closed door between the two rooms, and, with the baby pressed close to her bosom, she wildly battered against it. No notice was taken: who cared for her voice? She urged Mrs. Dorset to speak, and that tone and expression peculiar to white

ladies produced its effect,—the door was opened by
Mr. Cardon himself.   His hat was on his head, but
he doffed it in a moment, and assuming at once that
courteousness to the sex which he never forgot, even
under the most irritating circumstances, he advanced
to lead his guest away to the saloon.   But Laurine,
with a cry of desperation, grasped Mrs. Dorset's arm,
and forcibly drew her into the study.

The floor was strewn with instruments of punishment,—manacles, ankle-rings, chains, and above all, a
heavy bar of iron with a ring and padlock, for fastening
round the neck of incorrigible fugitives.   There were,
besides, a cowhide on the table, and a 'knife.   Mr.
Cardon's face, as he returned to the room and looked
towards the culprit, bore the dire expression of anger
and despotic will.   As for the slave, if there had been
any hope of obtaining mercy by inducing submission,
it vanished at the first glance; for what hope could
be entertained of one on whose brow the pride of
Lucifer sat enthroned?   Nevertheless his appearance
was one of extreme suffering: his hair was matted
with gore, his clothes were torn and stained, his fine
eyes were haggard and unearthly in their expression.
Mrs. Dorset looked from him to his master implor-
ingly.   "I am come," she said, "to ask pardon for
him, in the name of Him who forgave his enemies on
the cross; as we seek mercy for ourselves from above,
let us deal mercifully to those who offend us; forgive
him, Mr. Cardon!   I beg, I beseech, I implore you,
forgive him!"

Before the planter had time to reply, two persons entered the room, one of whom went up directly to Mrs. Dorset.

"Anna, my dear, what can have induced you to come here? Did I not beg you would never come here? These are not scenes for you. Come away, I insist upon it. Mr. Cardon, I beg you will excuse the intrusion, we shall not trouble you long. Come, Anna, come!"

Mrs. Dorset replied by throwing her arms about her husband's neck, and looking up in his face, her eyes streaming with tears. Mr. Cardon politely advanced: "I am not one who would lightly refuse a lady's petition," he said; "let this wretch confess his crime, let him tell who it is that administers the Obiah to the slaves and destroys my property, and I will not touch a hair of his head."

Madame Angélique had thrown herself into an armchair, and was whining out most theatrically, "Oh, my children! Here at last is the monster who destroyed them. Alas, poor me!"

Don Duro thrust his hands into his pockets, and, looking profoundly wise, demanded that the prisoner should be made to tell where old Fanty was to be found,—"The crippled beast who ran away long ago, Señor: people say he is an Obiah man, and I remember he is this dog's uncle. I tried," said the Manager, pointing to the culprit,—"I tried to make him confess it, and I thought to compel him by jamming the door on his arm: but he is a dog!—a pig!"

The Overseer stood sneering and leering with his goggle eyes, for he anticipated a feast for his malicious heart; while the little infant, which Madame Angélique had attempted to take, clung fast to Laurine, for it was repelled by the angry voice and anxious face of its granddame.

The planter looked at the child, and looked at Laurine. How could he help it?——she was so beautiful,—trembling from head to foot, her headgear off, and her silken hair sweeping in waving tresses almost to her feet, while through her long and moistened lashes there gleamed the fitful flashes of her anxiety and fear.

"And she too," exclaimed Don Duro, pointing to her,—"I swear she has something to do with it. I accuse her, Señor, of harbouring that runaway *demonio*, and of carrying messages and philtres for him backwards and forwards to this place. Make her confess it, Señor."

Laurine looked piteously round; she knew and felt her utter helplessness.

"*Allons donc !*" said the planter, "we will look into that afterwards; she came here with Mrs. Dorset, and through respect for Madame, we will let her be for the present; let us despatch this wretch first. Come, Sirrah, and before this lady, who condescends too much, in feeling for a black criminal like you,—come, render an account of yourself. These Negroes here, and every one on the estate, I am sure, are all longing for their release from your infernal machinations: I want

x

no other proofs of your black deeds : speak, therefore, if you would hope to live another day."

"Oh, I am sure," cried Mrs. Dorset, with eager looks, as she disengaged herself from her husband and advanced a little in front,—"oh yes, he will speak, I know he will! Speak !—and Mr. Cardon will forgive you, he has promised it."

The prisoner was still silent, but, with the same stubborn, wild look, kept his eyes fixed on his master's face.

"Pah!" said Mr. Cardon, after pausing for awhile, "idle work this ! Why I tell you, Madame, that were I to set him loose, he would give you a dose of Obiah the first thing, as a token of his gratitude. I know the dog !   Ay, speak, dog !—open your mouth, dog !—or bark, you vicious cur !—or snarl, if you can't speak!"

With a long gasp the Mulatto lifted his fettered arm, laying bare as he did so a hideous wound, and looking upwards, as in appeal to eternal justice, he broke forth :—" Listen !," he cried : "he calls me dog ! then dog let it be ; dog, therefore, is my father ! *Your* pardon ?—I would not have it, I would throw it in your teeth if you gave it.   Ay, beat me ! bruise me ! hack me ! kill me !   The same blood that flows in your veins, colours mine ; in your conscience you know it.   Ha ! I laugh to scorn your laws and your systems ; they cannot alter that great law which God has written in our natures, nor make you one whit less responsible to Him for my welfare, than for that of the white child you pampered and taught to trample upon me. How will you answer to God for this? My degradation, my sufferings,—they cry to Heaven for vengeance upon you. My life—that blessing which God placed in your hands to endow me with—you have turned to a curse : take it ! drink it as it oozes with my blood—fit draught for your wine-cup ! and remember, when you slumber at night, that every drop will turn to Obiah,—Obiah ! do you hear me ?—and shape into demons to people your dreams : that is my curse for you! Now do your worst with me—I am ready."

A breathless silence followed this audacious ha-rangue : the words, the expression, the unparalleled boldness, had struck every one dumb with horror. Mr. Cardon convulsively grasped the knife, which lay on the table before him, and the two minions, the Ma-nager and Overseer, roused by this movement, sprang upon the prisoner, dragged him to the floor, and like tempting demons held up his foot for the crippling operation—the cutting of the tendon.

But Laurine, in terror, had thrown herself at the planter's feet : " Master ! Master ! oh, merciful, kind Master ! look at him, he is ill,—he is delirious, Master ! He doesn't know what he says; let your anger fall upon me—I will suffer it all."

St. Hilaire, in his rage, spurned her from him; his hand flew up with fury. What stayed him? Was it a touch of his better nature? Was it the little child, which, frightened by the distress of its favourite play-mate, chimed in with its cries as it strove to climb

the grandfather's knees? Was it the pale, sweet, beseeching face of Mrs. Dorset? or pity for the humble
thing which lay in crouching beauty at his feet, that
made him pause before he struck? Or was it the
consciousness that there stood behind him, watching
every movement, a white man, hating and deprecating
oppression? Or was it all these in quick succession?
It were hard to tell; but, quick as the changes of the
tropical skies, Mr. Cardon changed his purpose. He
seemed to reflect a moment, then turned to Mrs.
Dorset.

"Madame," he said, "out of courtesy to you, I will
give him yet another chance. Let Laurine tell all
she knows about the Obiah, and perhaps it may yet
save him."

"Please your mercy, on my knees this hour," exclaimed the young girl, clasping his knees with vehemence, "here before Almighty God,—I know nothing
about it, and Belfond is quite as innocent."

"On your oath," asked Don Duro, "did you never
carry messages, and bottles, and powders to the Negroes on the estate, under pretence of visiting your
mother?"

"Never! never! never, Master!" replied Laurine.

"Do you mean to say," continued Don Duro, "that
you never spoke to this young man, or never—?"

Mr. Cardon interrupted him. "Laurine," he said,
"if what you say is true, you will prove it to me
by your submission to the orders I am going to give
you. Your papers of freedom, Laurine, are reported

to be incorrect and informal, and your name still remains uneffaced among the slaves mentioned in the bill of sale, as pertaining to the Palm Grove Estate. If that be true, you are to all intents and purposes part of this property, which I bought, and I require your services accordingly. Your shop and everything in it, you are aware, belong to me. I require you to remain here till I examine the registry and papers; and remember, that on your good behaviour and submission to my orders will depend the fate of that wretch," he said, pointing to Belfond; "and now, miscreant, go!"

"I will not have your pardon!" roared Belfond, hissing the words through his teeth, and wrestling with the men who held him.

"See to him, Don Duro," said Mr. Cardon, with authoritative composure, "and take him away, lest I be tempted further; secure him in the dungeon."

"Now, Madame," said St. Hilaire, coming forward and addressing Mrs. Dorset, "let us withdraw to the saloon;" and he courteously offered his arm to lead the way, leaving his wife to settle with Laurine as to the nature of her new duties. Mr. and Mrs. Dorset however were not inclined to stay longer, and Mr. Cardon was fain to accompany them part of the way home.

"I scarcely like," he said to the lady, as he walked by her side, "to part with you on such terms as these. I am sure, Madame, you set me down as an ogre."

"Not exactly that," replied the lady, with a sweet low voice.

"But something like it, I suppose," he added quickly; "and for what? for securing that demon—that— that— Madame! Madame! do you know what a tiger I should let loose in that wretch? The compounder, the administrator of Obiah! You surely would not wish such a thing : why, I should consider myself responsible to the whole Colony for the mischief that would ensue. His fame would soon spread throughout the island, and every Negro who imagined a complaint against his master, would go to him to buy his infernal help; particularly now, since all this hypocritical fuss about Emancipation has made the Negroes fancy themselves injured."

"But how can you tell it is he? for, after all, as far as I have been able to understand, there exists no proof against the unfortunate young man."

"You heard him yourself speak something like a confession of it, Madame."

"Nay, nay," replied the lady persuasively, "you would not take the ravings of delirium for a confession;—you are too humane, too just, Mr. Cardon. You had only to look at his face to know how ill he was; besides, it was a threat of future visions, not of past offences, remember. And after all, what is this Obiah, which I hear so often spoken of?—I cannot comprehend what it is."

"Madame," replied the planter with a heavy sigh, "it is the Negroes' power; they say it is witchcraft, I believe it to be poison. The country abounds with deadly herbs, of whose properties we are totally ignorant, but with which the Negroes are familiar; they mix them, stew them, distil them, and then make their Obiah compounds. They give them to us to breathe, in the form of fragrance,—to eat—to drink—to touch; they make us take them through the pores of our skin, and we know nothing of it. The poison is either slow, and takes months to do its work—then the victim fades away, sinks without a trace of a cause to be discovered; at other times it is sudden—the victim foams at the mouth, reels, falls down, and dies. What can we do? We are at their mercy!"

" Strange!" ejaculated Mr. Dorset, who had not hitherto spoken; " have the bodies been properly examined?"

" I have said before, they have: no trace is ever found by doctor or chemist."

" Is there no suspicion as to what drugs they use?"

" We are not sure they do use drugs, or they use such as are too subtle for our detection. We know the Brinvilliers, it is true: here it is," he said, plucking a corymb of small red and yellow flowers from the foot-path, and presenting it to the lady; "you see it grows everywhere underfoot; it yields a poison as deadly as it is subtle, and has received its name from a celebrated poisoner of the reign of Louis XIV., who is supposed to have used it in the composition of the *acqua toffana* she used. We know also something of the deleterious properties of the root of the pomme-rose and the cockroach apple; *mais sacré!* Madame, how limited is this poor knowledge to theirs! We are entirely at their mercy."

"In short," said Mr. Dorset, "irresponsible power in the master is parried with as terrible a weapon on the part of the slave."

"*Peste, oui!* and, like an invisible demon, this Negro witchcraft crawls round the white man's domicile, seizing in its deadly grasp the fairest and sweetest: this is the Negro's injured innocence! *Corbleu!* the most arbitary master trembles before that!"

"To speak plainer," resumed Mr. Dorset, "the very chain he has fastened round the foot of his slave, the Negro in his turn has locked by the other end round the neck of his master."

"Bah!" exclaimed the planter, "I am in no mood for arguing."

"Well, well," interrupted the lady, endeavouring to turn the conversation to a less irritating topic; "tell me, what are you going to do with that poor girl Laurine? Her lot seems to me very hard: for no fault that I can see, she is about to lose her earnings, her means of living, and her freedom."

"Say but the word, my good lady, and I will give her two shops, and her mother's freedom to boot; but I must first keep her on her good behaviour, and make her tell me what she knows about this Obiah, and that devil incarnate whom we suspect of compounding it: that was my motive for speaking as I did, and for detaining her; I never intended to carry out my threat, and I shall be the more inclined to let her go, because I suspect that fellow, my Manager, has his eye upon her."

"God help her!" sighed Mrs. Dorset.

"Is it possible," urged Mr. Dorset, "that you could find no easier and readier means of discovering the secret? why, methinks any Negro, for the promise of freedom—"

"Not one, I tell you,—not for gift, or promise, or threat;—not even when he is dying will he confess a word which might throw light on the cause or the means. I will tell you what I saw myself in the year 1822 in Martinique. I went there on business, and remained long enough to witness the completion of the tragedy I am about to relate. The Obiah had spread its ravages to such a fearful extent, that a Court was instituted, to stay the progress of its crimes. The bloodthirsty Davoust was chosen to execute its decrees: he went about with two hatchets, —a large one for cutting off heads, a small one for cutting off hands, — summoning before him every Negro suspected; he then and there pronounced sentence, without hearing or appeal, and had such forthwith executed. Such terrific examples were intended to scare away the Obiah; but, like an evil genius, it only seemed to open still wider its dark and terrible wings over the island. Davoust became sanguinary with the practice of his office, and, weary of the too lenient execution with the hatchet, had sixteen of the most hardened Negroes caged up in the great Place Lamentin, and ordered them to be burned, one after the other. Twenty thousand slaves were called from all parts of the island, to witness the scene; a small drizzling rain fell the whole day, as though sent on purpose to render their deaths more slow and torturing; yet in the face of this not a word was uttered by the sixteen criminals, nor by the twenty thousand who looked on : they remained impenetrably silent. The square was like a black sea of human beings, silent, sullen, dogged. I saw them go away in the evening in the same gloomy mood, and during that night there was not an estate on the island where death from poison did not occur. The evil was in no degree arrested, and, wearied out and conquered by the persevering horrors of Negro vengeance, the Court closed its sittings in 1827*. And these are the innocent lambs for whom all England is sighing at this moment!—for whom the ladies are weeping,—pardon, Madame, I speak only of the misguided fools in England,—and for whom the gentlemen are ready to draw their swords!"

During all this time Mr. Dorset and his lady had not offered a word of remark; the latter, it is true, had two or three times looked round with an expression of horror, and a stifled exclamation had risen to her lips; the former walked on with his hands behind him, his mild eyes somewhat closed, and his lips pressed gently together, as if all surprise had passed into settled dissatisfaction and regret. Thus they proceeded, leaving St. Hilaire to speak without interruption.

* An account of these circumstances appeared in the Paris 'National' of November 9th, 1841.

"It is for these reasons," he continued, "from knowing their obdurate hearts, that I cling to the hope of getting something out of Laurine. She is a good girl, and attends to her religion. I can just whisper a word to her confessor; he will visit her, and if she does know anything about this Obiah, he will make her come and tell me; that is my only hope. When this is done, Madame, I promise you to dismiss her well rewarded."

They had now reached the turning of the lane which led direct from the high road to the dwelling-house of the Fountain, and St. Hilaire paused to take his leave. His tone and manner were greatly changed since they had met before: the loud, authoritative voice was subdued; his manner, so bold and proud, was now almost gentle, and there was something sad in the expression of his dark, manly eye, which even his continued flow of conversation did not remove. Now, about to part from his companions, he took both their hands, and held them long within his own. "I have been talking about my Negroes," he said, "and my plans, and, seriously, I may never see them accomplished—I came with you this evening for an entirely different purpose: it is to you, dear lady, that I now address myself in particular; you add to all the charms of lovely woman, those of the mind and the heart; and I have something I wish to say to you, Mrs. Dorset:—should anything happen to me, will you promise to be a friend to my poor little Léonce? —he may stand in need of your kindness."

" My good Sir ! " exclaimed the lady, startled by his earnestness, " why should you think of such a thing ? "

" *Parbleu !* I cannot tell myself; but I feel strange this evening : whenever my thoughts go forward to the morrow, they fly back like stones thrown against the wall; I look forward, and all appears blank; something hangs over me, I am sure. It is useless trying to laugh me out of it; if that were possible, I should have done it myself. I only wish you to re-member well my words to you this night; and," he added, shaking their hands again and again, while he turned from the lady to the gentleman, remember as long as you live this my parting advice :——never inter-fere with another's affairs, or suffer another to inter-fere between you and your Negroes, for you do not know what mischief may come of it, nor where it will end. Suppose, now, you had children, and had plans of your own for governing them : severe as your rules might occasionally appear to a casual visitor, you would not like him to create a scene before them pro-claiming you cruel, would you ? No, *parbleu !* I am sure you would not. It would ruin your authority and the order of your establishment; it would destroy all respect for you in your children, and produce con-fusion in your household. *Eh bien !* so it is with those Negroes of mine. Yesterday morning they respected me as a sort of king,——a despot, maybe; but all kings are despots;——well, they will never respect me again : the *prestige* is gone which protected me, I feel it and know it; God only knows what hangs over me."

"If I thought such a thing," exclaimed Mr. Dorset quickly, "I should never forgive myself."

"Ah, *n'importe! I* forgive you," said the planter hurriedly; "and now, Dorset, another thing I have to say to you in particular; if you had not come to me so unexpectedly this evening, I should have gone to you to say it—I had so intended. I wish to give you this paper; it is a formal acknowledgment of the money advanced to me by Pelham the other morning at the slave-market: you remember the circumstance; give it to him. I have mentioned the debt again in my will. I have left you, together with my brother-in-law, executors; let this debt be the first paid off, should I never see you again, for I would not have a word breathed against the name I leave to the little boy. So good-bye! adieu, adieu, Madame! Remember my poor Léonce!" and, waving his hands, he walked away quickly towards his home.

CHAPTER XXIII.

PRESENTIMENT OF DEATH.

ST. HILAIRE had nearly reached the avenue which led to his home. He was walking very fast, and looking up at the sky, absorbed in thought, when suddenly he was awakened from his reverie by a rough voice addressing him. " I say ! holloa, Mr. Thing-a-me ! holloa !" and a bulky figure came up the road, waddling and blowing ; no longer with the fawning manner of the mate on board the brig ' Venus,' but with a triumphant, familiar manner, such as suited Higgins as the possessor of wealth. " Blow me !" continued he, " but you are a fast-sailing goer, my jo ! and you are deaf, I should think, for I have been behind the hedge, bellowing my breath away to you. Odds, man ! can't you stop a bit, and let a fellow know what's doing on your side of the world ? I've got a bit of news for you."

The planter turned and stood erect, as the speaker advanced.

" Now, Mr. Cardon, don't be looking so proud at me; arn't I a white man, like yourself? I tell you, I'll bring your Mulatto slave to you before another day is out."

" He is found, and caught, and secured," was the concise reply.

" Is he though?" exclaimed the other, starting; "'sblood! where did you get him?"

" Just here, in one of the Negro-huts; and without your help after all, you see."

" Zounds! that's queer. How the devil did he get out of that 'ere thorny prison? He's the very devil! but he's caught, you say. Hem! but have you found the Obiah man—the real Obiah man? What will you give me if I find him for you?—it's the real Negro priest poisoner, who did all the ruin on your property, as true as I am here; and for that I will give you my word as a gentleman, and the word of Tim Higgins, Esquire, I hope, is as good as any of them there jackanapes what sets up for nobs in Port Spain, and harn't as good a right to hold up their heads as me. Howsomedever, I'll bring him in tow tonight, all bound and chained for you; but first I must have a room, and the manager and overseer must hang up their hammocks by the side of mine, in case I should want help. Mind, I say, in case only; for my jobs is waluable to me, and I don't like meddlesome hands a-hauling of my nets. You mind, I haven't them dogs of the captain's with me, for you see they're never to be trusted when you want to keep a sly look-out; so you must let me have a shooting-gun. You needn't go sneering along that way, Mr. Cardon; I can tell you, white men needs keep a sharp look-out, when they has got those hell-hound Koromantyns to hove-to."

St. Hilaire heard no further, for they had now reached his own door; and as, according to the hospitable custom of the Colonies, a stranger, however disagreeable his manners, never enters a house in the country without meeting a generous and kindly welcome, this Higgins was freely admitted into the sociey of persons who, if in Europe, would hardly have allowed him to sweep their stables. St. Hilaire, after recommending his visitor to join his wife, who was taking chocolate in the sitting-room, left him, and retired to spend the evening in his own room,—not in writing or smoking, as was customary with him, but at his desk, looking over papers. He seemed to have spent many hours at this occupation at some previous part of the day, for he drew forth from a wardrobe sundry boxes of letters loosely thrown together, and a basket by his side was nearly filled with square scraps of torn letters. It was already late, and every one had gone to sleep before he locked his desk for the night. This done, and his papers arranged in their respective places, he went to look at his little grandson, the only being left him on earth, of all those on whom his hopes were once fixed. The child was sleeping in a small closet adjoining its grandmamma's room; it lay in a crib, softly cushioned, and all curtained with flowing net. He lifted the light drapery: sweetly, calmly the little innocent slumbered, with its plump hand beneath its cheek, which lay shaded with clusters of raven ringlets; and over that cherub face he bent, fervently to bless it, coaxing its smooth forehead, and tenderly kissing it again and again. The child moved a little, then heaved a baby sigh as it recomposed itself to sleep, St. Hilaire echoing the sound with a heavy, heavy heart; then he dropped the curtain again, and left it. He next retraced his steps, proceeding through various intervening apartments to a small pavilion at the end of the house, which was fitted up as a little chapel, where the priest celebrated mass at such times as he was called to the Palm Grove to officiate.

St. Hilaire was not habitually a pious man; like most Frenchmen, he usually left devotion to the ladies of his family, jocosely declaring that, provided they were good, he was pretty certain of getting into heaven by holding tight to their skirts at the gate. To-night however, as he entered the chapel, he made the sign of the cross, and knelt down to offer to Heaven a short but earnest prayer for mercy. Then again he rose, and passed through a side-door to an inner room used as a vestry. Approaching the further wall, he drew aside a heavy silk curtain, which hung from the ceiling nearly to the floor, and looped it over a peg on the wall, so as entirely to uncover a full-length family picture: it was in the best style of one of the great painters of the day, and was one of those

Y

rare works of art which fix themselves on the memory when thousands of contemporary scenes have faded away. The group consisted of four figures : a girl about sixteen, pale-browed and pensive, was seated on a rustic chair, and, with drooping eyelids, was tastefully arranging some flowers which she held in her hand ; at her feet was a sweet, intelligent, dark-eyed Hebe, whose lap was laden with flowers, some of which she had selected, and was looking up and presenting them to her sister : a third, a slender, smiling, ethereal-looking nymph, was seen tripping towards them on the right, bringing garlands and branches of rose and jasmine : behind these, to the left, stood a young man with his hand resting on the back of the chair,—his brow was serious, and his deep and thoughtful eyes indicated much of the elements of good, yet in his young and handsome face were visible traces of dissipation and European revels. St. Hilaire took a chair, and seated himself opposite the picture, folding his arms and gazing upon it with all the earnestness of his soul,—for those were the portraits of his children.

The thoughts that were hurrying through his active brain paused before the reminiscence that was rising, and the turbulent feelings that were rushing and eddying through his heart, slackened their impetuous course, to group, unite, melt into one strong holy yearning after treasures received into the bosom of eternity. His whole mind seemed to gather itself up in contemplation of the objects before him. Moments

——minutes fled; the great clock struck the quarter, the half-hour, the three-quarters, and still the father gazed, until nature imperceptibly merged into that state in which the soul, loosening as it were the ties which bind it to the earth, enjoys for awhile the liberty of spirits, and, heedless of the boundaries of time and space, setting at nought the order of earthly things, it revels in the past, the present, and the future. He dreamed; and the magic of art, which had fixed the likenesses with a permanence denied to the originals, blending with the magic of fancy, the figures one by one stood out from the canvas alive. The downcast eyelids rose, revealing the sweet, soft, full orbs which they overshadowed. "Louise!" exclaimed the bewildered father, extending his arms to the resuscitated dead; but the exclamation died away on his lips, and his arms dropped again, as the transformation before him continued: the flowers drooped, faded, blackened, fell; in their place, living eyes of Afric's children seemed to multiply unceasingly around, and each pair, with its respective expression of misery, became a voice, and shrieked its unutterable woe; and with that intuitive perception which belongs to the soul in dreams, the father knew that this was the eternal doom of his beloved for neglected opportunities of helping the fallen ones entrusted to her care. The face of the second turned itself towards him; alas! its Hebe expression of glee was gone, giving place to wan despair, for around her too those terrible moving eyes extended, coiling like the folds of a serpent, eating into her form, till nothing appeared but the face writhing with torture. Vainly the father struggled to get near them, to brush away those shrieking eyes,—he was immoveably fixed to his chair. And those types of ruined souls—he saw them extending on one side to his youngest, and on the other to his son—his eldest-born—the pride of his house; but here were mingled other forms from other climes—souls destroyed, not by omission, but commission; their shrieks were shooting like chains about his neck, about his person, and the father saw him dragged downwards—downwards—downwards. The strong frame of St. Hilaire was convulsed with horror, and he woke with a start—the effort he had made to save his son. He rubbed his eyes, spoke aloud, walked about the room, to free his mind from the fearful impressions it had received; then he went to the picture, and felt it all over, touching each figure in turn, to assure himself it was painted canvas. But human nature, encased though it be in iron, can bear only to a limited point. Exhausted with mental agony, and overwhelmed with the accumulated sorrows stirred up anew by his terrible dream, he sank upon his chair, and this strong, bold, wilful man wept like a little child. His head drooped upon his chest, the large cold drops stood upon his brow, his limbs shivered, the agonies of a hundred lives tortured him in that one short hour,—the despot was subdued, and he bowed before the power of Almighty God. Then did the angel of mercy, which is for ever hovering over the unfortunate, droop its wings over this suffering mortal, and touch him with its wand of peace; he slept, this time sinking into obliviousness and repose. A short time elapsed, and he half woke up with a strange consciousness of a coming change. There was a sound as of rushing floods, and a din of voices, which in vain he strove to understand. Then he woke up entirely, and found it was no dream, but a terrible reality. In a moment his mind was clear, and, heedless of the suffocation of the rolling smoke which was filling the rooms, he rushed from one apartment to another, till he came to the crib of the sleeping babe,—it was gone! He hurried forward to Madame Angélique's apartment; it was empty, only at the open window was Laurine, crying to him in agony—" Master! Master! fly for your life! I have the child; he is here, I have saved him. Fly, Master, they are seeking to murder you,—for God's sake, fly!"—and the flames, crackling through the dry wood of which the house was built, rolled swiftly along the walls to enclose him.

CHAPTER XXIV.

LET us now go back a few hours, and see what was passing in the Negro-huts. It was Saturday, the day usually granted to the Negroes for cultivating their grounds; on this occasion however, excited by the events of the morning, they had left the fields early, and had retired to their huts to talk. They were now assembled in the one which had been apportioned to Talima, who lay stretched on a mat, resting her chin on her elbows, as she gazed admiringly at the antics of Quaco, who was setting the company in a roar by turning the white people into ridicule. The power of mimicry is strong in the Negro—with Quaco particularly so; and as he slouched along like the Overseer, or strutted like the Manager, the imitation was so like, yet so ridiculous a caricature, that the assembly were in fits. His critiques on the personal attractions of the white ladies were not less relished;

and as the lad became more and more excited by the
plaudits of his hearers, he detailed many a spicy
anecdote of the white people in their own country,
which Belfond had formerly related to him. Others
again were grouped round Laurine, giving her sympathy and comfort; they wiped her eyes, threw their
arms about her, kissed her forehead, and wept; then,
in terms of warm affection, they gently urged her to
come among those who longed to comfort her and
divert her grief by friendly converse.

Very different was the temper of another individual
who here interrupted the proceedings of the assembly,
and at the sight of whom they looked cowed, huddling
together in the corners. "A good-night to you, my
children!" said Fanty as he entered: there was a
general murmur of response; but all stood aloof, save
Coraly, who immediately placed a stool for him, and
offered a pipe. "Woman!" he cried, as he pushed
the pipe aside, "*an empty bag cannot stand;* give me
to eat, and hot!" A fire was instantly made with
dried twigs and branches, and a pot set to boil, while
a round calabash was got ready, together with a long,
narrow gourd, to serve as a spoon or scoop. The fumes
rose savourily through the room, and, to judge by the
relaxing expression of the sorcerer's face, were fast
softening his heart; indeed, when the mess was ready
and duly poured out, the old man ate as though he
not broken fast for three days before.

The meal over, Fanty returned the calabash, carefully
wiped his lips, looked round at the company, and

spoke. " Countrymen," he said, in his native tongúe, "*when the head quarrels with the feet, the back must break.* . The white men no longer stand together as they used; they must fall, and we children of Africa must rise. I come here tonight to tell you how the King of the white people has called us children; how two smaller tributary kings, Buxton and Wilberforce, have confessed to loving us, and to make war upon other white kings to make us free. Time was, my countrymen, when the Negro might long for freedom till his mouth ran water like a river; now the thing will come before we know how to swallow it. Time was, countrymen, when *only the shoe could know whether the stocking had holes;* now the white man's shoe slips off, and the holes are bared to all Negroes' eyes. Did you mark the gentleman here the other day?——you see I know all that happens. What did he come here for?——just as a spy, to see whether Master flogged his Negroes. Time was, countrymen, when *cork-wood was not mahogany,* but now *wood is wood everywhere,* and the white man's back shall smart before he dares to do with us again as he likes."

Quaco had been listening attentively; he did not however share in the awe inspired by the presence of the sorcerer, but freely broke the silence, and advanced to argue. " Hey, Daddy Fanty," he exclaimed, " wharra talk so for?——*Grand talk neber wise talk,* and *eggs mustn't dance 'mong de stones.* We know, Daddy, you be one sabey man,—but go 'way ! Quaco always listening at master's door knows somefin too.

Now, da white man come here toder day,—he be one foolish man, so white people call 'em."

"Neber mind!" murmured many voices ; "he good heart to niggers, and *who throws kindness in de fire, will find 'em in de ashes :* he be good to niggers, niggers will be good to he."

"Cho!" exclaimed the lad, looking round contemptuously, "hold your mouth, and let me and Daddy Fanty talk. Me know bery well Massa Dorset no spy: he foolish man and good heart, dat's all : and as for free law, go 'way, dat neber come for nigger, nor for nigger children : *when cattle die, dem leave misery to 'em skin,*—dat's de way wi' poor niggers. Now, Daddy, you are a sabey man, so do jist tell us what for white man so grand, and nigger so low, hey ?"

Fanty gathered himself up, took the pipe from his mouth, and related a legend current among the Africans, which, put into clear language, runs thus :—When the Great Spirit, Accompong, made all things in the sky and on the earth, he made two men,—one in the day, and he was white, the other in the night, and he was black. The next day the Great Spirit called the white man and the nigger before him, that they might choose their future lot ; and in one hand he held forth a calabash full of gold and perfumes, and in the other only a book. Foolish nigger took the calabash, and, with the gold, the fruit, and the rich things, he sat down under a palm-tree to sing. The white man took the book ; then he washed himself, and looked about him; and the book taught him the secrets of all things, and he learned how to get the calabash, the gold, all the rich things, and lastly, the nigger himself. "So that is the way, countrymen, that the niggers got to be slaves, and the white men to be so great."

A groan went through the assembly;—"Oh, hey! is nigger neber to come right again? Oh! hey! oh! Didn't same spirit make the two?"

"Assarci," continued the old man, "he, the good spirit of regeneration, has long ago promised that the time shall come when the white man shall be glutted, and, in his feeble state, the calabash, the gold, and the rich things shall fall upon him and crush him. Then shall the Negro come and hold out his hand to his fallen brother, and shall lift him up, and together they will walk upon the earth in peace. That is what I have learned by the magic of my country; but, my children, I come here tonight, not for tales like these, nor yet to send you back to far bright Africa on the wings of death; I come to 'free that child of my dead sister, the Mulatto Belfond. The sun must not shine tomorrow, my children, before that boy is free;" and, with a shout, the old man stood upon his stool, and with outstretched arms and excited gestures called to the people before him to approach, for the administration of the Wanga Obiah oath of secresy, adherence, and obedience. They piled wood upon the ground before him, and the gathering flames shot upwards, as he uttered in his strange dialect the incantations of his craft : the whole group might have stood for a scene in the dark kingdom below.

Meantime, the object of Fanty's concern was lying quietly on the floor of his dungeon. This place had not been built expressly for the purpose of confinement; it was merely the lower part of the house, or, to speak more correctly, an enclosure formed by the foundation-walls, about four feet in height, on which rested the wooden superstructure of the family dwelling. It had formerly been used for stowing away barrels, boxes, old furniture, and wood ; but as, of late years, rumours of rebellion had become rife, it had been found desirable, on large estates, to have a stronghold for securing unmanageable Negroes, and Don Duro had long ago ordered the lumber to be removed. Into this place Belfond had been thrust ; his wrists and ankles were fettered, and secured by a chain to a ring in the wall, probably to prevent his reaching the door, which was not very strong. Belfond however was not inclined to give trouble now : from the moment he left his master's presence, he neither uttered a word nor attempted resistance, but, composedly and quietly sitting upon the ground, submitted at once to his fate. Here his tyrants left him ; and the long afternoon passed, and the evening came and went, and then he wearily saw the night advance. He could hear the loud voice of his master, when he returned from his walk, and the detestable twanging tones of Higgins, which made his blood boil; then the shrill tones of his mistress, reprimanding some unfortunate delinquent of the household, or the sweet laughter of the little child. One by one these sounds died away, for night was come, bringing rest to all but him.

He stretched himself upon the ground : it was damp and noisome, and huge rats scampered fearlessly over his body. He tried to sleep, but could not ; his thoughts grew busy, and he seemed to live again amid scenes long since forgotten, dwelling with painful distinctness on the happy hours he had passed. Little incidents, which years of activity and adventure had blotted from his memory, came forth in lines of bold relief, with every little touch and shading fresh as though impressed but yesterday ; then his days in France, his stealthy acquisition of knowledge, his intense delight when he effected his escape from his young master,—from which his thoughts passed to his second escape from Captain Hill's vessel to the wilds and woods of Trinidad, and, as a crown to all, the blissful moments he had spent with Laurine. But when he remembered how he had last beheld her, he groaned aloud and gnashed his teeth ; he writhed upon the ground, and cried to Heaven in pity to strike him, an impotent worm, which could not even turn upon the foot that crushed him. "I am of a race accursed upon the earth," he cried ; "what was life given me for? I did not ask it : I am alone in the world, useless and helpless,—no one cares for me, not a soul !" and then, by some train of emotions, his thoughts reverted to his mother. "Oh, my mother! African, black, humble as you were, you loved me! Where are you now? Does peace dwell where you are, my mother? does my voice reach you? do you sometimes look down upon me from your starry abode?" And, as if in answer, a light upon the ceiling caught his eye; he gazed at it,—it was the gentle green light of a little firefly; but his heart hailed it as a signal from her he called upon,— a guardian spirit, come to watch over him, and bear him company in his solitude. Think not meanly of him, kind Reader, for this superstitious feeling; the stoutest heart will yield to such in times of deepest wretchedness, when the mind vainly seeks for comfort in common things,—when reason holds down her head defeated, and religion itself only serves to excite the imagination.

Here however his meditations were interrupted by the barking of the watch-dog; its fury seemed to increase, then it yelped, gave a dismal howl, and again all was silent. "Some thief," thought Belfond, " prowling about to carry off our master's things— cursed be the day I learned that ugly word, I can never unlearn it! Well, I don't blame the thief, why should I? I am a thief myself; I would not take a straw from my fellow-slave, but I have run away from my master, and carried off his capital vested in these bones and sinews. Poor limbs! bruised and torn, and, still worse, guided by a head most hopelessly rebellious! who will care to use their worthless

labour again?   I am to be murdered, as an example
to the gangs,—a valuable example, if they will take
it! Oh, Negroes! poor, degraded, crawling things,
without spirit, without a wish to be free!"

Suddenly his reflections were cut short by an inde-
scribable sensation of something extraordinary outside; there was a rushing, a smothered sound of footsteps, which his hearing, rendered keen by solitude,
soon detected to be those of a multitude; then a smell
of fire, and almost immediately after clouds of smoke
came rolling through the crevices in suffocating thickness.   The wretched prisoner crawled as near to the
door as his chains would allow, and dismally, implor-
ingly cried for help; but, remembering his condition,
he checked himself: "They are burning me alive,"
thought he, "and they are doing it in the night, to
avoid detection.   Well! my sufferings will soon be
over; what can it matter, an hour sooner, or an hour
later? I will lay me down, and bid it welcome."

But the movement outside increased; a sound like
the distant roar of the sea, now in whispers, now rising into louder murmur, starting into shrieks, rolling
in hoarse remonstrance, burst upon his ear.   The
door of his dungeon was attacked; stones and ham-
mers were striking wrathfully, the doorposts cracked,
the door was wrenched open, and in the midst of
flame, and heat, and smoke, dark figures hurriedly
grasped the prisoner.   They forgot that he was fettered; but, perceiving their mistake, a lantern was

brought, the chains were knocked asunder, and in another moment Belfond was dragged into the air,—the free, fresh, blessed air of heaven !

Bewildered by the glare and the uproar, Belfond was at first unable to stand upon his feet ; his eyes were blinded with the light, his head reeled, and he fell ; and when he rose, he gazed upon the fire before him, and watched the rushing, gathering multitude with the air of a dreamer, bewildered and stupefied. With rage and fury the snake-like flames ascended ; they but touched the dry roofing, and the thatch was in a blaze, and a waving column of dazzling fire rose high, making red the clouds above. The noise increased ; there were cries of females and shrieks of alarm, savage screams of laughter, hoarse sounds of angry contention, and one mad roar of triumph : the Negroes had proclaimed an insurrection.

Amidst this tide of human voices there was one focus of deafening tumult ; but, rising above it all, was the voice of St. Hilaire, furiously contending with his rebel slaves. The sound acted upon Belfond like an electric shock ; his whole frame was nerved with instant vigour. Was it triumph ? was it rage ? was it vengeance ? At first it was all of these, but, only for a moment effervescing, they quickly settled down into a holy compound of the heart's natural pleadings. Seeking the tyrant whom he knew to be his father, bruised, broken, wounded as he was, he rushed forward to defend him, knocking aside all who opposed his way. " Comrades ! comrades ! don't kill him, for God's sake !" he cried, as the Negroes pressed closer and closer upon their master.

Cardon had already with his single arm laid Negro after Negro upon the ground, dealing blows from side to side with the butt-end of his gun ; but as he caught the words of Belfond,—" You miscreant," he cried, " curse you ! do you think I am to owe my life to you?" and with fearful strength aimed a deadly blow at his head. Before the words were ended, a hand had pushed Belfond beyond his reach—it was Fanty ; and Cardon fell beneath the weight of a hundred blows.

It was now impossible to restrain the Negroes : they were maddened with the deed. It was in vain that Belfond shouted to them, reasoned with them, warned them ; that he ran about from place to place, calling them to order, and to a concern for their own safety. They had given themselves up to the desperate delirium of their conscious guilt. Without plan, or chief, or immediate confederates in the island, these demented creatures rushed to destruction ; and when the house fell with a tremendous crash, their cries of triumph reached for miles, like an alarm-bell to the plantations around, and, as the showers of sparks flew about, and the bright roaring blaze grew wilder and brighter with the fall of every crumbling beam, the whole formed a huge bonfire, round which these infuriated savages danced and exultingly shouted, like the raging spirits of the element itself. As to Fanty, he was entirely lost in the confusion. If chief there was, it must be Talima, the warlike daughter of

Anamoa; for she had seized a horse, and with a torch in her hand was seen galloping off in the direction of the cane-fields, with a large detachment of the furious herd at her heels. But our hero did not follow; his heart was heavy: "He would not let me save him!" he kept repeating to himself,—"He would not let me save him!" and, weary and desponding, he turned to the Negro-huts to be alone. He was making his way thither, with his head down and his hands in his pockets, when somebody ran against him,—it was Quaco. "Hey!" said the youth, recognizing him by the glare of the fire, "me been a look for you; me just hear alarm-bell 'pon de Fountain Estate; you better look sharp, Belfond!"

"I had better," was the reply; "a pretty business you have made of it! Better have left me where I was."

"Yah! hey! how you talk foolish!" exclaimed the youth. "Go, hide yourself, that's all! leave all de rest to we niggers. They neber go punish us all,—too many dollars lost, eh? Yah! go 'way!"

"My poor master, you have murdered him!" said Belfond, "and most likely mistress too." ·

"Hey!" put in Quaco, with kindling eyes, "Missis, manager, oberseer—all! and, what you tink,—Mas'r Higgins too, da white Obiah man! Yah! hey!" and he finished his sentence by acting in strong caricature a state of terror and a running for life, and then he leaped up and laughed with glee.

"Where is the little child?" interrupted Belfond.

z

Quaco grew serious immediately. "We had got 'em," he said, "and somebody mad nigger throwed 'em in de fire, when Laurine shoved up and saved 'em,—then away, and nobody seen 'em since. Come, good-bye, Belfond! Da Talima be fine gal! let me go see what all of 'em be go down yonder!" and before Belfond could stop him, he was off.

CHAPTER XXV.

ESCAPE.

THE Negroes on the Fountain Estate, although orderly and obedient to their master, yet, as was natural, displayed a good deal of restlessness. They kept out of sight of the white people as much as they could; but ever and anon young ones would cross the hedges, to hear and see what was going on, and there was questioning and commenting among the older heads, too nearly interested in the event to conceal it. Nor was there less anxiety at the house; for here the inmates of the Palm Grove had taken refuge, bringing with them their confusion and terror, and good Mrs. Dorset had a great deal to do. There was Madame Angélique fainting at every instant, and she had to be attended to and comforted. She was just recovering from one of these fits, when Laurine rushed in, bearing in her arms the little Léonce, thought to have been murdered by the infuriate Negroes. Placing the frightened babe, not with the grandmamma, but

z 2

on Mrs. Dorset's lap, and without waiting to give a
word of explanation, Laurine fled as precipitately as
she had entered.   Eager and loving were the caresses
the ladies bestowed upon the child, who was rendered
tenfold more interesting by the mysterious way in
which it had been recovered.

The anxiety of the ladies was great; Mrs. Dorset,
especially, was anxious about her husband, who had
gone to the Palm Grove at the very first signal of
alarm.   By good luck Don Duro happened to be in
the way, looking for a strong place wherein to secure
his prisoners.   Yielding to the entreaties of the ladies,
he mounted his horse, and went in the direction of
the fire, which had now extended to some fields of
sugar-cane on the outskirts of Mr. Cardon's estate.
Thither now were the Negroes thronging, headed by
the warlike daughter of Anamoa.   Columns of rolling
clouds were rising, with a trail of fire raging, roaring,
streaming after them.   All the neighbouring white
people, for miles around, were galloping to lend assistance ; the militia too were there, with their uni-
form and arms.   There were hoarse voices swearing,
mules tramping, water streaming, and black figures
on foot, and white men on horseback, moving to
and fro against the red glare, like demons in Pande-
monium.

Just on the path, as Don Duro was hurrying to
the spot, stood a Negro woman, shouting and laughing at the scene ; she showed so little sense of self-
preservation as not to heed· the coming ·horse, nor to

get out of the way even when it was close upon her.
With a terrible oath Don Duro led the animal trampling over her, and when the horse stumbled, he
lashed the creature that lay writhing beneath the
horse's hoofs. His brutal phrases however were cut
short by the voice of Mr. Dorset, calling for help,
and to this, of course, he immediately attended. Setting his horse at full gallop, he found that gentleman endeavouring, with great difficulty, to support a
wounded white. The Manager alighted to lend assistance, but what was his horror when, by the light
of his lantern, he recognized the objects before him!
Higgins lay ghastly and dying,—not from any visible
wound, but, clinging round him, like a beast of prey,
was the crippled body of the sorcerer Fanty. Faithful to his promise, the old Negro had sought the
sailor, and then and there, in the midst of the confusion and terrors of the rebellion, regardless of the
shots and the blows which assailed him on all sides,
he had leaped upon him, and darting his long and
poisoned nails into the ears of his enemy, he clung to
him with a strength and pertinacity which no effort
could overcome. It was a hideous spectacle: the
old man's glassy eyes were wide open with a fixed
stare, while a demoniac grin on his shrivelled lips
showed the last working of his soul before it took its
final leave of earth's trials and wrongs. It was impossible to disengage him, and Higgins cried piteously for water; but ere they could bring it, the
words thickened in his throat, and, before many mi-

nutes, he lay a blackened, loathsome corpse, just as the sorcerer had foretold.

Leaving the gentlemen to settle between them as to the propriety and mode of burying these two, thus locked in the embrace of hate, we may direct our eyes another way, to a different scene.

Weary, disgusted, and desponding, Belfond had turned from the spot where St. Hilaire fell, and endeavoured to gain some place where he might be alone, and away from the tumult which his soul abhorred. He was thinking of his father;—" He would not let me save him," he repeated to himself; " He would not let me save him !—I, his own son, cursed even in that !" and with his head resting on his bosom, he bewailed his unhappy fate, and wept over the untimely death of one whom he would have loved had he been permitted. He had instinctively taken the direction of the Negro-huts, and had turned abstractedly to look at the progress of the fire, when he thought he heard the voice of one sobbing. He followed the sound to Madelaine's dark hut, where, not without a suspicion which at once awakened all his tenderest feelings, he found Laurine, like a frightened bird come back to the deserted nest for protection. In one moment all was forgiven, all was forgotten, for, at his soft, whispered call, she sought her lover's wing at once, and, throwing herself on his bosom, cried as if her heart would break. " Oh, Belfond, Belfond, help me ! they trod my mother down, I saw her fall; I saw him, that terrible white man, trample upon her;—I heard her groans, and I heard the whip whistling as it lashed her, and she dying beneath the horse's feet!"

"Hush! my Laurine, hush!" replied her lover, "our trials are nearly over. Say, will you come with me now? or will you stay here, and give away your precious freedom, and more than freedom—all that makes you dear in my eyes, Laurine?"

"Take me! take me! I will go with you anywhere," said the maid, in smothered accents.

"Then God bless you! God bless the hour and the day that hears you say these blessed words, Laurine!" said the young man, touching the ground with his knee; "it is the dawn of brighter, holier times for me,—days that no cloud can ever wholly darken."

"Oh, Belfond!" whispered the young girl, throwing her arms about her lover's neck, "to hear you speak so is such a happiness for me! I was so wretched at hearing you deny the goodness of God."

"Ah, well, it was of no use preaching to me then; my heart would never acknowledge a God in any place where Laurine lived a slave;—but free! ah! heaven shines in every ray of light; the holy goodness which surrounds you will be to me a beacon-light to lead me upwards. Oh, Laurine! did you but know the hell that worked within me while I saw the chains doubling and doubling about you, and I— impotent wretch!—unable to move a hand to save you!"

In such sweet converse they left the Palm Grove,

and plunged into the woods beyond. The fires disappeared behind the dense foliage of the forest-trees, and the din of voices of the terrifying and the terrified died away behind the hills, which the lovers now rapidly traversed ; and, as the wild thorns and prickly bushes thickened on the untrodden plain, Belfond was forced to carry the maiden, were it only to husband her strength for the long journey of flight before them.   The night had deepened, and had spread her mantle in solemn majesty over those wild solitudes, when it occurred to Laurine to ask timidly, whither they were going, and whether her lover was taking her to the runaway camp.

"What ! take you, my treasure, to the runaway camp?——nay, my brightest star ! what was pleasant to think of, the other day, will hardly do for us now ; but first set my mind at ease concerning one subject, ——what has become of little Léonce ?"

"I took the child," said the young girl, "and at first hurried off with him to my mother's hut, thinking to keep her quiet at home ; but she was off with the rest, and no entreaties of mine could bring her back ; and the poor little thing I had in my arms was so terrified, and clung to me with such a low, piteous wail, that I bethought me to run on to the Fountain Estate, and there leave it,——and so I did.   Then I fled as for my life, to try and get my mother home.   I was just a few trees from her, when, oh, Belfond ! Don Duro, galloping forward, trampled her down under his horse's feet ; they killed her before my

eyes !—my poor mother !—my poor helpless mother !"
and the young girl hid her face in her hands. " And
then, Belfond," she resumed, " when he rode away
and left her, I went to carry her home, and the Overseer came on hallooing to me, and telling me to stop,
or he would shoot me. How cruel, cruel, cruel they
are !"

" Laurine," interrupted Belfond, " we won't stop
to talk upon that point now, for I suppose we shall
never quarrel about it again. You asked me where I
was taking you : brighten up, my star, and I will tell
you : there, beyond the sunny islands across the
water,—there, where none are slaves, where Bolivar
has given to all equal rights,—there am I taking you,
Laurine ; where you can share my uprising, and bless
me as I go ; where our children will be a glory to us,
and our union sanctified, and held sanctified by the
people among whom we live ;—there, Laurine, am I
taking you. And first you shall teach me to be good,
my sweet flower. It is many a year since I said a
prayer, and you shall bless me ; you will see how
good I shall be when I feel I am free for ever ! All I
wanted was to feel myself something in this great,
beautiful world,—something responsible to God. Do
you see, Laurine, that fallen tree, lying prostrate on
the ground ? see the little twigs it sends shooting upwards—those are its endeavours to rise, but a power
greater than all its force keeps it chained to the
ground : such is the poor slave, and such are his
impotent yearnings to rise. Believe me, blessed

Laurine, the very spirit of rebellion I exhibited, my disgust and discontent, were but so many proofs of my worship of the Supreme."

Thus they journeyed, till, about two o'clock in the morning, they reached the eastern side of the island, where the Tamana joins its sparkling tide to the ocean, where the crescent forest of palms spreads its waving heads along the shore, and the Indian fishermen spread their nets in the shade. Belfond paused, and looked around him. "Here," he said, "they know me; they will not mind my waking them up; they will give me a canoe and provisions, and we shall be off." As he said, so it was done: the Indians asked but few questions, for they were used to helping the wretched fugitives who came that way, and such provisions as they possessed they freely gave to those who needed them.

Fortunately, some fishermen had their canoe ready to put out, and, glad of the company, they stowed in their provisions, intending, as they said, to make a good voyage of it,—up the Orinoco, for turtle-eggs and wild turkeys, to exchange at Port Spain for knives and fire-water. When all was ready, and Laurine comfortably seated, Belfond stood up a moment by her side, and looked back at the beautiful island he was leaving. "Farewell!" he said, waving his hand; "no spot on earth is more lovely than you. God might have chosen you for Eden when first he created man; angels might have lived among your gardens. What dreams of prosperity, of glory, have I not had about you,—all spoiled, corrupted, poisoned by the white man! Farewell, then, sweet island! the best I can wish you is that you may daily send forth slaves, flying, like myself, to be free."

The Indian on the shore smoked his calumet as he listened, and waved his hand in response to Belfond. Now the skiff is off; and the moonlight dances brightly upon the waters, and the breeze rustles softly among the palm-leaves, and the surf breaks in gentle cadence on the beach,—the hymn of nature's joy, the mingled song of sea and forest.

CHAPTER XXVI.

CONCLUSION.

My readers may perhaps wish to know something concerning the fate of the other personages who have figured in the preceding pages. Mr. Dorset demanded and obtained pardon for the Negroes of the Orange Grove Estate,—the more easily, as the implication of guilt affected them all, and the circumstances of the times rendered it advisable to hush up all such evil examples; the planters therefore agreed among themselves to tell no more than they could help to their wives at home. Mr. Cardon's death was attributed to the fall of the roof of his house upon him as he was rushing about to put out the fire, which was stated to have originated accidentally; the misconduct of the Negroes was explained by the confusion which ensued, and, in courtesy to Mr. Dorset's pleading, they were let off, after a sound flogging to each. A few of them were knocked down to Mr. Dorset at the sale of the estate, which took place shortly after, and among these were Quaco, Talima, and Beneba. Coraly was quietly smuggled off to Martinique, and has never been heard of since. Madame Angélique Cardon in due time married the Manager, and, up to the year of the Emancipation Act, the Palm Grove was a thriving estate. Léonce, the little child, was taken great care of, and was said to be fonder of being with Mr. and Mrs. Dorset than with his grandmamma. A certain love of rule displayed itself in his character at an early period. When we heard of him last, he was at school in New Orleans, whence he wrote word, that as soon as he was at liberty to act for himself, it was his intention to join the American army to put down the Texan "rebels."

Some little time before the Emancipation Act, a slaver was seized off the coast of Trinidad. The slaves, mostly children, where apprenticed to various individuals in the island, and the gold-dust and ivory sent to England with great ostentation. It was whispered among many that this was Captain Hill and his smuggler again, but that his name and former dealings in the Colony were for obvious reasons suppressed. How far this was true, I know not; but it is believed he may still be found stealthily carrying on his trade across the Atlantic to Cuba, and he is considered on the whole a very prosperous man.

The Overseer I know nothing more about; no doubt he went the way of all such, and ended as he had begun,—grovelling in everything that was low.

Enough has not yet been said, however, of our good

friends Mr. and Mrs. Dorset. They ought to have been prosperous, but they were not. With enthusiasm they commenced a system of teaching and reforming among their slaves, which on all occasions ended like the experiment of the wheelbarrows—in failure. On slaves that were African born they invariably succeeded in making some impression, but on Negroes born as slaves in the Colony, never; these were all hardened, cunning, and corrupt. A single voice, judiciously raised, may overthrow a system, but no single effort can counteract it effects. Mr. Dorset made the mistake of expecting that his individual action, through a small space of time, could efface the evils of an unrighteous influence which had been working for centuries upon a whole race. As he never allowed flogging, his slaves were of course the laziest among the lazy. "*Master,*" they would say to him, "*when we dead, and we go in a heaven, we go sit down softly* (idly),"—that was their idea of supreme happiness. His crops, as may be imagined, were never good; and when the Emancipation Act was passed, the Fountain Estate, small as it was, had so many encumbrances that it was put up for sale, and Mr. Dorset, in a new country and without friends or relatives, fell into distress. But a little time after this the writer received a letter concerning him, which told of better prospects; it was to the following effect :—

"Some days ago I was called to the door to see two *vendors;* you remember what they are,—Negro-women with trays upon their heads, going from house to house with articles for sale. The first who accosted me was a pleasant-faced girl—she had fruit and vegetables; and, as she placed her heavy tray upon the floor for my inspection, I had a full view of the other vendor behind, a magnificent-looking creature, black and shining as Newcastle coal; strong, too, or she could never have borne upon her head such a ponderous heap of silks and cottons and laces as she soon prepared to display. 'What is your name?' said I to the first, 'for I don't recollect seeing you before among the vendors of the town.' 'It is only lately I have set up,' she said (they disdain to say Missis now), 'and my name is Beneba; I used to belong to the Palm Grove, and afterwards to the Fountain.' 'Oh,' said I, 'to Mr. Dorset; I am sorry to hear he is so poorly off.' Whereupon Beneba tossed back her head with a look of scorn; 'Not so poor,' she said, 'while they have got friends like us.' After a pause, and for the sake of saying something, I ventured a question as to where they were. 'In a nice house,' said Beneba proudly, 'and living like gentleman and lady, as they are, and we are working for them and for the little piccaninny that is born; all I get for my tray is for their living, and what Talima there behind me gets by her tray, and what her husband Quaco gets by the two carts he has got on the wharf, is to get a heap of money to set him up as merchant, for we all think he would not like to be always living this way; he would like to do for himself.' "

A few years afterwards an opening occurred in New

York, and thither Mr. Dorset removed his family. His success was first marked by a remittance to his colonial friends; but the good creatures sent it back, alleging that the money advanced was a free gift, and should remain so; they would be well paid in hearing that he was rich and happy.

These are the actions and sentiments of a people whom the leading journalists of the day profess to consider too ridiculous and puerile to enlist the sympathy of so great a nation as England. Well for us if we could find but one out of every hundred, as disinterested, as simple-minded, and as generous!

THE END.

JOHN EDWARD TAYLOR, PRINTER,
LITTLE QUEEN STREET, LINCOLN'S INN FIELDS.

nily.
᠂ his
ıck.
ınd
ing

ıle
ɩo
-
ȝ